Responses to #1 *New York Times* bestselling author Tucker Max's first book,

I Hope They Serve Beer in Hell

"We protest everything about Tucker Max and what he stands for."

"I had never finished a book—not even for school—until I came across yours. I had no idea writing could be this interesting or funny."

"People who like Tucker Max: Douchebags and Baby Rapists."

"Your book made me laugh so hard I pissed my goddamn pants. I literally pissed in my pants. I don't even do that when I'm drunk."

"For some reason professional creep Tucker Max wrote a book which became a bestseller just to prove that America, as a concept, is over."

"I usually like people. I truly pray something terrible happens to you. You will end up drinking fire as the devil fucks you in the ass. Enjoy the limelight you alcoholic walking Petri dish."

"I am a happily married mother of three wonderful young sons. One day I will ask them, 'Sons, what do you want to be when you grow up?' The first will answer, 'an astronaut.' The second will answer, 'the president.' The third will look me in the eyes and confidently say, 'Tucker Max.' He'll be my favorite."

***Assholes Finish First* is available from Simon & Schuster Audio and as an eBook**

Also by Tucker Max

I Hope They Serve Beer In Hell

ASSHOLES FINISH FIRST

TUCKER MAX

Gallery Books
NEW YORK LONDON TORONTO SYDNEY NEW DELHI

Gallery Books
A Division of Simon & Schuster, Inc.
1230 Avenue of the Americas
New York, NY 10020

First Gallery Books trade paperback edition October 2011

GALLERY BOOKS and colophon are trademarks of Simon & Schuster, Inc.

For information about special discounts for bulk purchases, please contact Simon & Schuster Special Sales at 1-866-506-1949 or business@simonandschuster.com.

The Simon & Schuster Speakers Bureau can bring authors to your live event. For more information or to book an event contact the Simon & Schuster Speakers Bureau at 1-866-248-3049 or visit our website at www.simonspeakers.com.

Designed by Diane Hobbing of Snap-Haus Graphics

Manufactured in the United States of America

10 9 8 7 6 5 4 3 2 1

Library of Congress Cataloging-in-Publication Data
Max, Tucker.
Assholes finish first / by Tucker Max.
p. cm.
1. Max, Tucker—Sexual behavior—Anecdotes. 2. Max, Tucker—Alcohol use—Anecdotes. 3. Sex—Anecdotes. 4. Drinking of alcoholic beverages—Anecdotes. I. Title.
CT275.M464713A3 2010
616.85'83300922—dc22
2010023159

ISBN 978-1-4169-3874-3
ISBN 978-1-4391-9869-8 (pbk)
ISBN 978-1-4169-5114-8 (ebook)

Contents

Author's Note

My real name is Tucker Max. All the events described in the following stories are true to the best of my recollection, though certain dates, characteristics, locations, and other trivial details have been altered.

I hope you enjoy reading about my life as much as I have enjoyed living it.

ASSHOLES

FINISH

FIRST

Tucker Goes to Campout, Owns Duke Nerds

Occurred—September 2000

I went to law school at Duke, and as you may know, basketball is huge there. The demand for tickets, even for grad students, far outstrips the supply. In order to solve this problem, the people in charge make grad students camp out in a field to get into the lottery for the chance to get tickets. They expect you to spend a weekend sleeping in dirt and checking in every time they blow their whistles, like a fucking homeless kindergartener.

You think I'm exaggerating, don't you? This is taken directly from the Duke grad student website:

> "Welcome to Duke! Let's get right to the most important issue on your mind: How can **YOU** get season tickets to this year's men's basketball games in Cameron Indoor Stadium? Eligibility to purchase tickets is determined via the **Graduate and Professional Student Council Basketball Ticket Campout.** Campout for Duke Men's Basketball season will be held starting at 7:00pm on **Friday, September 8**, and runs through **Sunday, September 10**, at approximately 7am.
>
> The rules are simple: make it through the weekend without missing two attendance checks and your name is entered in a lottery. Lottery winners are then drawn and each of these lucky individuals is eligible to buy one of the 700 graduate and professional season tickets. . . .

> But Campout isn't just about basketball tickets. With almost 2000 students representing nearly every program and department at the University in attendance, this is also **the premier graduate and professional student social event of the year.** Campout is an excellent opportunity to bond with your students in your own program and make friends in other programs."

The bolding is theirs, not mine. Not only do they want grad students to spend their limited free time toiling in a parking lot, they are condescending about it. Either that, or they're just fucking retarded—do they really think that being stuck in a parking lot with 2,000 nerds is **"the premier graduate and professional student social event of the year"**? Not going to a bar or to a party with your friends, or, God fucking forbid, ACTUALLY GOING TO THE GAMES. Nope, to them, the coolest thing a grad student can do is to root around in filth.

I want tickets, so I have to go. OK, fine. But if those Duke basketball tools are going to make me sleep outside for two nights, I'm going to make them pay. And not just by getting drunk and fucking their ugly girlfriends.

It took me a few days, but I finally figured out how to completely ruin the event for everyone who sucks, while concurrently making it awesome for me and my friends. About two weeks before the grad student campout was to start, I was in the law library, intently focusing on my computer screen when my buddy Hate walked up.

Hate "What are you up to?"
Tucker "Ordering something online."
Hate "What, a Russian mail-order bride?"
Tucker "Better. A bullhorn."
Hate "What for?"
Tucker "For Campout. Look at this one, dude: It has a one-mile range! And a 110-decibel siren! It's made for police use!"
Hate [*ten-second blank stare*] "Jesus have mercy on our souls."

I paid extra for 2nd day delivery. When the day of arrival came, I was so excited I stayed home from class. Waiting for the delivery guy felt like Christmas, except without the part where your parents drink all the present money and wrap up things from your room as your gifts. Credit and Hate stayed home that day too, not because they were excited about the bullhorn, but because they are dicks. They wanted to taunt me until it arrived, knowing the anticipation was slowly killing me. (That, and none of us ever went to class anyway because law school is ridiculously easy.)

Credit "Max, I haven't seen you this excited since Brad Pitt took his shirt off in *Fight Club*."
Tucker "Credit, you're Jewish, your best friend is black, and your girlfriend is a cheating whore. Even if I *were* gay, I'd still have it better than you."

When the FedEx truck finally showed up, I sprinted to the front desk. I scribbled my signature, ran back to my room, tore open the package, loaded the batteries I already purchased, then cautiously put the bullhorn up to my lips and whispered:

"Hello."

My voice boomed out of the bullhorn so crisp and loud it shocked me. I felt a strange new power surge through me. It was like I drank from the Holy Grail. I took a deep breath and bellowed:

"WOOOOOOOOOOOOOOOOOOOOOOOOOOOOO!! CREDIT, I AM THE GREATEST MAN ALIVE!! HATE, I'M FUCKING INVINCIBLE!"

I ran out of my room into the living room. Hate was jolted forward in his recliner, white-knuckling the armrests with a look on his face like he'd just seen the devil. Credit had the same exasperated expression he got when he learned the student parking lot was a full mile away from the law school building.

Tucker "Holy shit! The volume's only at 6! It goes up to 10!"

Credit "Everyone is going to hate us."

Hate "Max, you aren't really taking that thing to Campout are you?"

Tucker [*into the bullhorn*] "We are friends and roommates, and yet . . . I feel like you don't know me at all."

I turned it down to 2—loud but still a manageable indoor volume—and spoke to everyone exclusively through the bullhorn for the next week. It became a part of me, a natural extension of my arm. I put it down only to shower and masturbate.

You know how when you pine after something really badly, like a cool toy or a new car or whatever, once you get it, it's never as good as you imagined it would be? This was the opposite. This was so much better than I could've ever dreamed. No possession of mine, before or since, has ever completed me the way that bullhorn did; it embodied all of the characteristics that I consider most essential to myself . . . and amplified them.

Arguing: I was pretty good at debating with people before, but now, I had a permanent trump card. How can you win an argument against someone who is louder than a chain saw? Even if you're completely right, you're wrong, because I have the bullhorn.

Humor: Everything you say becomes one level more humorous through a bullhorn. Stupid becomes passable, passable becomes funny, funny becomes hysterical, and hysterical becomes Dave Chappelle doing Rick James. I think this is because a bullhorn makes you so loud that it puts you on an imaginary stage. Just being the center of attention primes people to think you're funny—how else does Dane Cook get laughs?

Confidence: I was not lacking in confidence beforehand, but add a bullhorn and I became superhuman. It was like having a gun, except better. Walking around with a bullhorn gives all the authority of a gun, without any of the toolishness or danger of it accidentally discharging in your sweatpants. People just assume you're in charge and defer to you.

It was as if one internet purchase had suddenly made all things right in the world. Maybe the Duke nerds are right. Maybe this *will* be the premier social event of the year.

Campout started on Friday at 7pm, but me, SlingBlade, Credit, Hate, Jojo, and GoldenBoy got there about 5pm, so we could park our RV in a prime spot. As we pulled in and started to get situated—which for us entailed setting down the cooler and sitting around it drinking—I pondered my tactics:

Tucker "Alright fellas, what should my bullhorn strategy be?"
Hate "Break it. Or set it on fire. Anything that will get that fucking thing out of your hand."
GoldenBoy "Aren't you just gonna get drunk, yell at people, and not worry about consequences? Do you know any other way to act?"
Tucker "There is wisdom in your words."

At 7pm they blew the whistles for the first check-in. The Head Campout Nerd was giving instructions with one of those tiny little megaphones you can buy at Home Depot. He saw me and came over all excited, like we were friends:

Nerd "You have a bullhorn! I have one too!"

I immediately saw this encounter for what it was: my first chance to assert dominance over Campout. In the most condescending tone possible I said:

Tucker "Aren't you the cutest! And look at the toy Santa brought you for Christmas! You must have been a good boy this year!"

The dude visibly deflated. Here he was, hoping for a Bullhorn Buddy, and instead he got, well . . . me:

Tucker "What the fuck is that, a Speak & Spell or a See 'n Say? The frog says 'Ribbit'!"

He was about to say something, but I put my bullhorn right in his face and hit the siren trigger:

EEEEEERRRRRRNNNNNN

Tucker "Don't bring a knife to a gunfight, motherfucker. Take your Fisher-Price 'My First Megaphone' and get the fuck out of my face. This thing is made for riot control! I run Campout now, bitch!"

The dude sulked off like the old lion that gets his ass handed to him by the younger lion and won't be seeing any more lion pussy. It was awesome. Only minutes into the start of Campout and I had savaged the only challenger to my authority!

Tucker "To be the man, you gotta beat the man! And now I'm the man! WOOOOOOOOOOO!"

GoldenBoy "Rick Flair quotes? I know we're in North Carolina, but come on."

SlingBlade "Tucker is so proud of himself. He just bested a pimply, insecure 130-pound public policy student. Next up, *Romper Room Smackdown*."

The testosterone rush of my victory—on top of the beer I'd already drunk—put me into what could be called an "aggressive" state. Conversely, I was surrounded by the type of passive, fearful people who'd chosen to stay in school to avoid the conflict and consequences of real life. This meant I had in front of me a weekend where I could say or do anything I wanted, without worrying about anyone being able to talk over me. This must be what narcissist heaven is like.

Beer in one hand and bullhorn in the other, I began my symphony of awesome, starting off by verbally assaulting random passersby:

[*to a dude in a* Star Wars *T-shirt*] "Be honest, how many times have you jacked off to a picture of Princess Leia in her metal bikini?"

[*to a group of grad school students*] "You look like the type of people who would criticize a misspelling in a suicide note."

[*to this guy who had blond hair, was kinda fat, and wore thick glasses*] "If this were *Lord of the Flies*, you'd be dead already."

He foolishly turned to respond.

EEEEEERRRRRRNNNNNN

Tucker "Silence! I've got the conch now, Piggy!"

[*to some random nerd*] "How hard was it choosing between the midnight showing of *Rocky Horror Picture Show* and Campout?"

[*to a chunky girl*] "Have you been tested for hoof-and-mouth disease!"
Chunkygirl "What?"

SlingBlade, who at this point was warming up to the idea of the bullhorn, took it from me and piled on:

SlingBlade "Tucker, you have it wrong. Clearly she has mad cow disease."
Chunkygirl "Fuck you!"
Tucker "You're right! She's frothing at the udder!"

Some European-looking dudes in Diadora shorts walked by.

Tucker "Fact: Soccer is a game invented by European ladies to pass the time while their husbands cooked dinner. Go practice your throw-ins, you cheese-eating surrender monkey!"
GoldenBoy "You just seamlessly stole a *King of the Hill* quote and a

Simpsons quote to form one insult. I've never been this impressed by plagiarism."

Tucker "I'm awesome even when I steal."

Many beers later, I saw what looked like a hot girl far over on the other part of the parking lot.

Tucker "Man, look at her!"

Jojo and Credit looked over, and immediately started laughing at me. A lot.

Tucker "What? She's hot!"

As she walked closer, it became very evident she . . . was a he.

Tucker "Come on, he has waif legs and those tight skinny jeans and long hair—how was I supposed to know it was a douche Marxist and not a girl?"
Credit "He has a beard, Tucker."
Tucker "Does he? Shit, maybe I'm drunker than I thought I was."
Jojo "Yeah, that's it."

Everyone had a great time laughing at my expense. To this day, Jojo brings this up approximately once a month. It happened TEN FUCKING YEARS AGO. He's like a woman; he never forgets anything.

Tooling on idiots is fun, but I still have a penis, and it still demands its pounding of flesh, so we decided to see what good-looking—or at least willing—girls we could find at **"the premier graduate and professional student social event of the year."**

Dealing with grad school girls can be tricky. At Duke there were four distinct types: insecure, fearful types hiding from the real world; the super-serious ones so brainwashed by the unreality of academia they aren't even human anymore; the ones just looking for their Mrs. degree; and the sluts. Of all the types of women, I like sluts the best. Mainly because they are the most receptive to me putting my penis in their vagina.

A group of cute girls who looked like they might be game walked by.

Tucker "Ladies, you can't be the first, but you can be the next."

They looked at me suspiciously, as they should. Most of the time I don't know what's going to come out of my mouth, and sometimes, well . . . it's dumb. I've found the best thing to do when you stumble is to pretend that nothing happened and just drive forward.

Tucker "In addition to the bullhorn, we have beer! And we will share it with you!"

They laughed a little but didn't come over. I decided to go for the high-risk play. Nothing ventured, nothing gained.

Tucker "Look, here's the deal: If you're into immature, sexually compulsive men who drink too much and need to be the center of attention at all times, you are going to find me very attractive."

SlingBlade [*grabbing the bullhorn*] "Don't talk to this man. He has herpes simplex A, B and C. This was a public service announcement brought to you by SlingBlade."

Tucker "IT'S IN REMISSION, ASSHOLE!"

The fact that this exchange not only made them laugh out loud, but also got them to come hang out with us, should be all the info you need to know which grad school group they fell into.

But there was a bonus: They were in nursing school. We hit the slut jackpot! Slutty nurses not only want to fuck you, they want to take care of you too. They do you, then they do your laundry. This'll be better than Shark Week!

We talked for a while (without the bullhorn), when, just making conversation, I asked one girl about her favorite movie.

Girl "I love John Cusack, especially in my favorite movie, *Better Off Dead*."
Tucker "Oh no . . ."
SlingBlade "Did we ever establish why Lane Meyer couldn't be bothered to pay the paperboy? Why he tortured him for the entire movie, without any reason?"
Girl "That was funny. 'Gimme my two dollars!' I liked that."
SlingBlade "So you think that's cool, to take goods and services from people and not compensate them? Two dollars is a meal! That's two double cheeseburgers off the McDonald's dollar menu, which can be the only source of protein for those of us whose parents abandon all financial responsibility for their children at age 18."
Girl "Umm . . . calm down. It's just a movie."
SlingBlade "Whatever. You're clearly a selfish whore who would run over a puppy for a guy who shows the mildest interest. I'm sure you and Tucker will get along swimmingly."

The best part about hanging out with SlingBlade is he makes me look nice by comparison.

This girl wore a T-shirt that said FRONT LOADER on it. I couldn't figure out what it meant. She wouldn't tell me. This annoyed the fuck out of me, because I am smarter than she is.

Nurse "Well, if you're so smart, you should be able to figure it out."

Motherfucker. She leaves me no choice. Now I have to break her self-esteem, sleep with her, and steal the shirt.

I use a basic and well-worn tactic: I subtly disapprove of her for various reasons, so that she'll be forced to seek my validation. By sleeping with me. You know, the classy and mature way to get women. One particular exchange I remember:

Girl "I'm not a slut!"
Tucker "I mean, I want to believe you, you seem like a really nice girl, but . . . that's not what those guys over there said about you."
Girl "They did not! What guys?"
Tucker "I don't know, they left already."
Girl "They did not!"
Tucker "Well, let's try a little test. Now, you know everyone has their price, so how about this: Would you sleep with a guy for, let's say, 100 million dollars?"
Girl "Well, I mean, I don't know . . . yeah, probably . . . I guess."
Tucker "OK. Would you sleep with a guy for 10 million dollars?"
Girl "I don't know, maybe."
Tucker "OK. Would you sleep with a guy for 10 dollars?"
Girl "No, of course not."
Tucker "Why not?"
Girl "Are you kidding? I'm not doing that."
Tucker "We've already established that you'd sleep with a guy for money, now we're just haggling over the price."

I guess she doesn't have to learn history to be a nurse, because she thought my little Winston Churchill impression was funny and original. It went on like this for another several hours, me playfully disapproving, her seeking approval, until we snuck off to the back of my SUV and I gave her my full endorsement.

It was about 2am by the time we were done. After we finished, we both wanted to get back up and start drinking more. Plus, I think she was disappointed in my performance. That, or the fact I had been drinking, sweating, and blasting out meat farts all night made me smell like a Pakistani cabdriver. Whichever.

It had been pouring rain for over five hours, everything was soaked, and people were starting to go to bed. Which SlingBlade and I decided meant a prime opportunity to fuck with people.

But before I get into that, let me digress for a second to set the scene.

The most important thing you have to know about Campout is that it's not the same for everyone. There are two places to be: You can rent an RV or U-Haul, park it in the parking lot, and sleep in that, or you can pitch a tent in the field, which is at the bottom of a small hill. Even though the parking lot and field are only yards apart, they are very different worlds. RVs are nice; they have toilets, electricity, TVs, refrigeration, beds—all the comforts of modern life. Tents suck. They are nothing but walls made of thin fabric. You essentially sleep on the ground. Given the choice, most people would take the RV. But it takes money to rent an RV for a weekend, and the vast majority of grad students are broke.

Therefore, a divide develops naturally between the haves and the have-nots. The law students, business school students, and med students tend to be the ones with some excess money, so they rent the RVs and get to sleep in relative luxury in a nice clean parking lot. Pretty much every other grad school student—from political science to divinity school to environmental sciences—is stuck pitching a tent in the field below.

If it's a normal September weekend in North Carolina, this is not really that bad an arrangement. But this weekend it had been raining for days leading up to Campout, including that Friday. This meant the field the poor grad students were camping out in was completely soaked—quite literally a quagmire. It was like a huge mud-wrestling pit, except filled with loser nerds instead of bikini girls.

Which brings us back to the story: SlingBlade and I had, up until this point, spent all of Campout drinking and hanging out in the parking lot. We hadn't paid any attention to Tent City.

That was about to change. This was the moment I had been waiting for all week. I was Tucker Maximus: enslaved camper for an unwanted weekend, coerced supplicant for tickets that should rightfully be mine. And I would have my vengeance, in this life, right now.

Tucker "Tent City! Behold, you live in filth! Your refugee camp for poor nerds is a cesspool of poverty and excrement! You are dirtier than the abandoned children of Bowery whores!"

Some of the people who were out of their tents looked up at me quizzically.

Tucker "Tent City, do you realize how bad you smell? You are swimming in urine and feces. And for what? Crappy tickets to watch a shitty basketball team? You are a Christian Children's Fund commercial!"

One of them yelled out, "Shut up!"

Tucker "Tent City, query: Was it really worth it? Was it really worth the $30 you saved to spend the weekend mired in squalor and filth? [*sniff sniff*] I smell poop and bad decisions."

Someone yelled out from Tent City, "Shut up and go to bed!"

SlingBlade [*taking the bullhorn*] "Mom, is that you?!? STOP EMBARRASSING ME IN FRONT OF MY FRIENDS!!"

Four or five other law student friends came to join in. These weren't even my real friends, who were all asleep or being "mature." These were just guys who knew an awesome idea when they saw one, and they stood around drinking with us and laughing while SlingBlade and I continued to fuck with Tent City.

Tucker "Tent City, you are sleeping in mud and excrement. Don't believe me? I just pissed on this hill. Do you know what gravity is? Ask the physics grad students, they're down there with you because studying the underlying mysteries of the universe doesn't pay for shit!!"

Someone yelled out, "You know, there are things called BATHROOMS!"

Tucker "Toilets are for pussies and poor people!! I am a conquerer!"

Eventually some of the nerds had had enough and started congregating at the base of the hill. At its top, the hill is about 15 feet high and a good 15–30 yards from the people at the bottom. It was far enough away that you could see the people and interact with them, but not so close that you were near them in any physical sense.

RandomNerd "What gives you the right to keep us awake?"
Tucker "Because I have a bullhorn and you do not! Your fancy book learnin' should've taught you that the strong do what they want, and the weak endure what they must. Now bring me your finest meats and cheeses, and be quick about it!"

There were about six of them, and they all kept yammering at me. It was hilarious.

Tucker "I'm sorry, I can't hear you over the sound of how awesome I am. Please speak up."

They actually yelled louder.

Tucker "Again, I can't hear you, because . . . I HAVE A BULLHORN."

They kept jabbering at an even louder volume, and this one dude in particular was fuming. He kinda stepped forward wildly gesticulating at me.

Tucker "I want to keep doing this to see how long you will argue with a man who can speak 100 times louder than you. I bet you are sociology grad students; only an overdeveloped sense of justice can create this kind of indignation."

A few of them actually chuckled, and one girl nodded her head—I WAS RIGHT! Three of them, including the supermad dude, were soc grad students! And of course, this just made him madder.

There is nothing funnier than a disproportionate display of inappropriate and overwrought anger. You know, when someone really fucking loses their cool and completely explodes over something small? To me, that is the height of comedy, and I was determined to make this dude flip his shit.

Tucker "Oh, this is just awesome. Define 'post-structuralist' for me."

He actually started to define it! Like an idiot I laughed instead of letting him finish, and he immediately realized the joke was on him. Fortunately, all of us laughing at him must have taken him to his breaking point, because he walked a few steps up the hill and, shaking with anger, busted out this unforgettable quote:

SociologyNerd "'*Against stupidity, the gods themselves contend in vain!*' . . . Friedrich von Schiller!"

Tucker "HAHAHAHAHAH! Did you just quote a German philosopher at me? You're standing in mud and piss at 2am, and you just quoted a German philosopher at me?"

SlingBlade "I think he's calling you out."

Tucker "OK, I can play this game too. '*Stop ya cryin' heifer, I don't need all dat!*' . . . Mystikal!"

SociologyNerd "'*Wise men talk because they have something to say; fools, because they have to say something*' . . . Plato!"

I can quote rap lyrics until the sun comes up. But instead, I opted to come over the top and play the nerd trump card on him:

Tucker "Let's settle this once and for all. I'll give you the chance to save Tent City. Throw something at me—anything you want—and if you DON'T throw like a girl, I'll leave right now. I swear on my bullhorn."

The Sociology Nerd paused, thought about it, got a look of unbridled hatred on his face, adjusted his glasses, and stormed off in a huff.

SlingBlade "HAHAHAHAHHHAHA!!! IT'S LIKE LITTLE LEAGUE ALL OVER AGAIN!"
Tucker "You can run away to your burlap sack, but it won't save you from my bullhorn! I am the ruler of Tent City!"

All of the nerds got mad, but their anger never went beyond passive-aggressive complaining. People came and went, some people tried to yell over us, some tried pleading, some tried reasoning, and some just threw things (all like girls).

By about 3am, we'd woken up and pissed off enough people that something resembling a mob had assembled. But they STILL wouldn't do anything other than mill around and be angry. One tool in particular was fed up.

Tool "If we come up there, you're through!"

Unlike this bald-headed tool, I knew my Greek history, so I said the same thing to him that the Spartans said to Philip of Macedon when he sent them a message saying, "If I enter Laconia, I will level Sparta to the ground."

Tucker "If."
Tool "Yeah, IF, buddy, IF!"

It's frustrating when you make a smart joke, and even a nerd doesn't get it. OK, fine, let's see if he can detect condescension:

Tucker [*in baby voice*] "Who's dat widdle guy down dere making all dat big noise? He's jus so leetle! Coochie-coochie-cooo!"

That did it. Four of them got up their courage and ran up the hill. I know the one dude had just "threatened" me, but in the moment, it honestly didn't even occur to me that they would try to get physical. These grad students had taken our relentless mocking for hours because they were pussies. I mean, pussies *are* pussies—it's not just a word.

When they got to the top of the hill, they saw all my friends behind us that they couldn't see from down below, and they kinda stopped and milled around for a second, unsure of what to do. You know that scene in *Braveheart* where the two guys pretend to be lost so they can get the English to chase them, and the English take the bait, only to run into a huge group of Scots over the hill, and they become the prey? It was like that. Except with nerds.

Seeing their body language completely change, I figured this out . . . but was in such disbelief, I put the bullhorn down for a second:

Tucker "Wait . . . did you storm up here . . . thinking we'd run off?"

The embarrassed silence was all the confirmation I needed.

SlingBlade "HAHAHAHAHAHHAHAHHAHHAHHHAHAH! Oh my God, that's so precious!"

I fucking lit them up:

Tucker "WHAT ARE YOU GOING TO DO??? NOTHING!! YOU'RE GOING BACK DOWN TO YOUR MUDDY GHETTO! YOU CAN'T BEAT ME! I HAVE A BULLHORN, AND YOU HAVE NOTHING, BECAUSE I AM SMART AND YOU ARE STUPID!

NOW GET THE FUCK OFF MY HILL, YOU FUCKING PUSSIES!"

They milled around for a second more, then walked back down the hill. I don't know if I've ever felt more like a real warrior in my life.

Tucker "TENT CITY, YOUR PITIFUL ASSAULT HAS BEEN REPELLED! I AM YOUR CONQUERER AND YOU ARE ALL MY SUBJECTS! BOW BEFORE ME!!"

[*to SlingBlade*] "This is so awesome! This must be like what Alexander the Great or Genghis Khan felt like!"

SlingBlade "Jesus Christ, you are delusional."

Tucker "To be the man, you gotta beat the man! WOOOOOOOOO! And at Campout, I'M THE MAN! WOOOOOOOOO!"

I proclaimed sovereignty over Tent City for another ten minutes in various different ways, and after vowing to return the next day to continue my rule, we went to bed. After twelve hours of dedicated drinking, we'd finally hit our wall.

The Next Day

We didn't wake up until around 2pm. Once we beat back our hangovers with a 12 pack, SlingBlade came upon this one RV with an awesome spread of food—not just cheap hot dogs and sausages, they had gourmet shit. Judging by the quality and quantity, they were those rare type of grad students who actually had real money of their own, not just government loans. This can mean only one thing: business school tools.

In order to go to business school, you have to have worked for a few years and been good at it, so most of them have money saved. As a result, they not only have cooler stuff than the rest of us, they think they are better'n everyone. I decide to fix that for them.

I moseyed over, grabbed one of their bottles of wine, and started chugging it. A girl gasped out loud.

Tucker "Well, I'm sorry, your highness, but I happen to think wine tastes better out of a bottle!"

The entire group looked at me like I had just dropped a steamer in their shrimp platter, except one girl who laughed, so I talked to her.

FunGirl "So you're the bullhorn guys? I heard them planning your demise this morning in Tent City."
Tucker "I will crush their puny rebellion. Blood alone moves the wheels of history!"

As I housed their food and hit on the cute girl, SlingBlade tried to run interference before our inevitable eviction, but one bitchy girl was quite persistent:

BitchyGirl "Your friend brought a bullhorn to Campout? I mean, who does he think he is?"
SlingBlade "You must be lucky enough to not have met Tucker."
BitchyGirl "Why is he drinking our wine? And eating my pâté?"
SlingBlade "He has what the DSM IV refers to as Narcissistic Personality Disorder. Also, I believe that he is out of beer."

I think the fact that I was flirting with her friend actually pissed her off more than me drinking the wine and eating her goose liver. She was the type who would cockblock endangered pandas at the zoo.

BitchyGirl "Can I ask you a question?"
Tucker "If you wonder whether you're fat, you probably are."
BitchyGirl "Uhh . . . no, what I wanted to ask—"
Tucker "Yes, you could stand to lose a few pounds."
BitchyGirl "And you don't think you could stand to drink less?"
Tucker "Daddy drinks because otherwise he can't justify having sex with you."

BitchyGirl "Have sex with you? HA! You wish!"

Tucker "You can pretend you aren't into me to keep up appearances, but you know you're moist right now."

BitchyGirl "UGH! I could not find you more unattractive. You're slurring your speech, you have a shirt on that is two sizes too small, is covered in mustard stains and says FRONT LOADER on it, you reek of cheap beer and sex, and you clearly have a drinking problem."

Tucker "Drinking is a problem only if you're *not* good at it. To me, everything you listed is proof that I am *very* good at it."

BitchyGirl "You disgust me."

Tucker "I will not apologize for being awesome."

At some point we found ourselves at the Porta Potties. SlingBlade went into one, but I had to wait because the other was occupied. He came out laughing.

SlingBlade "I just dropped a deuce that could sink the Titanic."

Tucker [*I was so in shock, I put the bullhorn down*] "You took a dump in a Porta Potty? What is wrong with you?"

SlingBlade "Alcohol has made me impervious to your attempts at shaming."

The guy in my Porta Potty came out. As I opened the door to go in, I recoiled in terror.

Tucker "OHH! That is AWFUL!"

He started walking away, like everything was just fine and dandy.

Tucker "Hey you, come back here. Do you know what you just did in that bathroom?"

Guy "Yeah . . . I uh . . . sorry about that, man."

Tucker "Come here and smell this."

Guy "What?"

Tucker "DO IT NOW!"

Thus is the power and authority of the bullhorn: The guy actually walked back to the Porta Potty and took a sniff.

Guy "Yeah, so?"
Tucker [*angry astonishment*] "Yeah, so? That smell is not [*air quotes*] 'just went to the bathroom.' That is felonious assault on a toilet. You have raped my olfactory senses. Apologize."
Guy "What?"
Tucker "APOLOGIZE RIGHT NOW!"
Guy "OK, fine . . . whatever . . . I'm sorry."

Had we not been drinking for 24 hours straight, and had I not conquered an entire city the night before, I don't think I would have tried this. But the bullhorn had emboldened me:

Tucker "Now apologize to the toilet."
Guy "Dude, what?"
Tucker "Repeat after me: 'I am very sorry and greatly embarrassed that my excretory system could produce such a smell. I promise to eat more bran to prevent such things in the future.'"
Guy "Are you nuts?"
Tucker "I SAID DO IT!"

I was pretty much joking with the guy and fully expected him either to walk off or punch me in the face. There was no legitimate reason to obey me. I was just some drunk idiot yelling at him with a bullhorn . . . but he gave in and basically said it. After he left, I stood there in mild shock.

Tucker "Did I really just use the bullhorn to make a dude apologize . . . to a Porta Potty . . . for taking a smelly dump?"
SlingBlade "That thing is too powerful. It's like the One Ring that rules them all. After Campout, we have to find a volcano and throw it in."
Tucker "Let's make Hate do it. He hates the bullhorn, plus he's short like a Hobbit."
SlingBlade "Credit can go with him. He's a Jew, like Gollum."

We chilled the rest of the afternoon and evening, planning how we would fuck with Tent City again that night. But this time, the nerds had come prepared. They must have had spies watching us, because before we even got to the ridge to start our second assault on Tent City, they were standing there with a Duke cop. Still drunk on alcohol and the testosterone rush of the previous night, I decided to handle this the logical way, as I was Lord Tucker Max, Tent City Conqueror:

Tucker "What's the problem, Officer?"
DukeCop "You need to stop using the bullhorn."
Tucker "What? Why?"
DukeCop "The proper response to a lawful order is not 'Why?' "
Tucker "But Officer, I don't think you understand," [*I hold it in front of his face as if he hadn't seen it yet*] "I have a bullhorn."

You know that look a cop gives you when he's so confused that he doesn't even know how to respond? If you don't know that look, it means you haven't had enough fun in your life. He gave me that look.

DukeCop "You have to stop using the bullhorn for the rest of Campout."
Tucker "Officer, I can't stop. I am the ruler of Tent City!"

It was at this point the cop realized I wasn't crazy or stupid, just really drunk.

DukeCop "You're not in charge, you're not even on the Graduate Council. I am a law enforcement officer, and I am giving you a lawful command. You can obey it, or I can arrest you and confiscate the bullhorn."

I was not prepared for this gambit. I turned to SlingBlade:

Tucker "What do we do?"
SlingBlade "Stop using the bullhorn."
Tucker "Isn't there some way around this?"
SlingBlade "I don't know. I don't take Criminal Procedure until next semester. But I don't think so."

Tucker "Does it matter that he's a campus cop and not a real cop?"
SlingBlade "We're on Duke's campus. He also has a Taser. Taser beats bullhorn."
Tucker "Shit."

On Day 1, I subjugated all of Tent City. On Day 2, I was defeated by a single rent-a-cop.

To fuck with me, SlingBlade took the bullhorn from me and addressed Tent City:

SlingBlade **"You are safe to go back to sleep. Tucker has been bested and the bullhorn problem is taken care of. I repeat, the bullhorn problem has been taken care of."**
DukeCop "Hey! That means you too. NO ONE gets to use it again. If I have to come back, you're all getting arrested."

As I started to go back to my RV, head hung low in shame, I could faintly hear someone yell out from deep within Tent City:

"I guess the man got beat! WOOO!"

Motherfucker. Even ten years later, it still upsets me that my reign as conquerer lasted only a single night. I had so many people left to insult and piss off.

It's OK though, I got the last laugh. In the intervening years, my notoriety has made it so that all those people who were there, when they tell other people where they went to school, invariably have to answer this question, "You went to Duke? Did you know Tucker Max?"

I may have lost the battle, but I won the war.

The Sex Stories, Part 2

I had a section of stories in *I Hope They Serve Beer In Hell* called "The Sex Stories." This is how I introduced them:

> "The pen may be mightier than the sword, but I have found that the vagina is stronger than both. No matter what happens to me, no matter how many girls vomit on me or shit on me or screw me over, I keep hooking up with all kinds of women, seemingly without regard for the repercussions."

Pretty much every word of that still holds true. Here are some more of my funnier short stories that revolve around hooking up:

Whoredentification

Occurred—November 2002

One night out I get drunk and meet this girl. She seems only mildly into me, so I repeatedly tell her she shouldn't flirt with me. Of course she takes the bait, I play even more coy, the whole time we're drinking . . . you know how this ends:

With us eating each other's faces at the bar, while everyone else gets disgusted and leaves.

The rest of the night is a standard drunk blur. I wake up in my bed, sticky and sore, with her next to me. She looked QUITE A BIT better last night. I am honestly baffled as to how a woman can put on 30 pounds in one night of sleep.

I make myself some cereal and realize I can't remember her name at all (granted, it usually doesn't matter to me, but for some reason at the time I really wanted to get her name right). I rack my brain and genius strikes: Check her purse.

I find it on the sofa in the living room. I pull out the wallet, casually look into the side pocket, see $80, consider stealing it, but don't. I feel like taking her money AND her soul is not cool. One or the other.

I pull out her license. Her name is Stacey. Never would have guessed Stacey. Weight, 110? Yeah. During the Reagan administration. And goddamn, she kinda looks hot here. She's the first person I've ever met who looks *better* in her driver's license picture.

I put the wallet back in her purse and go back to eating my cereal and watching Springer. She eventually comes out of my room, looking like she got run over by the cum truck.

Tucker "Clearly *Sleeping Beauty* isn't your favorite fairy tale."
Stacey "You were funnier last night."
Tucker "Well, Stacey, that is one of the main reasons people drink."
Stacey "What? Who is Stacey?"
Tucker "Uhhh . . . that would be you. Stacey."
Stacey "My name is NOT Stacey!"
Tucker "OK . . . and my name isn't Tucker Max."
Stacey "Uhhh . . . Yes, it is. You showed me your stupid fucking website last night, your name was all over it."
Tucker "Well, Stacey is the name on your driver's license."

She looks at me with an expression that can only be described as "utter contempt." She walks into my room and from next to my bed, picks up a completely different purse, one I had not seen, digs through it, finds her wallet, and throws a driver's license at me. The name on the license is Jennifer, and the picture looks like the angry Yeti standing in front of me. I'm so confused.

Tucker "Well, who the fuck is Stacey?"
Jennifer "You tell me, asshole!"

I knew I shouldn't say this. It was mean . . . but she is being such a bitch, I just couldn't help it. Plus, she wasn't very attractive.

Tucker "I don't know, but her purse is on the sofa. Can you send her over? Because she's a lot hotter than you."

This might be why I always have to find new girls to fuck.

She dresses quickly. The whole situation is awkward and confusing, even for me. Well, confusing more than awkward, because I don't actually give a fuck. But seriously, why is there another purse in my apartment, and whose driver's license is it?

Oh my God.

I call TheRoommate. I hear his cell ringing in his bedroom. He answers in a groggy voice.

TheRoommate "What's up?"
Tucker "Dude, did you hook up last night?"
TheRoommate "Yeah."
Tucker "Oh shit! Dude, why did you do that to me? You NEVER bring girls home."

I explain to him what happened, but instead of laughing, his first question shows how well he knows me:

TheRoommate "Did you take any money out of her purse?"

Reduce, Recycle, Reuse

Occurred—January 2003

When I first moved to Chicago, it was to be a writer, so I refused to use my law degree to get a "real" job. I knew it would pay so much that it'd make me complacent and drain my creative energy. If I was going to become a writer, I was going to do it full-time. Anything else was a distraction from my goal, and a compromise I was unwilling to make.

That's great in theory, but in practice, not making any money means that at some point you can't afford to buy food. That's pretty bad. Then you don't have enough to buy alcohol. That's really bad. But when you don't have enough money to even go to $1 beer night, it's an emergency.

To solve this problem, I got a job with Princeton Review teaching the LSAT. The LSAT is the admissions test for law school, and is very difficult for most people. I on the other hand fucked that test so hard, Duke gave me an academic scholarship. Because of my high score, Princeton Review paid me $21 an hour to teach other people how to take it. I taught about 15 hours per week, which was barely enough to pay for my rent and beer, but I didn't have to go to an office or really even have a boss, so it wasn't a soulless job that sucked the life out of me, and it gave me time to write.

There was another benefit I hadn't anticipated to teaching that class: girls. Lots of cute girls want to go to law school. And most of them need help on their LSAT. I can do that. I can also have sex with them.

One of these girls was in my Oak Park class. She was Chicago-girl attractive—great face, big ass—a year out of college, and was way too impressed with my law school résumé. I guess she didn't mind the fact that I didn't have a real job or even enough money to pay for both food AND beer in the same week. She always stayed after class for help, and one day I suggested we go to a bar for further "instruction." Four hours later, we closed the bar, having talked about LSAT stuff for all of two minutes. Gotta love alcohol and sex hormones.

We went back to her place, pretty far out in the Chicago suburbs. It came time to fuck, I pulled a condom out of my backpack, put it on, and we went at it. It was awesome, some of the best sex I'd had in my life to that point. For whatever reason, this girl and I just clicked physically, so we both wanted to fuck again right away.

I started searching through my backpack and realized I was out of condoms. She didn't have any either, which meant I had to go out and buy some.

As annoying as it is to get dressed and go out in the cold after you've had sex, that wasn't my biggest problem. Here's the thing: like I already said, when I first put up my site and started writing full-time, I was poor. Not regular I-can't-afford-steak poor, I mean more like Bangladeshi slumdog poor. It's not a big deal now that I'm rich—I can even laugh about it in retrospect—but when it was going on, it really sucked. There were many days in 2002 and 2003 where I ate nothing but ramen . . . that I had stolen from my roommate. And other days that, had I not been really good with women and always had girls around who were willing to take me out or cook me dinner or buy me food, I might not have eaten at all. Seriously, I was that poor.

The truth isn't that I wouldn't go *get* more condoms: I was too poor to *buy* condoms. If you've ever been poor, you know what it's like to be at a 7-Eleven and swipe your debit card, not sure that a $3.25 charge will go through. I did not want to deal with that.

She was a spoiled daddy's girl, so she wouldn't go herself. I tried to get her to go with me, thinking I could play the I-left-my-wallet-at-your-place game, but she was too spoiled even to leave her house. I couldn't ask her for money, because being that poor is embarrassing. Great. I looked for another solution.

Tucker "Can't we just fuck anyway? I mean, what are the chances you'll get pregnant?"
Girl "NO! Seriously, I had my period two weeks ago."
Tucker "So?"
Girl "Don't you know anything about women? I'm at my fertility peak right

now. These are the three days I am MOST likely to get pregnant. I really want to have sex again, but we CAN'T have sex without a condom."

Tucker "What if I pull out?"

Girl "Pull and pray is not happening. I'm not on birth control, and I won't have an abortion."

Well, this fucking sucks. I rack my brain trying to think of something to do. I momentarily consider asking to use her car because there might be spare change in there. I ponder what it would take to steal money from her purse . . . when I look down and saw my used condom on the floor.

Tucker "Latex is pretty resilient, isn't it?"

Girl "What?"

Tucker "Hold on."

I go to the bathroom, turn on the faucet . . . and put the condom under it, careful to not tear the latex as I wash it out.

It was 3am, and there I was, a grown man washing out a used condom in a bathroom sink . . . because I was too poor to buy a new one. As I rolled up the wet condom to put it back on, I thought to myself: I had better end up making it as a writer, because this is about as bad as it gets.

She laughed at my ingenuity, inspected it, and gave it the thumbs-up, so we had sex. I pulled out as I came, just in case, but the condom was still there, unbroken, and caught my load without problem.

Apparently, this is a big no-no with a condom. From what I have been told since, the likelihood of a condom breaking on a second use is like 500% higher or something. Whoops. Oh well, to paraphrase Hunter S. Thompson talking about drugs and alcohol:

"I wouldn't necessarily recommend it for anyone else, but it worked for me."

The Shittiest Hookup Ever

Occurred—June 2003

This girl emailed me because she liked my site, and once we got together, the conversation eventually turned to the two topics that all my conversations are about: me and sex.

She told me she wasn't there to hook up—in fact, she'd been with only two guys in her life. This was not because she didn't like hooking up but rather because she was afraid of hooking up. Apparently, she had a very weak immune system, took forever to get over a sickness, and claimed that a VD could possibly kill her. Not just something like AIDS, mind you, which can kill anyone except Magic Johnson, but shit like genital herpes or chlamydia could knock her off.

I told her to immediately get away from me. I am almost certainly a supercarrier and she shouldn't even touch me, much less fuck me. I went so far as to tell her that I wouldn't hook up with her even if she wanted it, because even though every test I have ever taken has come back clean, I can't have it on my conscience that I killed a girl by giving her some random VD that hadn't been discovered yet.

I was kidding of course, but it worked: She ended up coming home with me. The harder you push them away, the more desperately they want in.

We started hooking up, she took off my clothes and her top, but refused to remove her jeans. Wait, what?

She said she had some injury or something, but she wouldn't elaborate on what it was or why it precluded her from removing her pants. She did have a bandage on her hip and I could sort of see it sticking out of her jeans, so I just let it go at first.

We made out some more and she got more into it. After her initial reticence, she decided she did want to have sex with me, despite her "injury" and risk of death from HPV. OK, condoms work great, let's get to the fucking, right?

Is it ever that easy for me? Well, yeah, most of the time it is . . . but I wouldn't write a story about it if it was just normal sex.

As she took off her pants, she decided that this was the appropriate time to let me in on a little issue she had. She began by telling me that she had Crohn's disease. I told her that a friend of mine has it so I knew what it was (FYI, a degenerative disease of the colon). Well, hers was pretty advanced. She kept dancing around the issue until, all of a sudden, it hit me:

Tucker "That's not a bandage on your hip is it? OH. MY. GOD!"

Great Holy Mother of Jesus, this girl had a fucking colostomy bag.

A COLOSTOMY BAG. ON HER HIP.

[In case you are lost, let me introduce you to the Webster's Medical Dictionary definition of colostomy bag: "A bag worn over an artificial anus to collect feces."]

About three inches to the left of her belly button a tube stuck out of a small hole and emptied into a bag—about the size of a small Ziploc sandwich bag—that was bandaged to her hip. I shit you not, there was a BAG FULL OF POOP—LITERALLY HUMAN SHIT—TAPED TO HER HIP.

This was quite the shock for me. I tried to be cool about it. I told her it was no big deal, that everyone has issues, hers just happened to be more out in the open than most, and that I would be supportive . . . all right, who am I bullshitting? I laughed like a fucking hyena, right in her face.

I mean, come on, the girl had a bag of crap on her hip, like some sort of old Western shitslinger. What do you want from me? Caring? Compassion? Sorry, we're sold out. I immediately asked the first thing that came to my mind:

Tucker "So if you shit in a bag, can we have butt sex and not have to worry about getting crap on my penis?"
Girl "Not exactly. My asshole has been sewn shut."
Tucker "GET THE FUCK OUT! YOUR ASSHOLE HAS BEEN SEWN SHUT?"
Girl "Uh, yeah."
Tucker "I want to see, right now."

I rolled her over and stuck my finger down there. Lo and behold, THERE WAS NO ASSHOLE. It was just all crack, from top to bottom!

She told me that since she never used it, her asshole was sewn shut to prevent infection. I couldn't hold off anymore. Sex be damned, there were jokes to be made:

Tucker "So I guess opinions aren't like assholes, at least not for you?"
Girl "Very funny."
Tucker "If I go too hard, could I fuck your shit right into that bag. I could literally fuck the shit out of you couldn't I?"
Girl "Tucker . . ."
Tucker "What happens if I'm too vigorous? Will the shit hit the fan?"
Girl "Well . . ."
Tucker "You're only a two-holer! I couldn't even three-hole you if I tried!"

She explained that as long as she was careful, she could do anything any other girl could do—except shit out of her asshole, of course. Not wanting to lose the opportunity to mark a new type of handicap off my Sexual To-Do List, I coaxed her back into a romantic mood. Just as we started hooking up again, she whispered:

"Be gentle, you don't want this thing to break."

Tucker and His First MILF

Occurred—April 2002

At this point, the majority of my friends are married. Most of their weddings were in places like Vegas or the Outer Banks. One of my boys decided to buck the trend and get hitched in Akron, Ohio. Really. If marriage is hell, I guess he figured it was fitting to have the ceremony at its gates.

He's a college friend, so I meet up the day before the wedding with my other college buddies and we head out to find the "nightlife" in Akron. What an awful experience. It was like looking for a clean spot in a dirty ass. Leaving some bar, an attractive girl with two other girls and a guy walk by me. I give it a shot:

Tucker "You want to go to a wedding with me tomorrow?"
Girl [*stops, looks me up and down*] "Maybe. Where are you going right now?"
Tucker "Wherever you are."
Girl "You can come with us." [*motions to her friends getting into a taxi*] "We're going to get something to eat."
Tucker "Don't offer if you're not serious."
Girl "I'm very serious. Come with me."

I wish I could bottle the seductive look she gave me so I could sniff it when I jack off.

I hop into the car with them, don't even say good-bye to my friends, and head off. We go to some shithole bar/restaurant, but actually have a great time. The girl who invited me is very into me, and I've got the perfect amount of alcohol in me, so I'm lighting up the table with jokes about any and everything: our obviously coked-out waitress, the Akron nightlife, and the other single girl at the table, who told me, and I quote, "My boyfriend is with his wife tonight."

Eating time over, we go back to her place, she puts on Indigo Girls or something, lights about six candles, and we have all kinds of great sex.

The next morning, I wake up at 9am and call one of my college buddies to find out when and where the pre-wedding golf game is supposed to be that morning. He gives me directions, and I wake the woman up to drive me there. As she is getting ready, she asks me to write down my number so she can call me that night to meet up again.

I cannot find a pen in her room, so I venture out to the other rooms on the top floor. No pens, but the rooms are filled with toys, coloring books, very small beds, Powerpuff curtains . . . oh no.

Tucker "Do you have kids?"
MILF "Yes, but they're with their dad this weekend."

Relieved, I search the rest of the house and cannot, for the life of me, find anything normal to write with.

I end up writing my number on a piece of yellow construction paper . . . with a red crayon. That I found in her daughter's room. So I could fuck her mommy again that night, in the butt.

Sometimes I disgust even myself.

Not Another Teen Hookup

Occurred—January 2005

One of my teenage fuck buddies (yes, she was 18) calls me at 1am:

Girl "I'm at a party and it's lame and I'm baked and my genitals are burning for sex. Can I come over?"

The only thing that shocks me about this is that she uses the voice line instead of texting. When she gets to my place I'm busy with something important, so I make her wait.

Girl "UH! Come on, let's fuck."
Tucker "Not until this is over."
Girl "This is *IRON CHEF*?! WHO CARES? I am offering you PUSSY!"
Tucker "I know. And your pussy will wait. Chairman Kaga doesn't wait for shit. The man takes bites out of raw peppers for fuck's sake."

She huffs and pouts. And waits. The funny thing is that I had a TiVo at the time, but fuck her if she can't take a joke. Teenage girls need to learn patience, anyway.

We eventually have sex and it is great—for me, because I cum. Afterward she is still baked and wants to hang out and talk or eat Sour Patch Kids or whatever it is young stoner girls do. I don't. I want to go to sleep. She keeps annoying me.

Tucker "You need to shut up before I call your parents and tell them that you just fucked a 28 year old."
Girl "You know, you don't have a big dick, so I thought you'd make up for it by being good in bed. You aren't good in bed, so I thought you'd make

up for it by being a nice person. You aren't a nice person, so I don't think there is any reason for me to hang out with you."

Tucker "AAHHAHAHAHAHAHAHA. Awesome! That means you can go. Bye."

Girl [*after a long pause*] "Uh . . . that did not go the way I intended."

Tucker "It never will. You aren't as smart as me. Just admit defeat and submit."

Burn, Baby, Burn!

Occurred—March 2005

When I was living in Chicago, this one girl was so into me she paid for my ticket to come see her in Atlanta for a weekend. She was a cute Southern girl but probably needed to realize that her metabolism wasn't the same as in college and she couldn't drink five nights a week anymore. But, hey—free trip to Atlanta!

She picked me up outside security at Hartsfield, holding a sign that said SEXIEST MAN ON EARTH. When we got to her car, she threw me the keys.

Tucker "You want me to drive?"

Girl "Well, I have something for you, and I can't give it to you if I have to focus on driving."

I've seen this movie many times before, but it's a classic, and very rewatchable.

We weren't even out of the parking structure before she has her face in my crotch. The best part was that she didn't stop when I pulled up to the pay booth. The second-best part was the lady working the booth glanced down, barely raised an eyebrow, and calmly gave me my change. Nothing shocks old black women.

I should have told her that I hadn't showered in like two days (long story) and had swamp ass from sitting in a middle seat on a hot plane for three hours, but whatever. You play crotch roulette, you're gonna hit double zero once in a while.

We get on the highway to where she lives to the north of downtown, and it's rush hour on a Friday. If you know anything about Atlanta, you are laughing right now. If you don't, let me explain: The I-75/85 corridor runs through the middle of Atlanta. Without traffic, it's a 15 minute drive across the city. It's NEVER without traffic. In fact, that section of road has some of the heaviest and most persistent traffic in America.

I'm not a patient driver. I could give you a hundred examples of my road rage, but perhaps the most telling is that on a weekly basis, my dog crawls to the back of my SUV, cowers and gives me her pitiful face, because she thinks my yelling at the idiot drivers is directed at her. Poor Murph.

So here I am, navigating the most aggravating stretch of road in America, getting a nice relaxing blowjob. Who is going to win this battle? Road or Head? It's like Road Head Thunderdome: TWO MEN ENTER, ONE MAN LEAVES!

Start-and-stop traffic at 5 miles per hour on a 12 lane highway was hard enough. Being cut off by shithead drivers multiple times made it much harder. Still, I maintained my calm. But the accident that was already off to the side, yet still causing delays because ALL THOSE FUCKING RUBBERNECKERS WON'T JUST FUCKING DRIVE... that was too much for me. The road won. Despite the efforts of the hardworking lips on my dick, I got so angry I forgot I was getting road head.

I gunned the accelerator and swerved violently to get around the rubbernecker in front of me. As I did this, I lurched forward in the seat, pushing the girls' face into the steering wheel as I yanked on it, and I heard an awful screeching squeak—sort of like the sound flesh makes when rubbed against hard plastic.

Girl "OWWW! That hurt!"

She popped up from my lap, and I started laughing so hard, I forgot my road rage.

Girl "What's so funny!?!"

I managed to point to it in between fits of laughter, and she twisted the rearview mirror so she could see herself.

Girl "Oh my God! We are supposed to go out with my friends!"

On her right cheekbone was a huge, shiny red friction burn.

It was bad. Like, so bad her concealer didn't even work. The next morning it had a nasty yellow scab on it, like a severe rug burn. She was so distressed about this we stayed in all weekend.

Good thing, too. She was much chunkier than the pics she sent me, which is fine for fucking in private, but not so much for going out in public.

I'M A ZIT, GET IT?

Occurred—July 2005

One time in Chicago, I was at a bar watching some complete tool try to hit on a cute girl. He could not have been any more of a douche if his chest cavity was filled with vinegar and had a plastic nozzle sticking out of his head. He was like an Axe Body Spray commercial, but without the plot or character development. It was obvious she was not into him, so I tried to see if I could flip his failure into my success.

Tucker "Hey, dude, I have a bet with my friend. Could you help me out?"
Douche "Uh, yeah, I guess."
Tucker "Exactly how many shirtless pics do you have on your MySpace page? The over/under is 10."

She cracked up laughing. I went in for the kill.

Tucker "Don't worry about it dude, I'm sure you'll make a Porsche dealership very happy when you turn 40."

I stood between him and her, smiled at her, and ordered beers for her and myself.

Tucker "Sorry, you might be disappointed by me. I don't think I have his game."
Girl "You're doing OK so far."

He left, and it was pretty much cruise control from there. A few hours of drinking, a few goofy jokes ("I like it when girls say harder, but not when they say deeper" and "I had a dream that I was in a horrific plane crash, and when I woke up I had an erection"), and we were back at my place.

We started making out, then foreplay, then got down to business. She told me she likes it from behind, so I flipped her over and slid it in. As I was fucking her doggy-style, I reached down to grab her hair—for romance and leverage—and as I did so, I looked down at her back and noticed something so shocking it almost took my breath away:

Right there, in the middle of her back, was the biggest zit I'd ever seen in my life.

It was astonishing. Like looking at the snow-capped peak of Mount Fuji from a plane. I couldn't get over it. I was so distracted by the fact that this cute, otherwise clear-skinned girl had this single, massive carbuncle on her back, I actually forgot I was fucking her.

Girl "Tucker, are you OK? Why'd you stop?"
Tucker "Oh, sorry. I was . . . uh . . . thinking about . . . um . . . butterflies?"

She kinda made this weird face so I pushed her head back down, thrust myself back into her, and refocused on fucking.

I kept pushing into her and tried to avoid it, but I just could not get this epic boil out of my mind. I looked around the room for anything else I could focus on, but sadly, I am something of an ascetic in terms of home decoration, and there was literally nothing else in my room to distract me. Trying to count the number of kernels on a popcorn ceiling can keep you occupied for only so long. And it could not compete with the siren's call beckoning my eyes back to that cyst's craggy shoals.

Eventually, I could resist no longer. I looked down, and it was still there—staring at me, mocking me, daring me to have the courage to do what must be done. I held off as long as I could. I even tried to make myself cum so I could get away from it, but I didn't have the dick discipline to pull it off.

I finally just said fuck it and gave in. Knowing I would have only one shot at this, I grabbed the zit and squeezed with all my might.

Girl "OW! That hurts!"

I squeezed the zit so hard, and there was so much pus, it exploded out with such force that the pus HIT ME IN THE CHEST!!

Here's the strangest thing: I wasn't grossed out. At all.

In fact, this weird sense of accomplishment and satisfaction came over me, like I had just set right a grave wrong. That zit had been camping out on her back, fucking up the property values for all the nice clean pores around it, stealing her body's resources to make pus, and I just broke up its criminal enterprise. I had done a legitimately good deed and I was kinda proud of myself.

And nothing was going to convince me otherwise, not even her histrionic yelling.

Head Doctor

Occurred—April 2007

When I lived in NYC, I came home from a night of drinking and called one of my semi-regular booty calls. I didn't really like her personality, but it was late and I was horny . . . so, you know.

She was asleep, but I convinced her to come over by telling her something romantic like, "You're my number one dick sucker." I started watching TV while I waited, but the liquor was strong, and I was tired . . . fading, fading, fading.

I woke up the next morning to 8 new messages on my voice mail:

> Message 1, 3:21am [*excited*]: "Tucker, I'm downstairs, come down."
>
> Message 2, 3:25am [*anxious*]: "Tucker, I'm here! This isn't funny, you need to come down here right now, hurry up, it's cold and rainy!"
>
> Message 3, 3:29am [*angry*]: "I hate you so much. Answer the fucking door, you asshole. I know you're there, stop playing this stupid game with me! Come down here and get me!"
>
> Message 4, 3:35am [*confused*]: "I cannot believe you are doing this to me. I don't know what I did or why you are acting like this. Tucker, please, PLEASE just answer the door. It's cold and raining, this isn't funny anymore, please just come down and get me, I'm sorry I yelled, but just come get me."
>
> Message 5, 3:39am [*exasperated*]: "YOU FUCKING ASSHOLE! I spent the last cash I had on the cab coming over

here, now I have to walk back home IN THE FUCKING RAIN. You don't even care, you fucking asshole, I cannot believe you are fucking doing this. I HATE YOU!"

Message 6, 3:45am [*serious anger*]: "I am completely disgusted with you. I can't believe you would do this to me. I cannot believe it. You are such a fucking prick. I am so fucking pissed off right now. I hate you so fucking much."

Message 7, 4:08am [*sobbing*]: "Why would you do this, Tucker? What did I do? Why would you be so mean to me? I love you so much, and you treat me like this? Why? How could you do this to me? I just . . . I can't understand it at all."

Message 8, 4:19am [*hurt*]: "I'm back home. I don't know what happened or why you did that. I just wish you had let me in. Well . . . call me tomorrow I guess, I still want to see you."

I called her the next day. Normally, I wouldn't want to deal with all of this drama, but she is a Head Doctor. She has honed her craft to an art form, and one does not discard a dick-sucking artist lightly. Take note, ladies.

Earth First

Occurred—April 2010

As I was finishing this book, I lived in Austin, Texas (I still live there, actually), and one of the girls I was fucking was really sweet and nice but ridiculously crunchy. She liked to say she was "environmentally conscious." OK honey, fine, but when you're recycling your own poop to use as fertilizer in your garden, that crosses the line from "environmentalist" to "crazy hippie." Fortunately she was hot and fun (and she introduced me to the best new liquor I've had in ten years, Deep Eddy Sweet Tea Vodka), so I kept fucking her.

To her, I was like her naughty vacation sex. All her friends hated me, so by being with me she felt like she was transgressing. Of course, this didn't bother me at all, because her friends were those annoying pretentious fucks who think that being vegan makes them better than everyone else. Tell it to the cow who died for the leather seats in your Lexus, you fucking hypocrite. At least I have enough respect for the animal to eat the resulting ribeyes.

She always wanted me to go with her on hikes to see some collection of rocks or look at some old tree. Normally, I would rather jump ass-first into a dildo factory than do that shit, but my dog Murph loves hiking, so I would bring my goofy pup and go with her.

One day she took me to some park that must have been extra full of nature or something, because she was super horny. I'm always horny, so once we got a little ways down the trail, I grabbed her, pulled her about two feet off the trail—you know, for privacy—and started to take her pants off.

EarthGirl "No, we can't, I'm on my period."
Tucker "So? Shouldn't you be into that? It's natural and shit."
EarthGirl "No! That's gross!"

I just pushed her head down to my crotch, and since she loved that, we were on. The key to being good at fellatio is not skill; anyone can watch a decent porn and figure out the proper technique. The key is enthusiasm, and this girl LOVED sucking my dick. As she got more into it, she adjusted so that her crotch was on my shin and she could rub her clit back and forth as she sucked me off. This got her more excited, which made her better at head, which turned me on more, and so on, creating this awesome positive-feedback loop. But after about five minutes of this, she'd had enough.

EarthGirl "Bend me over and fuck the shit out of me."

She pushed her shorts to her ankles and started to pull me inside her. She remembered before me:

EarthGirl "Oh, wait."

She pulled out the tampon and flung it on the ground. Thank God; I've already done the "fuck a girl with a tampon inside her" thing. It's not fun.

Tucker "But . . . what about the environment?"

I don't think she was listening to me anymore as she yanked me inside of her. In nature's ultimate bitch fight, Mons Venus trumped Mother Earth.

We finished up and got dressed. She picked up a leaf, found the tampon—the one she pulled out of herself with her pussy blood all over it—wrapped it up in the leaf, then put the period burrito in her pocket.

Tucker "What are you doing?"
EarthGirl "I can't leave that out here."
Tucker "You can't put it in your pocket either. It's a used tampon."
EarthGirl "That's littering!"
Tucker "You're kidding, right? It's just cotton and blood. That's how they made South Carolina!"
EarthGirl "No." [*in her most indignant tone of voice*] "I leave the Earth like I found it."

[*Long pause*]

Tucker "I can't believe I'm fucking you."

The Capitol City Clown Crawl

Occurred—June 2003

I was in Austin for a few months in the middle of 2003. While there, I got an email from a lawyer named J.D. Horne. He invited me to an event called the Capitol City Clown Crawl:

> "Me and 50 of my closest drinking buddies are dressing up as clowns, renting a yellow school bus, and going on a bar crawl. We plan to get drunk, yell at strangers, fuck with an improv comedy troupe, and generally be the most obnoxious clowns possible. You should come."

I could not imagine anything more appealing. I collected a group of friends—Nils, Stydie, and B-Ski—to go with me. We decided the appropriate way to attend this event would be dressed as the most offensive clowns possible.

B-Ski went as Hitler Clown. It was as bad as it sounds. Stydie went as Postal Clown, with toy gun and blood splatters. Nils went as Monsignor Pedophile Clown, complete with purple shirt, priest's collar, a child's T-shirt covered in blood and, tucked into his waistband, a pink insulated lunch bag with BAG OF INDULGENCES written on the outside and condoms and broken glass sloshing around on the inside. And of course, big red clown shoes. I mean, just because he's a pedophile doesn't mean he has no clown pride.

I took a different approach and picked a nonsensical outfit—Lifeguard Clown, complete with floaties. I knew the best way to be offensive is not with an outfit, but with actions, and I could think of no other clown outfit that could justify me carrying the greatest bar crawl accessory ever: my beloved bullhorn (the one I still had from the Duke grad school campout).

We started that fateful day at B-Ski's apartment:

5:00pm: Wake up from hangover nap. Everyone else is still asleep. I gently put the bullhorn in B-Ski's ear, the volume only at 4 (to be nice), "WAKE UP SHITBIRD, WE'RE LATE FOR DRINKING!"

5:01: He puts a pillow over his head. I kick his bed until he takes a swing at me.

5:02: Turn on very loud rap music.

5:04: Neighbor bangs on the wall. I turn it up louder and crack my first beer.

5:06: Neighbor bangs again. I bang on the wall back. "I don't even live here, bitch!"

5:10: Nils, Stydie, and B-Ski wake up. We crack beers and start putting on clown makeup.

5:12: Nils doesn't want to paint a clown face on. He is full of bullshit rationalizations. I ruthlessly question his manhood until he agrees to apply his makeup.

5:15: I have never put makeup on. It's hard. "You assholes are crowding my mirror space. Gimme some room, I keep smearing my blush." Everyone glares at me. I feel like a gay homosexual.

5:16: I shotgun two beers, piss out the bedroom window, catcall passing girls, burp violently, put cage fighting on TV, and play with myself. I feel manly again.

5:30: I remember past bar crawls. It can be difficult to get beer because everyone descends on the bar at once. This worries me greatly. "Nils, do you think they'll have enough alcohol for us?" He is dismissive. "Tucker, we are going to BARS. All they do is serve alcohol."

5:35: I keep imagining 50 clowns clamoring around a single, harried bartender. I crack another beer, "I don't know, man. What if I don't get drunk enough?" B-Ski is dismissive, "Tucker, when have you ever not gotten drunk enough?" I yelp, "Can I really risk it?"

5:45: I am obsessed. I cannot get past this issue. I decide to bring insurance: I fill my CamelBak with ice, a liter of vodka, a quart of Gatorade, and several cans of Red Bull. I call this concoction Tucker Death Mix.

5:50: I take a pull from my CamelBak and choke at its potency. It tastes like bad decisions. It's perfect.

5:52: Walking to the bar, I let everyone else take a pull from my CamelBak. They reel. Nils refuses, "God only knows where your mouth has been." I tell him if God knew where my mouth had been, he'd retire.

6:10: We pass a mother with stroller and child. She seems to think we're real clowns. She tells us her baby loves clowns. Trying to be helpful, I put the bullhorn in the baby's face and ask if it wants "to reach into the Bag of Indulgences?" The baby starts crying. The mom looks worried. I offer to help her make the baby stop. Stydie is skeptical: "Tucker, you don't know what to do with a crying baby." I scoff at him: "Of course I do. You put it in a trash can."

6:13: The mother scampers away. I giggle at myself.

6:30: We arrive at Opal Divine's. There are already a dozen clowns there. "CLOWNS, REJOICE, YOUR SAVIOR IS HERE! WE'RE GOING TO PARTY LIKE RUNAWAY AMISH KIDS ON RUMSPRINGA!!" Everyone cheers. I am the Lord of the Clowns.

6:50: I ask a large female clown if she came as Pregnant Clown or Fat Clown. She gets mad and storms off. "You're never going to find a husband acting like that." I giggle at myself.

6:55: Fat Clown is apparently already married. Her husband is now also mad. He starts throwing around phrases like "kick your ass" and "who do you think you are?" I casually use my bullhorn to inform him who I am—"THE GREATEST CLOWN ALIVE"—when J.D. steps in. "Tucker, let's direct the abuse outside the group. Then we can ALL join in mocking them. No one can withstand 50 clowns laughing at them. We'll break them." I see the wisdom in his logic.

7:15: The clowns get on the bus. This picture was taken:

7:30: We arrive at Hula Hut. I see two of my regular Austin booty calls. Apparently, both work here as hostesses. And both are on shift. At this moment. I decide this is a great omen and tell everyone about how awesome I am.

7:31: Nils is disgusted, "Both those skanks are fucking you? Make sure they wash their hands before they bring us our drinks." I will not stand for disrespect toward my whores. I point out that perhaps Nils is angry because he is too ugly to have even one skank, much less two. Nils gets angry with his ugliness. He misdirects his anger by pushing me very hard.

7:32: There is broken glass all over me, and I am staring up at the roof. From the outside of the window. It takes me a second to realize what happened, then I understand: Nils has pushed me through the window. The fact that it took me a few seconds even to realize this makes me pause. Perhaps I should not drink my alcohol so fast.

7:34: Nils is dumbfounded by his strength: "Sorry, I didn't mean to do that." The taller of the two girls I'm fucking comes running over to help me. The shorter one stands there, shaking her head in dismay. The taller one is now promoted to FuckBuddy #1.

7:35: As new FuckBuddy #1 tends to my wounds, Nils writes out all his information so the manager can send him the bill for a new window.

7:40: I look at what he is writing. His name is not Larry Ellison. I am confused. Nils whispers, "This is my fake ID from college. It still comes in handy." Nils is a genius.

7:50: Everyone in the bar thinks our clown pub crawl is the coolest thing ever. They are correct. They buy us rounds of shots and toast us. I steal someone else's shot and do it along with mine as they toast me (and the other clowns too, I guess).

8:00: The girl whose shot I stole is mad at me for some reason. She has a lazy eye. It mesmerizes me. I focus all my attention on it. I ask her if she knows her eyeball is off center. She seems annoyed. I ask her why it's like that. Her good eye glares at me. I suggest that perhaps it's trying to escape from her face. She leaves. I giggle at myself.

8:08: A woman comes over and sighs loudly, fishing for attention. She is ugly. I don't give a fuck what's wrong with ugly girls.

8:10: UglySigher loudly tells me I am not as cool as I think I am. I correct her mistake: "I am awesome. Some people may disagree. Those people are wrong and/or queer." She is stumped by my impeccable logic.

8:12: She recovers and starts talking about more things I don't care about, like "respect" and "decency." I notice her sweatshirt. "Is that the bullshit they taught you at Texas State? Is that even a real school? Why'd you go there, couldn't get into the University of Phoenix?" UglySigher angrily lectures me about pointing out the flaws of others. She tells me that people who live in glass houses should not throw stones. I tell her they should also not use the bathroom. She tells me I am missing the point. I tell her she is a pompous cunt. She is aghast. I make a concession, "Maybe we're both right."

8:20: Management asks the clowns to leave. Because of me. Apparently breaking windows is OK, but refusing to put up with sanctimony from an ugly fat bitch is not.

8:21: As we walk out, I hear someone say, "Those clowns are jerks." I beam with pride.

8:32: We get to the next bar. It is a dive bar, full of old people.

8:35: Old people aren't impressed by clowns. This angers me. I use the bullhorn to loudly inform them that clowns are the greatest drinkers on earth, way better than crusty, decrepit old people. They refute this claim. I question their sexual preferences. They seem confused. I accuse them of enjoying farm animals in a nontraditional manner. Their anger suggests my social artillery strike has hit their private shame.

8:40: I notice one old man hunched over his drink, shaking. Stydie suggests he might be afraid of clowns. Stydie thinks we should leave him alone. "No Stydie, when someone is upset, the best thing to do is to yell at them until they come out of it. Tears mean the sadness is leaving."

8:45: I ask the old man if he is afraid of clowns. He nods. "HEY, EVERYONE COME OVER HERE. THIS GUY IS AFRAID OF CLOWNS!!" 50 clowns walk over to greet him.

8:50: The old man's knuckles are white around his pint glass. His shaking has become alarming. He is about to snap. I think maybe provoking him was a bad choice.

8:52: One girl does not perceive the signs of danger. She gets very close and asks him how he could hate her. He throws his drink in her face and pushes her down.

8:53: At first I am mad at him. He hurt a clown. Then I see that she is a titless hippie clown. I decide she deserved it.

8:55: We decide it is time to leave the bar. The bartender wants me to settle the tab. "I don't have any money. I'm a clown." He gets angry. I tell him I'll be right back with his money.

8:56: I walk through the kitchen, out the back door, around the building, and get back on the bus. I'm sneaky.

9:00: The CamelBak is empty. If I were sober, I would think that drinking a liter of vodka in three hours was a bad idea. Thankfully, drinking a liter of vodka in three hours means I am no longer able to think.

9:20: We arrive at the next bar. I am slow off the bus and end up behind 50 clowns at the bar. I decide to be a good clown and wait patiently for my beer.

9:21: I am still waiting patiently for my beer.

9:22: I am waiting for my beer.

9:24: I am not happy.

9:25: I scream across the bar, "NILS, YOU ASSHOLE, I TOLD YOU THIS WOULD HAPPEN!"

9:30: The call comes for everyone to get back on the bus. I am enraged at the slow service from the bartenders and curse them abusively, loudly informing them that they are incompetent retards.

9:33: They *are* competent at calling the large bouncer. I quickly scurry away.

9:34: I scurried the wrong way. There is a door, but it won't open. The bouncer is coming, and he is bringing an ass-whooping with him. I kick the door until it crashes to the ground, landing in a shitheap of wood and glass. The fire alarm goes off. Everyone panics. I run to the bus, giggling to myself.

9:35: I am the last clown on the bus. I tell everyone why I'm late. They think I may have gone overboard with the door. I think they don't understand the context of the situation.

9:45: We are dropped off at the next bar. I can feel the six-pack of beer and liter of vodka sloshing around in my stomach. I think perhaps my fears about not getting drunk enough were misguided.

9:50: Nils buys a whole pizza for me. I take a slice and accidentally drop it on the ground. I drunkenly stare at it for a second, then pick it up and eat it anyway.

9:51: Nils knows that when I eat street pizza, it's time for me to pass out in a bathtub. He tries to flag down a taxi to send me home.

9:55: Nils can't get a cab. He gets angry. One taxi slows down, sees a large, angry Pedophile Clown, and starts to pull off. Nils flings the entire pizza box at the cab as if it were a Frisbee. The box flops open in midair, vomiting pizza everywhere, like a drunken cardboard Pac-Man. My last clear memory for over an hour.

10:00–11:15: [MISSING FROM MY MEMORY]

11:15: I wake up. I am face down on a hard, metal grate-type surface. My hands are bound behind my back. I have never been more confused in my life.

11:18: The floor is moving. I look around. I am in a paddy wagon. Nils is sitting on the bench above me, "We got arrested." This is not good. Maybe if I go back to sleep, everything will be better when I wake up.

11:20pm–2:15am: [MISSING FROM MY MEMORY]

2:15: I wake up. I am face down on hard plastic. I can barely move. I feel like I've been in a multi-car accident.

2:18: I sit up. I'm in a plain white room, linoleum floors, lots of plastic chairs. There is a sea of brown paper towels on the ground in front of me. My bullhorn and my floaties are gone. This is the second time in one night I've been the most confused in my life.

2:20: I look around. There are many drunk Mexicans sitting around me. They do not look happy. This might be a bad sign.

2:22: I hear someone say, "Well look, Tucker's awake." It's a cop. When you wake up in a police station, surrounded by drunk Mexicans, and a cop you've never seen before knows you by name, it is VERY bad.

2:24: He tells me to clean up my vomit. I don't see any vomit. I see only hundreds of paper towels on the floor, in a circle around me. The circle is at least twelve feet across.

2:25: I pick one of them up. It is soaking wet. My vomit is underneath the paper towels. ALL the paper towels have vomit under them. I must have done this. My emotions conflict: I am simultaneously impressed and mortified.

2:30: After five minutes of putting paper towels into the trash can, I am no longer impressed or mortified. I am pissed off and disgusted. I consider paying one of the Mexicans to do this for me. This plan is thwarted when I can't find my wallet.

2:33: The cops make clown puns as I clean. "So, these two cannibals are eating a clown, and one says to the other, 'Does this taste funny to you?' " and "Hey man, stop clowning around so much." They think this is the most hilarious thing they've ever heard. I want to punch them in the face.

2:35: I have to use another entire roll of towels to wipe up all the vomit. I consider that I may be personally responsible for massive deforestation. I don't care anymore. Fuck trees.

2:40: I have to piss. I look at myself in the bathroom mirror. There is no clown makeup on my face. Not one single speck. This confuses me greatly. I seem to remember putting clown makeup on earlier that day. Where is it?

2:45: I still have no idea why I am in jail. I ask the desk cop:

Cop "Let me check . . . says the charge is Pedestrian in Roadway."
Tucker "Pedestrian in Roadway? What the hell does that even mean? Don't pedestrians have the right-of-way on roads? I can't be arrested for being in one!"
Cop "Tell it to the judge, Bozo."

3:15: They are satisfied that I am awake, conscious, and relatively sober, so they release me. The property clerk gives me back my bullhorn. It is broken into several pieces. "Yeah, that kind of thing happens sometimes when you're a shithead to cops." I angrily tell the property clerk to dispose of the bullhorn in his rectum. He asks me if I want to go back in the jail. I quietly leave.

3:16: I am standing outside the Travis County Jail. I have no idea where I am. I remember that I puked up everything I'd eaten the past 18 hours. I am starving. I start walking aimlessly.

3:44: I see lights. A place called Katz's. The sign says KATZ'S NEVER KLOSES. I am overjoyed.

3:45: I see myself in the mirror as I walk in. I look like a used condom on the floor of a public restroom. The hostess gasps when she sees me, "We can't serve you."

3:46: I am so famished, dehydrated, exhausted, and hungover I can no longer control my emotions. I sit on the curb and start crying.

3:47: I stop crying. I start getting mad.

3:48: I am really pissed off. I decide they are going to close. If I can't eat, no one can eat.

3:50: I find a brick in the alley behind the restaurant, smash the lock off the circuit breaker, and pull it down. All the lights go off. You're closed now, Katz's. That'll teach you to refuse to serve drunk, dirty, disgusting clowns that don't have any money.

3:51: Petty vengeance makes me feel better. I wander around for a few more minutes, until I realize I don't know where B-Ski lives. I give up on everything, find a bench, and go to sleep.

Postscript

I got home the next day by wandering around asking people where all the assholes lived, until I saw a building I recognized. I eventually talked to everyone and put the missing pieces of my night together. J.D. Horne filled me in on how I got arrested:

> "You want me to revisit this? Never mind the fact that you decided to kick down the door at one of the first bars completely off its hinges and I had to go back the next day and pay for it. Or, when dancing with an old lady on the street, you spun her around so many times she fell over and you just walked away from her like nothing happened, as she lay on the ground writhing in pain. Or that you offended 52 of the 54 people on the clown bus and 97% of the persons at the first 5 or 6 stops. Oh, no. The defining moment of this evening was when you were arrested after you walked dead into the middle of Sixth Street on a Saturday night, still wearing your floaties and with your bullhorn—something akin to walking on the Hollywood freeway at 6:00 pm—and ordered all traffic to stop, declaring, "I AM Tucker Max." As I watched from the doorway of the pub, two cops approached you from the other side of the street. Your reaction? You turned the bullhorn on the rather portly male and barked, "Don't fuck with me, tubby! I wouldn't want a donut store to lose its best customer." To the female officer, "Honey, you might have nice tits but I can't tell underneath all that polyester. Let's have sex in your patrol car and find out." Cuffs and the clink for you—although I swear I thought I saw the female cop actually laugh."

I legitimately don't remember dancing with an old lady, or any of that shit with the cops, which sucks. It'd be one of my proudest memories.

Nils explained what happened from the time I passed out in the paddy wagon until I woke up in jail:

> "The most amazing part of our bumpy ride to Travis County Jail was the arrival, when the cops opened the back of the paddy wagon to let us out. I walked out easily. You were face-

down on the corrugated metal flooring, with your feet splayed out and your hands cuffed behind you, and the cops would not help you. They just shouted at you to "get the fuck out of the wagon."

What you should have done was shimmy your way down the length of the floor on your stomach and basically slide out backward until your feet hung over and you could land upright. Instead, you were intent on getting to your feet INSIDE the paddy wagon but without using the benches or the wall to help. And that's exactly what you did. You somehow used your face to balance yourself as you slowly got to your feet. It was the most amazing thing I'd ever seen, drunk or sober. Even the cops were impressed.

After staring, then laughing at us as we made our way through booking, they had us take our clown makeup off for the mug shots. I think you used up the remainder of your cognitive ability with that Houdini paddy wagon move, because by this time the only actions you were capable of were the involuntary ones: breathing, blinking, farting. The guys behind the counter recognized this and allowed us to go into the bathroom together (apparently against policy) so I could help you remove your makeup and prevent you from faceplanting into the sink.

This was the first opportunity I had to look at myself in the mirror. The amateur application of clown makeup always leaves something to be desired. After 8 hours of drinking, eating, laughing, sweating, and yelling, you stop looking like happy-go-lucky fun clown and start looking like live-in-the-sewer-and-gnaw-on-small-children's-bones clown. Your makeup was equally streaked, but when I went to scrub it off, it sloughed off into the paper towel in a single layer, like the charred skin of a 3rd degree burn victim. It was remarkable.

Once they took our mug shots, they set us down in a large, open holding area filled with rows of white plastic chairs and other nonviolent offenders. For the most part, everyone kept to themselves, and you fell over passed out on a vacant row of chairs.

Nothing of note happened for the next 45 minutes or so. That's when you started puking. EVERYWHERE. I'll never forget it. It was this viscous, dirt-brown mixture that rocketed out of your mouth like someone was jumping up and down on your stomach. You never woke up, I don't think you even made a sound, you just puked. And puked. And puked some more. It just kept coming. Watching you from across the row of seats, it felt like staring into the mouth of a sewage runoff pipe spilling toxic sludge into a white linoleum lake.

Lake TuckerPuke. Right then the desk sergeant came over with a giant brown roll of industrial-strength paper towels.

DeskSergeant "He's your friend?"
Nils "I guess."
DeskSergeant "Then you're cleaning it up."

The desk sergeant handed me the paper towel roll and walked away. There was no way I was actually cleaning that shit up. I wasn't the one who thought it was a good idea to deep-throat a CamelBak full of vodka.

I did the next best thing. I unrolled nearly the entire roll and gently laid layer upon layer of towel on top of the stagnating pool of TuckerPuke. This must have satisfied the desk sergeant, or he didn't bother to check back with me, because he didn't call my name again until it was time for my release, sometime around 2am. You were still passed out."

I present to you the actual mug shots from that night:

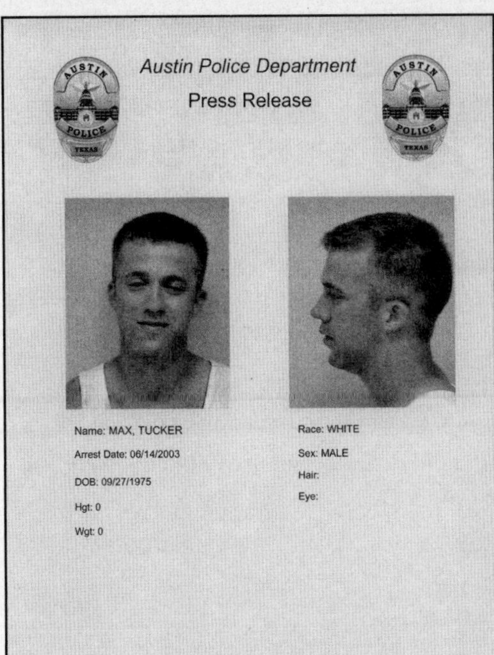
Austin Police Department

Press Release

Name: MAX, TUCKER
Arrest Date: 06/14/2003
DOB: 09/27/1975
Hgt: 0
Wgt: 0
Race: WHITE
Sex: MALE
Hair:
Eye:

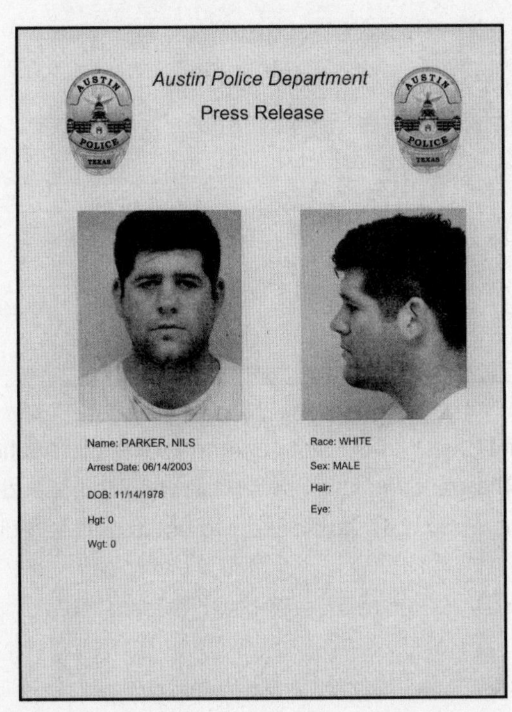
Austin Police Department

Press Release

Name: PARKER, NILS
Arrest Date: 06/14/2003
DOB: 11/14/1978
Hgt: 0
Wgt: 0
Race: WHITE
Sex: MALE
Hair:
Eye:

And the funniest police report ever written:

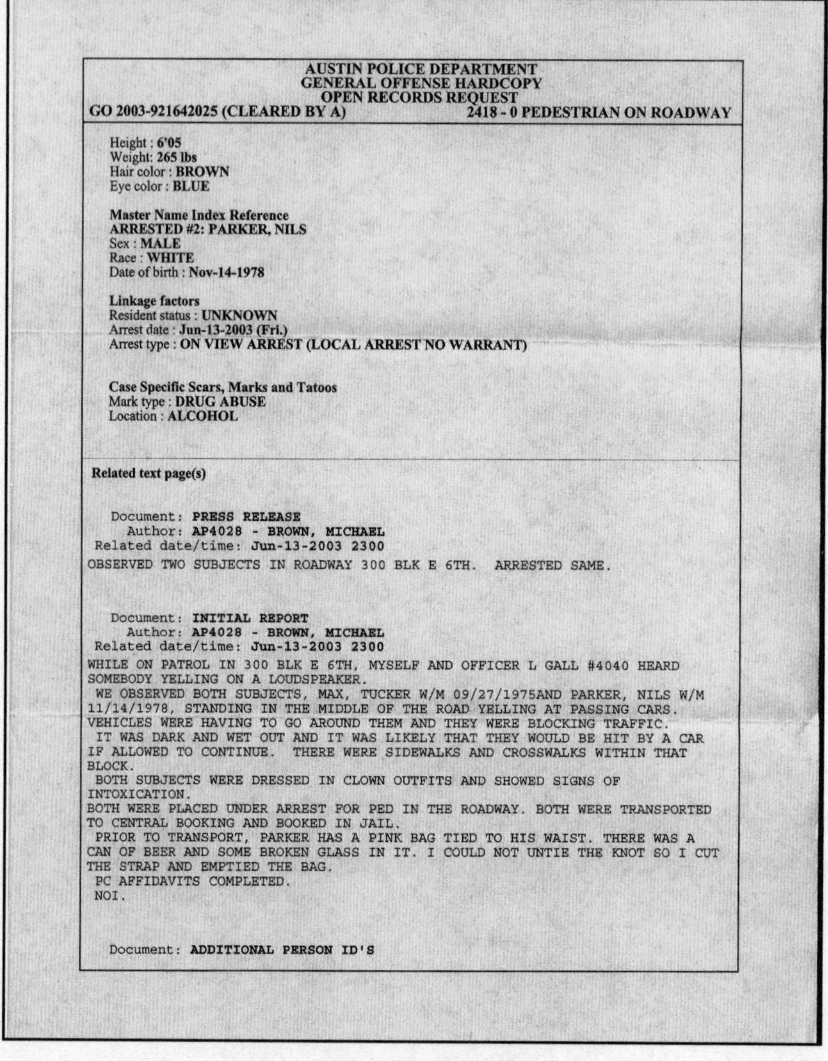

AUSTIN POLICE DEPARTMENT
GENERAL OFFENSE HARDCOPY
OPEN RECORDS REQUEST

GO 2003-921642025 (CLEARED BY A) 2418 - 0 PEDESTRIAN ON ROADWAY

Height : **6'05**
Weight: **265 lbs**
Hair color : **BROWN**
Eye color : **BLUE**

Master Name Index Reference
ARRESTED #2: PARKER, NILS
Sex : **MALE**
Race : **WHITE**
Date of birth : **Nov-14-1978**

Linkage factors
Resident status : **UNKNOWN**
Arrest date : **Jun-13-2003 (Fri.)**
Arrest type : **ON VIEW ARREST (LOCAL ARREST NO WARRANT)**

Case Specific Scars, Marks and Tatoos
Mark type : **DRUG ABUSE**
Location : **ALCOHOL**

Related text page(s)

Document: **PRESS RELEASE**
Author: **AP4028 - BROWN, MICHAEL**
Related date/time: **Jun-13-2003 2300**
OBSERVED TWO SUBJECTS IN ROADWAY 300 BLK E 6TH. ARRESTED SAME.

Document: **INITIAL REPORT**
Author: **AP4028 - BROWN, MICHAEL**
Related date/time: **Jun-13-2003 2300**
WHILE ON PATROL IN 300 BLK E 6TH, MYSELF AND OFFICER L GALL #4040 HEARD SOMEBODY YELLING ON A LOUDSPEAKER.
WE OBSERVED BOTH SUBJECTS, MAX, TUCKER W/M 09/27/1975AND PARKER, NILS W/M 11/14/1978, STANDING IN THE MIDDLE OF THE ROAD YELLING AT PASSING CARS. VEHICLES WERE HAVING TO GO AROUND THEM AND THEY WERE BLOCKING TRAFFIC.
IT WAS DARK AND WET OUT AND IT WAS LIKELY THAT THEY WOULD BE HIT BY A CAR IF ALLOWED TO CONTINUE. THERE WERE SIDEWALKS AND CROSSWALKS WITHIN THAT BLOCK.
BOTH SUBJECTS WERE DRESSED IN CLOWN OUTFITS AND SHOWED SIGNS OF INTOXICATION.
BOTH WERE PLACED UNDER ARREST FOR PED IN THE ROADWAY. BOTH WERE TRANSPORTED TO CENTRAL BOOKING AND BOOKED IN JAIL.
PRIOR TO TRANSPORT, PARKER HAS A PINK BAG TIED TO HIS WAIST. THERE WAS A CAN OF BEER AND SOME BROKEN GLASS IN IT. I COULD NOT UNTIE THE KNOT SO I CUT THE STRAP AND EMPTIED THE BAG.
PC AFFIDAVITS COMPLETED.
NOI.

Document: **ADDITIONAL PERSON ID'S**

The Capitol City Clown Crawl is still an annual event in Austin, and though J.D. Horne no longer runs it, he and I still attend, dressed as clowns of course. If you ever go, I would advise you not to act like I did.

Unless, you know . . . you're an asshole.

The DC Halloween Party and the Worst Girl I Ever Fucked

Occurred—October 2001

My friends and I graduated from Duke in May of 2001. After graduation, our jobs took us to different cities. Everyone else worked for various law firms and I worked for my dad's restaurant business in Florida. Within a few months, we independently came to the same conclusion: Work sucks.

The biggest difference between school and work is not free time, not responsibility, not money, not even access to college bars and parties. The biggest difference is hope. When you're still in school, no matter what is going wrong or how bad it gets, you know it's going to end. You know school will eventually be over and you can move on to something different. You know you have another chance, because your "real life" is still in front of you.

It's not like that with work. Once you are done with school and get a job, that's it. That *is* real life, that *is* what you've been working toward in school . . . and if you hate your job or what's going on with your life, there isn't an obvious end to it or an obvious escape. I mean, besides alcohol. We were slowly realizing that the "real life" we'd chosen really fucking sucked. A lot.

As a way to relieve this post-school malaise, we decided to pick a city and all travel there to celebrate Halloween as a group. PWJ suggested Washington, DC. His little sister was having a huge Halloween party at her house in Arlington (just across the Potomac in northern Virginia), and she was going to have so many girls at her party that she actually asked PWJ to invite his guy friends:

> "PWJ, please bring your friends. I'm worried that this will be like the 4th of July party I had. There were 100 girls and only 25 guys. All my single friends were bored."

PWJ added that his sister's friends fell into two groups:

1. Elementary school teachers (her current occupation)
2. Sorority girls recently graduated from Southern colleges (her previous occupation)

Plane tickets were purchased post haste.

I arrived in town a day before everyone else. It wasn't for an extra day of drinking, though I can always use that. I came early to cheer up Hate and SlingBlade. As much as the rest of us were starting to hate our lives, it was WAY worse for those two, because they didn't even have real jobs to hate. When we graduated, they were the only two of our group who didn't have law firm jobs waiting for them. Now, six months later, they still hadn't found permanent law firm jobs and were relegated to doing document review to survive (essentially legal temps, REALLY shitty work).

They tried to joke about it, but you could tell it was not good. Two months before Halloween, in an email chain where we were all bitching to each other about our lives, Hate sent this email:

> From: Hate
> To: Tucker Max, PWJ, GoldenBoy, El Bingeroso, Credit, Jojo, SlingBlade
> Subject: Depression
>
> Ah yes, I would like to welcome all of you to the world of depression. I know it well.

I would be happy to conduct a seminar on how to cope with depression for those of you newcomers to the scene. The price of admission will be one case of domestic beer. In the biz, we call this "medication."

Also outlined in the course will be proper masturbation techniques, clinically known as "a reason to get up in the morning." And finally we will teach basic rugby techniques, also "legalized assault."

As for getting out of your dead-end jobs, I have no tips, as I cannot even get into one.

That was bad, but it was this email from SlingBlade that made me book the early ticket:

From: SlingBlade
To: Tucker Max, PWJ, GoldenBoy, El Bingeroso, Credit, Jojo, Hate
Subject: re: Depression

These are actual quotes from a conversation Hate and I had last night concerning the state of our lives. You can judge for yourself how we are doing (bonus points for matching the quotes to the person):

"The problem is I have no beacon, nothing to look forward to. Or even any hope that anything good will happen to me . . . ever."

"One of us needs to get laid."
"Just one of us?"
"What are the odds of both of us getting laid?"

"The problem with this interview is that I have to get them to like me, and at this point, I don't even like me. They'll ask,

'What do you have to offer us?' The answer, of course, will be I have nothing to offer you or anyone else."

"I've decided to compile a list of reasons why I shouldn't kill myself. As you can see, the paper is blank."

"I could never kill myself. What if it doesn't work? Then I'll have failed at the only thing that could save me from my failures. Where do you go from there?"

Oh yes—did I mention that Hate and I tried out for *The Weakest Link* last week? We were rejected. Apparently, when pitted against unemployed steelworkers in a competition of intelligence, we come up lacking.

I pulled up to their place about 4pm on Friday. Describing the awfulness of what I found will be a struggle, but let me try:

The apartment was in one of those shitty, beat-up complexes that was probably cool when it was built in the late '60s but now looked like it was one drive-by shooting away from converting to Section 8. The piles of animal shit everywhere were a nice touch, but what really seemed to tie everything together for me was their apartment screen door hanging by a single hinge. With a little more artful disrepair, it could easily be used for a movie set in a postapocalyptic world. I half expected to see packs of stray dogs fighting over decomposing carcasses and feral children scurrying into sewers.

Inside, I was momentarily impressed, because it looked like SlingBlade and Hate had painted their apartment in really cool shades and designs. Then I realized those shades and designs were not interior design—they were huge water stains in the cheap drywall.

SlingBlade and Hate were in front of the TV, sitting in those fabric camping chairs you can buy for $15 at Walmart, playing Tetris against each other. There was no other furniture in the apartment. Unless you count SlingBlade's action figures on all the ledges as furniture.

As he got further and further behind in the game, Hate was becoming more and more enraged, and of course SlingBlade was talking shit to him about it: "Hate, your spatial-reasoning skills are inferior to mine" and "Do the pointless spinning geometries of Tetris remind you of anything?"

As Hate's bricks stacked perilously close to the top of the screen, SlingBlade got the four-block single piece and cleared his screen. This was the final straw; Hate could no longer stomach failing in both the real world he lived in and this virtual world he was trying to escape into. He threw his controller at the TV and left for rugby practice.

SlingBlade "Beating him at Tetris is the only reason I even get anymore. I'm not sure what keeps him going. Rugby, I guess. Or anger."
Tucker "You ready to start drinking?"
SlingBlade "Whatever."
Tucker "What, am I interfering with your masturbation schedule? Is your 4pm jack-off session usually a good one?"

He ignored me, as if that's ever worked.

Tucker "I'm curious. Do you hold the action figures in your off hand when you masturbate, or do you just stare at them from across the room?"
SlingBlade "I masturbate in the shower. My action figures judge me. Especially the Justice League."
Tucker "Come on, let's get out of this shithole and go to a bar. Alcohol helps alleviate depression."
SlingBlade "Go away. I'm not going to a bar."
Tucker "Look, I know everything is shitty right now, but if you don't stop acting like such a bitch, someone's gonna fuck that pussy on your face."
SlingBlade "Why don't you go back to your regularly scheduled program of shame fucking retards and crying yourself to sleep, and leave me alone."

Tucker "Get up, you're coming with me. There are sluts at the bar, but they aren't going to wait for us all night. Early bird gets the worm."
SlingBlade "What if you're the early worm?"
Tucker "It means be the bird, not the worm, so then you get the worm."
SlingBlade "Worms are blind, brainless, dirt-eating shit tubes."
Tucker "You're still coming with me."

We ended up at a pretty cool bar—hot girls everywhere, great vibe, everyone having fun. I go to the bar, and see this girl with an O'Doul's. She was not just holding it—she was actively drinking it. Legitimately pouring the liquid from the bottle into her throat so she could then swallow it. I didn't know people actually drank those things; I thought they were just for show.

Tucker "Why would you drink a beer without alcohol? That's like dating a woman without a vagina."
Girl "Do I know you? You think you can just come up to me and say 'vagina'?"
Tucker "Well, sorry Miss Manners. Maybe if your beer had some alcohol in it, you'd think that was funny. Now, if you'll excuse me, I have to go talk to the hot girls."

One girl charmed, rest of the bar to go.

I eventually got two homely girls to come over and talk to us. I picked them because they seemed very nice, and since they weren't great looking, I assumed they would be desperate to talk to us. What SlingBlade needed right now was some kind of affirmation. I should have known better than even to try.

Girl1 "So what do you guys do?"
SlingBlade "Oh, this is precisely what I needed, Tucker. More people who can judge and reject me."
Tucker "He's a lawyer."
Girl2 "That's a cool job."

SlingBlade "I'm a legal temp. I do document review in a windowless office in the basement. In my firm's pecking order, I'm below the paralegals and secretaries."

Girl2 "It's OK. We've all had crappy jobs."

SlingBlade "When I need a pep talk from a dim-witted receptionist, I'll be sure to look you up."

Tucker "Don't pay attention to him, ladies, he's just in a bad mood."

Girl1 "Well, uh, what do you do?"

Tucker "I'm an inventor."

Girl2 "That's so cool. What things have you invented? Anything I would know?"

SlingBlade [*dripping with sarcasm*] "Oh, this'll be good."

Tucker "Not yet, but my big invention is coming out soon, I think it's going to do really well."

Girl2 "Oh, what is it?"

Girl1 "Is it cool?"

Tucker "You know those cones that dogs have to wear around their necks after surgery to keep them from chewing the stitches?"

Girl1 "Yeah, of course."

Tucker "Well, I invented one for babies."

Girl1 "For babies?"

Tucker "Yep. It's not for surgery, obviously, that would be ridiculous. It's a party game."

Girl2 "A party game? What do you mean?"

Tucker "You put it around the baby's neck just like with a dog, but then you fill it to the top with some sort of liquid—water or apple juice or pretty much anything drinkable—and then he has to drink it as fast as he can. It's called: Baby Drink or Die."

Girl1 "Baby Drink OR DIE?!?"

Girl2 "WHAT?!?"

Tucker "You think Baby Drink or Drown is a better name? The investors thought it was more marketable. Should I have listened? Fuck, I should have."

They didn't think that was funny, for some reason.

I eventually quit trying to cheer up SlingBlade and started talking to a group of Georgetown undergrads, because one of them was hot and into me. SlingBlade could not have been more disgusted with them. They were self-absorbed, spoiled sorority girls who thought that because their daddies were rich and powerful they could do whatever they wanted. To SlingBlade, these girls represented everything that was wrong with the world, and he wanted nothing to do with them. To me, they represented fish in a barrel. Though their daddies may have spoiled them with material things, they also ignored them emotionally. These girls were going to find male attention somewhere, and I was more than willing to vigorously and enthusiastically hump it into them.

After an hour of "validate then withdraw," plus a lot of vodka, I had missile lock on the one I wanted to fuck. Well on the way to rubbing our genitals together, she decided to be playful and call me out.

Girl "I think I can outdrink you."
Tucker "Please. I woke up this morning drunker than you've ever been in your life."
Girl "You're a big talker, but are you a big drinker?"
Tucker "Line'em up."

She returned quickly with two brown shots. I smelled them.

Tucker "What is this?"
Girl "Three Wise Men."

FUCK. This is not good. I'm allergic to whiskey. I think maybe I should explain this to her, and request a different alcohol. Then I remember that I am awesome. Even fighting through anaphylactic shock, I can STILL bury this emotionally unstable, bulimic undergrad.

We do the first shot, and for the second, I think I'm going to be OK. Then it's like I took a hit of acid: I get dizzy, everything slows down, people's words begin to slur, and I just know I'm going to puke. I am about to make a quick trip to the bathroom, but before I can do it, she hands me the next shot.

Girl "We're not done yet, Mr. Big Drinker."

Just smelling the shot, my knees buckle. If I was smart, I'd throw the shot in her face, run out of the bar, and punch a drifter. But I want to get laid, so I stupidly dump it down my throat and hope for the best.

My body went into involuntary convulsions and immediately rejected the shot. I had one of those small reaction vomits where just the top layer of your stomach comes out. I was holding a cup of beer, and about 8 ounces of brownish, watery vomit sloshed into the cup and on my hand. For a second I tried to play it off casually, like it was a totally normal thing for me to vomit back into my cup—you know, to save my drink for later.

It didn't work. The girl and her friends looked at me like I was a Mexican busboy who'd just propositioned them. I don't think they could believe a grown man just puked into his own cup, after only two shots. Before anyone could say anything, SlingBlade tied a nice bow on the incident:

SlingBlade "You make me ashamed to be a man."

We left immediately after that. Alone, obviously.

In the middle of the ride home, I abruptly commanded SlingBlade to pull the car over, and proceeded to vomit all over the street. Literally all over the street—I ran across the road as I was throwing up, puking the whole time. And for some strange reason, I was waving my arms above my head, like one of those women on Maury Povich who sprint backstage after finding out that none of the three men is the father.

SlingBlade "Why were you flailing your arms like that?"
Tucker "I needed to alert the oncoming cars to my presence."
SlingBlade "Well, why did you run across the street vomiting?"

Tucker "If I understood why I do the things I do when I'm drunk, I'd be . . . rich . . . or less drunk . . . or something."

The Halloween Party

The next day, we all bummed around and played video games until it was time for the party. About 7pm we started putting on our costumes, but SlingBlade just sat there.

Tucker "Dude, what are you going as? A morose, underemployed video game nerd?"
SlingBlade "I don't have a costume. You think I spent even a millisecond thinking about that nonsense?"

If he doesn't get a costume, I know exactly what's going to happen: Everyone will pester him about why he doesn't have a costume, and he'll spend the entire party sulking and pissed off, which will ruin any chance he has of having a good time. Not on my watch.

On our way to the party, I made him stop at a costume store. Ever been to a costume store at 7pm on a Halloween weekend night? It's like the Superdome during Katrina. The store was packed with all the people who'd missed Halloween being on the calendar for a whole year. The employees, who are completely bored 364 days, were freaking out, and there was basically nothing left except the picked-over carcasses of the shittiest costumes.

We ended up with two options: a Batman costume—very sweet except that it was sized for a 10 year old—or a pirate costume that was nothing but a parrot, an eye patch, and poofy pants.

SlingBlade "So I can either be a pedophile or a gay animal trainer? How about neither, thanks."

Then I had an inspired stroke of genius:

Tucker "Dude, just take the parrot. Put it on your shoulder and use it to talk shit to people all night. It can be like your version of Triumph the Insult Comic Dog. I poop on your costume!"

He seemed to like the idea. Well, more like he was indifferent and just wanted to leave the store, so I bought the parrot and we went to eat. On the way to dinner, the tide started turning in SlingBlade's favor.

SlingBlade was driving when, out of nowhere, a hot blond woman in a Mercedes accelerated past him and cut him off, then slowed down. She just brazenly pulled her car in front of his, forcing him to hit his brakes and swerve out of the way, and then had the temerity to continue on as if nothing happened. She didn't give an apology wave or make even the slightest acknowledgment that she committed such a serious breach of highway etiquette. It was as if his existence was completely meaningless to her.

Oh boy. If you know anything about SlingBlade, you know he has a finely tuned sense of justice. One time in San Francisco he saw a cop run a red light for no reason, and tried to pull him over to make a citizen's arrest. Dude takes the law seriously. Add to this the fact that he despises entitled, uppity-rich-girl types, then mix in his current state of depressed self-loathing, and you've got the recipe for emotional Semtex. This incident became the detonator.

He started flashing his high beams, honking, and finally, when she still refused to acknowledge him, stood on the accelerator of his beat-up eggplant purple 1993 Saturn. It took a few seconds, but eventually he got it up to 35 miles per hour and pulled up on her passenger side.

He was red-faced, veins bulging out of his neck, as he screamed curses at her and jabbed the driver-side window with his finger. She didn't notice him at first, then glanced over, saw the commotion, and from inside the safety of her huge luxury sedan, she gave him that type of contemptuous sneer that only the landed, Southern socialite gentry can muster. It was a glare that said, "You are beneath me, how dare you waste my time."

He got real quiet and, for a split second, I really thought he was going to swerve his car into hers. I started praying to every god I could think of (to hedge my bets) and braced for impact. But he had something even better in mind.

He hocked up the loudest loogie I've ever heard, rolled down his window, pulled slightly ahead, and spit it right at her car. It hit dead center on the passenger side of the windshield. I estimate it had the circumference of a golf ball. It immediately started spreading, like the concussion from a bomb blast. Being that it was allergy season in northern Virginia, SlingBlade's hay fever had made it gooey and thick with just the right amount of greenish yellow tint. It looked like a pterodactyl took a dump on her windshield.

Mortified, she quickly hit her windshield wipers. Big mistake. Instead of wiping away the loogie, it smeared his phlegm across her windshield. Because she had one of those fancy Mercedes with the one big wiper blade, it turned SlingBlade's spit mortar into a perfect arc of lung butter, and every trip the wiper made across the windshield spread it larger.

It was a beautiful, retributive rainbow of karmic justice.

We both exploded in laughter. I was tearing up and snorting, and SlingBlade almost had to pull over he was laughing so hard. This was probably the most he'd laughed since we graduated law school.

Instantly, he became a whole new person; it was like he had hope again. Yes, she would still be a spoiled, entitled bitch. Yes, she would just go to a car wash and have it cleaned by some underpaid migrant worker who she wouldn't even tip, then return to her McMansion, standard-issue trust fund husband, and life of unearned privilege. And yes, SlingBlade would still be a depressed, underemployed lawyer living hand to mouth in a shithole with stains on his walls, driving a purple Saturn. But for one brief, fleeting moment, his world was just. Sometimes you have to take the little victories where you can get them, and on this day, SlingBlade got one.

Still floating on the wings of SlingBlade's moral victory, we met up with everyone else for dinner. It was a relatively uneventful meal, except when the manager came over and asked Hate if he could stop cursing so loudly, because the Mormon family behind us was complaining. Can't blame the Mormon. If I had to wear "magical" underwear that covered my whole body and deal with four wives simultaneously henpecking the shit out of me while not sucking my dick, I guess I'd be high-strung too.

Costume-wise, we were not blowing the doors off. I was in scrubs I'd stolen from a nurse I hooked up with the week before, with some vague notion of being a doctor or orderly or something. Credit had a police outfit that was nothing more than a plastic badge and a cop hat. Hate was a rugby player. PWJ put on a skirt, painted half his face blue, and went as William Wallace. And Jojo just had on a gray hoodie that he pulled tight over his head, so that he looked like the Black Unabomber. And of course SlingBlade had his parrot.

Whatever. We don't conquer people with fancy costumes or clever outfits. We do it by being better at the things that matter: drinking, fucking, and funny.

We arrived at PWJ's sister's house, frothing in our anticipation over the bevy of hot and nubile young ladies who were desperately eager for our attention, only to walk in and find . . . a fucking disaster. You should have seen this party. Seriously, it looked like Lane Bryant and Jenny Craig had a knife fight in there.

SlingBlade "PWJ, I have a theory about why your sister had no guys at her last party."
Tucker "Who are these girls, the caterers?"
Jojo "Do the hot girls show up later?"
Credit "I think they ate the hot girls."
Hate "Where's the bar? This is the type of problem liquor was designed to solve."

We immediately went to get drinks. There was NO LIQUOR, only a pony keg of cheap beer. For a party that was expecting seventy to a hundred people to show up.

Hate "Gentlemen, this is not good. This is NOT GOOD AT ALL."
SlingBlade "This must have been what it was like on the Titanic, when they realized they didn't have enough lifeboats for everyone."

Our first group party since law school and we were presented with a Halloween party that had:

1. mostly fat girls
2. unattractive skinny girls
3. not enough alcohol to last an hour of purposeful drinking

No. NO. This would not stand. There are many different ways for a party to be epic, and even starting so far behind the 8-ball as this party had, it could be saved. We could make a great time anyway, but for that to happen, we needed to get rip-roaring drunk, and that necessitated LOTS of alcohol. So what the fuck would I do now?

I remember I am Tucker Max, and I am awesome, and regardless of what obstacles fate puts in my way, I can go through them, over them or around them to get my way. I WILL make this party great, one way or the other. It only takes me a second to come up with a plan.

Tucker "Jojo, PWJ—you two are making the most money. Come with me. Everyone else: we'll be right back. Prepare the women for our triumphant return."

The ABC store was ten minutes from closing when William Wallace, the Black Unabomber, and Gaylord Focker stormed in, grabbed a cart and started tossing bottles in. Everything that looked remotely potable, we bought.

Cashier "I ain't never seen no one buy this much liquor at once. This gonna be one hell of a party, eh?"

Tucker "No, it's mostly fat girls. Takes more to get 'em drunk. And even more than that to drink'em pretty."

Since Virginia has government-controlled liquor stores, and because we bought an irrational amount of alcohol, the guy had to fill out this special slip for us so we could transport it. If we got pulled over without that slip, we could be arrested, even with all the bottles closed, because we were carrying THAT MUCH ALCOHOL.

I crashed through the front door, box of alcohol in one arm, the other hand brandishing the pink alcohol transportation slip like it was one of Willy Wonka's Golden Tickets.

Tucker "Now THIS is how you throw a fucking party!"

We left an awful, dying party and returned from the liquor store as conquering heroes. Of course our triumphant return demanded that we do shots, and some of the girls were in fact eager to drink with the party champions. One was a tad overweight, wearing an all-white nurse outfit, and her friend was a butterface in some sort of Girl Scout costume.

Hate "Ladies, what are your costumes?"
SlingBlade "Let me guess. The Michelin Man and . . . a victim of child abuse?"
SluttyGirlScout "I'm a slutty Girl Scout."
SluttyNurse "I'm a slutty nurse."
SlingBlade "You look more like a slutty marshmallow."
SluttyMarshmallow "Hey!"
Tucker "That's what I've never understood. Why do women go to Halloween as a slutty nurse or a slutty cat, or whatever? Just cut out the middleman and go as a slut. The slutty part is what's key—no one gives a shit about the rest. You could be a slutty tree for all we care."
SluttyGirlScout "You can't go as just a plain slut, everyone will judge you!"
SlingBlade "Oh, I think you are well past the point of being judged."
Hate "Don't you understand Tucker? Halloween is the only day of the year a girl can dress like a slut and not be considered a slut."

SluttyMarshmallow "I know, that's true, it's such a double standard, and it's unfair!"
SluttyGirlScout "Seriously, if a guy fucks a different girl every week, he's a legend. But if I fuck two guys in a month, I'm some slut."
SlingBlade "Two guys a month is 24 guys a year. That's zooming well past slutty and crashing straight into whoredom."
Tucker "You fuck two new guys every month? Have you hit your quota this month? Because I'll be drunk soon, and you'll make a good backup plan."
PWJ "Tucker, be nice. Look, the double standard makes perfect sense, you just have to see it in the proper perspective. My grandfather put it to me this way: If a key opens lots of locks, then it's a master key. But if a lock is opened by lots of keys, then it's a shitty lock."
SluttyGirlScout "That's actually really smart."
Hate "I've always looked at it this way: Being a stud as a guy is hard. It's not easy to sleep with a bunch of girls; you have to have game. There are not many fat, ugly, stupid studs. Being a slut is easy. There are plenty of fat, ugly, stupid sluts."
SlingBlade [*points to the girls*] "Exhibits A and B."
SluttyGirlScout "Don't be a dick!"

I noticed that SluttyMarshmallow had a wandering eye. Target acquired.

Tucker "Why won't you look at me?"
SluttyMarshmallow "I am."
Tucker "No, with both eyes!"
SluttyMarshmallow "FUCK YOU!"
Tucker "Can you see around corners? Do they move independently? Show us!"
SluttyMarshmallow "SHUT UP!"
SlingBlade "Was it hard, growing up with one human parent and one chameleon parent? I bet you were teased mercilessly; interspecies kids always are. Children can be so cruel."

They both stormed off.

Tucker "The buffet is the opposite way!"
SlingBlade "She already knows that, she never took her eye off it."

This other girl was standing nearby, covered head to toe in sparkly gold paint. She made the unfortunate mistake of injecting herself into the conversation. I honestly don't remember if she was mad at us or thought we were hilarious; when the jackals are in a frenzy, they snap indiscriminately.

SlingBlade "What are you supposed to be? The victim of a paint truck accident?"
Hate "A spray-can blew up on you?"
Tucker [*in a singing voice*] "Goldfinger, da-da-da, he's the man, the man with the Midas touch . . ."
PaintGirl "I'M SUPPOSED TO BE THE STATUE OF LIBERTY! YOU KNOW WE WERE JUST ATTACKED BY TERRORISTS!"
SlingBlade "The real Statue of Liberty doesn't look like C3PO."
Tucker "Are you rooting for the terrorists?"

She stormed off just as PWJ's sister came over.

PWJSister "Tucker, did you make that girl cry?"
Tucker "It's her fault! She's the one who hates America!"
Credit "She should consider herself lucky that he didn't try to take her home."
Hate "HAHAHAHA. Gentlemen, it begins."

While we were out getting alcohol, SlingBlade had put on his "costume." The attachment on the feet of the plastic parrot was useless in terms of keeping it on, so he duct-taped it to his shoulder. He was walking around the party with a plastic parrot duct-taped to his sweater. That was his entire costume.

SlingBlade "I shall name him Mr. Peepers."
Credit "SlingBlade, that really is the worst costume ever."

SlingBlade turned his head and leaned into the parrot, as if it were whispering in his ear. Then he nodded in agreement and said in the sort of baby voice I use to talk to my dog:

SlingBlade "No Mr. Peepers, unfortunately Hitler didn't get them all."
Jojo "Credit may be Jewish, but at least he spent more than $2 on his costume."

SlingBlade cocked his head and raised his eyebrows at the parrot, chuckled as if to an inside joke, nodded, and said:

SlingBlade "I know Mr. Peepers, I wish Lincoln hadn't signed that document either."

SlingBlade is, on a normal day, the funniest person I know. But with Mr. Peepers as his friend and comedic foil, he was in a zone like I'd never seen before. Mr. Peepers was the alter ego he'd always wanted and the friend that would always have his back. SlingBlade authentically bonded with this plastic bird in a way that he never has with another human. Mr. Peepers became a way for SlingBlade to emote, a mouthpiece for the hurt, angry little boy inside of him to lash out at a world that had been so cruel.

I followed him throughout the night, as he took his new prop on a self-esteem-robbing adventure through the people at the party. It was amazing. At the time, I wasn't writing full-time but I was keeping a quote list of funny things said by my friends and me. The next day on the plane, I wrote down as many of his jokes as I could remember, and I probably forgot at least half. And those were just the ones I heard. Some of the best examples:

—He walked up to a group of girls, looked them all up and down, and started walking away:

SlingBlade "You're right Mr. Peepers, there aren't any good-looking girls at this party."

—One girl was kinda cute, but boring, so we found a way to make her interesting:

SlingBlade "Wait, what's that? Yes, I agree Mr. Peepers, you'd never know she's had three abortions unless her friend told us."
CuteBoringGirl "What?!?"
Tucker "How many abortions have you had for real?"
CuteBoringGirl "None!"
Tucker "OK, how many babies have you had and then thrown in the Dumpster?"
SlingBlade "Mr. Peepers calls them 'prom babies.' "
CuteBoringGirl "I have NEVER had an abortion or a child."
Tucker "Are you at least pro-abortion?"
CuteBoringGirl "It's called pro-choice, and yes, I am."
Tucker "Too bad your mother didn't share your politics."
CuteBoringGirl "WHAT!?!"
PWJ "Tucker, be nice. What if her mom is dead?"
Credit "What if she died during an abortion procedure?"
Tucker "AHAHHHAAAHHAHAHAHHHHAHA—THAT WOULD BE AWESOME! THE JOKE WOULD BE TEN TIMES FUNNIER!"

—We were talking to some girls, and one of them was not very bright:

Girl "Who is this Mr. Peepers you keep talking about?"
SlingBlade "How dare you! He is my best friend." [*He affectionately pets Mr. Peepers on the head.*]
Girl "What are you supposed to be, like a pirate or something?"
SlingBlade "I know Mr. Peepers, some people don't get the genius of our costume. Yes, the world needs hotel maids and massage therapists too."
Girl "What IS your costume? You're just talking to a fake parrot! This is stupid!"
SlingBlade "I agree with you Mr. Peepers, she needs to be turned upside down and have her vagina filled with concrete."

—I had been talking to a girl I thought was kinda cute, but SlingBlade was not having it:

SlingBlade "Yes Mr. Peepers, if she were a dog, she'd have been put to sleep a long time ago."

Tucker "Shut up dude, she's not that bad."
SlingBlade "Mr. Peepers thinks that if you painted her black and white and took her to the beach, the seals would run for cover."
Tucker "She's not even fat!"
SlingBlade "I guess it's true, Mr. Peepers: There is always someone as drunk and horny as you are ugly."

—Girl in an argument with SlingBlade:

Girl "I like your friend Credit. He's cute too."
SlingBlade "Good call Mr. Peepers. If Beaker from the Muppets was Jewish and terrified of public speaking, he would be Credit."
Girl "I don't know what you're talking about, he's better looking than you. You aren't even wearing nice clothes. Where did you get your clothes, from a homeless person?"
SlingBlade "I've bought some of my favorite outfits off of hoboes."
Girl "And what is with the parrot?"
SlingBlade "I know why God gave women mouths Mr. Peepers, but I am not sure about why they got vocal cords."

At some point, Jojo came over to us with two bottles in his hand and the type of devious look that makes you understand why old white people cross the street when they see a young black man coming toward them.

Jojo "Gentlemen. Thug Passion is going to make an appearance at this party."

Thug Passion is made from cognac and Alizé. Jojo introduced the drink to our group years ago (shocking, I know, the drink with two types of cognac in it is a favorite of the black friend). Thug Passion is the break-glass-in-case-of-emergency drink we bring out when it's time to kill what little inhibitions we have left and do *really* stupid shit. It is Special Olympics in a bottle.

Thug Passion had a different effect on each of us. For me, it just created an amplified me—I'm already pure id anyway. For PWJ, it turned the nice guy of the group into a predatory sex lion; dude was ruthlessly hitting on every girl at the party, using his sister to introduce him, then playing the "brother of my friend must be a nice guy" game. Jojo pulled his hoodie tighter around his head and became even more shady looking, if that's possible. Hate got more aggressive and angrier. Credit eventually just sunk into a puddle of pitiful, drooling on himself and counting down the minutes until he started puking.

Strangely enough, it made SlingBlade open to female companionship. Thirty minutes after we did our Thug Passion shots, I found SlingBlade talking to a girl. You can usually tell by his body language how it's going: If his arms are crossed or he's turned slightly away from the girl, it's going badly. If he's looking at her, with his head to the side, he doesn't think she's a whore yet, and with this girl, his head was cocked like a confused dog.

SlingBlade "Tucker, have you met Joanne?"
Joanne "My name is Jolene."

SlingBlade looked over and raised his eyebrows to the inanimate bird, nodded knowingly, and looked back at Jolene with bemused condescension:

SlingBlade "Mr. Peepers seems to think that your name isn't very important."

She thought he and Mr. Peepers were hilarious, which was awesome. But it was obvious that this was a Thug Passion casualty. Granted, she did have a really good body, but her face had so many craters it looked like the moon. But SlingBlade seemed into her as much as she was into him, so I kept my mouth shut.

Tucker "That cheerleader costume is good. Where'd you get it?"
SlingBlade "Oh, we already went over this quite extensively. It's not a costume. She was a college cheerleader, and this was her uniform."
Tucker "You wore your college cheerleading outfit? To a Halloween party?"
Jolene "I couldn't think of anything else to come as!"

SlingBlade "Mr. Peepers, you shouldn't call her that. The politically correct term is 'developmentally disabled.'"
Jolene "Mr. Peepers!"
Tucker "Well, can you at least do some cheers for us?"

Right in the middle of the party, she started doing all kinds of cheers, jumping up and down, and then did a fucking backflip! It was awesome.

SlingBlade "Mr. Peepers and I are impressed with your flexibility."
Tucker "Can you put it to use, though?"
Jolene "I don't know, I guess I can."
Tucker "What's your favorite sex position?"
Jolene "I like pretty much all of them."
SlingBlade "Mr. Peepers wants to know if 'dead girl' is an actual position or just a medical diagnosis?"
Jolene "Mr. Peepers, that's terrible!"
SlingBlade "Mr. Peepers likes dead girls the best because they don't say 'no.'"
Jolene "That's awful!"
SlingBlade "Mr. Peepers has a dark past. He doesn't like talking about his conviction."
Jolene "Mr. Peepers went to jail? For what?"
SlingBlade "Wait—what's that Mr. Peepers? Oh, I see. Mr. Peepers says she's a lying tramp, that he didn't rape her, he beat her until she consented, so technically, that should have only been assault."
Jolene "Oh my God!"
SlingBlade "I don't think Mr. Peepers understands the legal principle of duress."
Jolene "Mr. Peepers seems very bitter."
SlingBlade "Yes. I think perhaps Mr. Peepers didn't make optimal use of the rehabilitation aspect of his time in the clink."
Jolene "Forgiveness is the first step to acceptance, Mr. Peepers, and acceptance is how you heal."

I don't think she was kidding when she said that. I think she was trying to give actual advice to a plastic bird.

I saw this HOT girl standing next to PWJ, dressed as a slutty Indian. I have no idea what she was doing at this party, as the invite clearly stated the girls were supposed to wear as much fat and ugly as they could find. Since she was dressed as an Indian, I figured alcohol was the perfect in:

Tucker "Have some firewater, Chief Buffalo Fucker. Then we'll sign a lopsided treaty that I'll reneg on, so I can steal your lands and ship you off to Oklahoma."

She looked at me like I asked her if she wanted to fuck on a blanket full of smallpox, and walked off.

Tucker "What the fuck? That may not have been the best Native American joke ever, but it was pretty funny."
PWJ "No Tucker, it wasn't. And she isn't dressed as a slutty Indian. She actually IS an American Indian."
Tucker "She's actually wearing the crap from the set she's claiming?"
PWJ "She's not 'claiming a set' you idiot. She is dressed as a squaw from her tribe."
Tucker "Wait a minute. THAT outfit is what the women in her tribe wore? What tribe is she from, Frederick's of Hollywood?"
PWJ "Tucker, shut up dude. She is Native American, leave it alone."
Tucker "You think if I tell her that I'm related to George Custer, she'll forgive me? After all, the Indians killed him, so it's equal. We can commiserate about our victimhood!"
PWJ "That is your worst idea in a long line of awful ideas. Don't talk to her again."

I tried my luck with another girl. She was a veterinary assistant.

Girl "I just love working with animals."
Tucker "I love animals too. Except cats. Cats are evil."
Girl "No they are not!"
Tucker "When I was a kid I used to go around the neighborhood collecting stray cats in a bag, then tie the bag up and toss it off the bridge. I

stopped, though. Apparently, some people didn't think this was funny. They started throwing around fancy words like 'animal cruelty' and 'felony charges.' Don't you hate it when people don't have a sense of humor?"

Her look of disgust told me that she didn't have one either.

A few minutes after this, some dude dressed in a SpongeBob SquarePants outfit started yelling at me from across the party:

SpongeBob "Who the fuck do you think you are! I've seen you and your friends go around and insult every girl at the party!"

I honestly didn't know what to do at first. I mean, how do you even react to an angry face sticking out of a cartoon character's body? Then, as soon as people got between us, that's when he got all tough and tried to come at me. When there was no one getting between us, he was content just to yell from across the room. There is nothing worse than a fake tough guy, and this just set me off.

Tucker "YOU FUCKING PUSSY! DON'T ACT LIKE A FUCKING TOUGH GUY BEHIND ALL THOSE GIRLS! COME OUT FRONT AND FIGHT ME LIKE A MAN, YOU FUCKING BITCH! COME OUT FRONT RIGHT NOW!"

I stormed out to the front yard, took off my shirt, and yelled at him to come out and fight me. For 15 minutes. Really, I stood outside, in the freezing cold, bare chested, for 15 minutes, screaming for SpongeBob SquarePants to come out and face me like a man.

Did I mention I was 26 years old at the time? Thug Passion is no joke.

Eventually, PWJ came outside and told me SpongeBob left by the back door. I got a drink and wandered around until I saw SlingBlade; he and Jolene were still deep in flirty conversation. SlingBlade leaned into Mr. Peepers, got a shocked look on his face, popped Mr. Peepers on his beak, and pointed at him as if he were a naughty dog that had piddled on the carpet.

SlingBlade "Mr. Peepers, don't say that!"
Jolene "What did he say?!?"
SlingBlade "No, no, I can't tell you. It's terrible. He's being cruel again."
Jolene "Tell me! Tell me!"
SlingBlade "Well, how can I say this diplomatically? Mr. Peepers said he feels really smart around you."
Jolene "Mr. Peepers, that's mean!"
SlingBlade "You think that's mean? See that girl over there? Mr. Peepers said she looks like she got hit with a bag of hot doorknobs."
Jolene "Mr. Peepers! You can't say things like that about people!"
SlingBlade "He seems to think that one over there got ambushed by a shit grenade."
Jolene "Mr. Peepers! We need to have a serious talk about your attitude!"

As she said this, she actually faced Mr. Peepers and addressed him directly, pointing at him and gesticulating in his face. I couldn't help myself:

Tucker "Are you actually talking to a plastic parrot?"
Jolene "Yes! NO! I DON'T KNOW! Come on Mr. Peepers, let's go outside!"

She took SlingBlade by the hand and led him to the backyard. Later on that night, I went outside to get more beer, and on the swing set in the backyard, Jolene and SlingBlade were kissing. Mr. Peepers was still taped to SlingBlade's shoulder, and because of the way they were sitting, Mr. Peepers was essentially a third party to the kiss. Possibly the weirdest threesome I've ever seen, and that's saying a lot.

It was getting late and time to find some pussy. Well, unbeknownst to me, Hate had gone around the party and told EVERY SINGLE GIRL that I was a player. Two girls I had made inroads with earlier told me in subsequent conversations that they weren't into me anymore because of this.

Girl "I was told you're a player. You are. You're too confident. I don't want to talk to you, because I've been played many times."
Tucker "No, no. I don't want to play you. I just want to have sex with you and then not talk to you anymore after that. That's not playing you; that's being honest."

For some inexplicable reason, this just made her madder.

Normally when people play the "stay away from him he's bad news" game, that actually helps me—girls love the asshole, after all. But not the girls at this party. PWJ's sister had indeed invited many females who were recent graduates of Southern schools. But here's what she didn't tell PWJ: They went to smaller Southern schools with evangelical leanings, like Furman. These aren't the fun Southern Baptist "sinner on Saturday, saint on Sunday" types. These are the no-sex-before-marriage types. One girl told me that she couldn't stay at the party because she had to go to church in the morning. I told her to go to the night service. She told me she goes to both.

How was everyone else doing? Let's see.

Hate

Hate was his usual charming self. This exchange typifies his approach. He would storm up to a group of women much too aggressively, and introduce himself in his stadium voice:

Hate "LADIES! HAVE YOU TRIED ANY OF THE THUG PASSION??"
Girl [*to Credit*] "Your friend is scaring me."
Credit "Yeah, he does that to all of us."

Jojo

At some point, a young lady in an angel costume arrived at the party. About an hour and fifteen minutes after that, she disappeared into a bedroom with the Black Unabomber.

Jojo and FallenAngel did not emerge for quite some time. After about twenty minutes of this clandestine interaction, Credit, who drank one and a half Thug Passions and was in their grip, got wind of this and walked in on them four times in the next hour. (He did this not only because he was drunk but also because he and Jojo are ridiculously co-dependent. It's awesomely hilarious.) Sometimes he knocked, sometimes he demanded they stop what they were doing, sometimes he brought Hate or me with him. Strangely, Jojo did not seem to lose his shit over this. That's probably because his shit was at the bottom of a cognac bottle in the backyard, but whatever.

Anyway, Jojo found a way to lock the door, they committed their acts of miscegenation in private, and an hour later, they came downstairs. Being the good friends we are, we were cool about it:

Hate "THE FALLEN ANGEL ARISES!!!"
Tucker "THE SNEAKY BLACK GUY DOES IT AGAIN!"
Credit "YOU HAD SEX WITH HER!"

FallenAngel didn't understand why we kept calling her that, so Jojo spent an hour on the stairs having a heart-to-heart with her about whatever it is drunk girls like to talk about. She thought he was a sweet guy who was listening intently to her but discovered otherwise when she looked over and found him leaning against the railing, asleep.

PWJ

PWJ was smitten with a girl in a white, dressy outfit:

PWJ "What are you supposed to be?"
WoodNymph "A goddess."
PWJ "You should tell people you are a wood nymph. Did you ever read mythology? Mortals who hooked up with goddesses always came to rather unpleasant ends."
WoodNymph "Well, we wouldn't want that happening, would we?"

His sister had earlier made him promise not to go home with Wood-Nymph, and he had agreed. Well, WoodNymph convinced him to walk her to her car, parked on a major street. On the way there he remembered that he was a smart lawyer who could parse his logic and still get what he wanted. He had promised not to go home with WoodNymph. He said nothing about hooking up with her in her car.

He started kissing her neck, she gave him a lap dance, and things started going really well . . . until the passing cars started honking. That's when she realized she was standing outside her car on a busy intersection with her shirt up to her chin, bra undone, with a guy's hands down her pants, while she was reaching back around with his dick in her hand.

For some reason this embarrassed her. She got in the car—shirt still up—and sped off.

Credit

I found Credit completely fucked-in-half drunk, to the point where he might have qualified as dead in several states. He was sitting next to a very, very unattractive girl in a Catholic schoolgirl outfit:

Credit "You better watch out. I'm a red belt in tae kwon do."
Fattie "Oh yeah? I'm a third-degree black belt."
Credit "I don't believe you."
Fattie "I'll count to twenty in Korean."
Credit "I'd rather you broke my neck and left me for dead than continue this conversation."

She actually started counting in Korean. I know a little Korean, because in boarding school I tutored all the FOB Koreans in English and chemistry. In return, they gave me bowls of kimchi noodles and taught me a little Korean. So when I say she had a GOOD accent, I know what I'm talking about. This wasn't some bullshit she learned off the internet. Ugly or not, a white girl counting in Korean intrigued me:

Tucker "How the fuck do you know Korean?"
Fattie "I work in intelligence. Korean is my specialty."
Tucker "Intelligence? For who?"

Fattie "The NSA."
Tucker "You work for the NSA? Get the fuck out of here, you do not."

She showed me her government ID card. I can't remember if it said NSA on it or not, but I don't think it did, because I still didn't believe her. I called one of my friends who knows about these things and asked him how I could confirm this. He gave me a question to ask her, something I can't remember and made no fucking sense to me at the time. Her answer, which also made no sense to me, sold him, though, "She's a legit spook."

Holy shit. Fattie works for the National Security Agency! That is the largest spy agency in the world, five TIMES bigger than the CIA. "Fuck a spy" is on my Sexual To-Do List, directly after "Fuck a midget." I've hit the jackpot!

Except for one thing—she was not attractive. On a scale of 1 to 10, she should have hung herself. Her body looked like a nesting doll made of owl pellets. She did not have a redeeming physical quality about her, maybe aside from her vagina, if in fact she had one of those.

It quickly became obvious she would fuck me. And I desperately wanted to fuck a spy. But she was so unattractive . . . I almost could not look at her. Seriously, some of the women I've fucked should have THIS SIDE TOWARD ENEMY stamped on them, but if I fucked her, she'd be the worst. EVER.

I didn't know what to do. Since my friends were around and would see me leave with her, I would not be able to disassociate the memory and pretend she was hot when I told them the "I fucked a spy" story later on. But this might be my only chance to mark spy off my list. I needed advice. I went to the bar and discussed my options:

PWJ "Dude, not good. Not good at all."
Tucker "She's not that bad. She's fuckable at least, right?"
SlingBlade "Yes, I know Mr. Peepers, Tucker would fuck a beehive."

Tucker "When I get to the bottom of this drink, she'll be fuckable."
SlingBlade "No, Mr. Peepers, I don't think that's a bottomless drink."
PWJ "If you wake up next to her, you're going to scream in terror."
Tucker "Dude, she's a spy! In the NSA! That's big-time."
Hate "You realize if she takes you home, she'll never let you leave. She can make you disappear, Max."
SlingBlade "That is, in fact, the only justifiable reason to hook up with her: if you decide you don't want your penis anymore."

Jojo, either understanding my dilemma and wanting to be a good friend, or more likely wanting me to do something so awful he would have blackmail material on me for the rest of my life, handed me a full glass of Thug Passion.

Jojo "Drink this."

As shit-housed as I already was, chugging the Thug Passion was like throwing jet fuel on a tire fire.

Tucker "Cognac is rough. Is this why rappers act so stupid all the time?"
Jojo "Quit your bitching. Are you going to make history or not?"
Tucker "I don't know man . . ."

Jojo grabbed me by the shoulders, looked me in the eye, and in his best Mystical Negro voice, said:

Jojo "Tucker, you're a single, 26 year old man. At this point in our lives, it's all about the story."
Tucker "You're right! I'm gonna do it!!"

I confidently marched off to secure my place in history . . . by fucking the ugliest, fattest spy on earth.

PWJ "If we have to go save him, we'll need to use the reflections in our shields to conquer her."
Hate "Gentlemen, I think this makes it official. We have lost our religion."
Credit "We had religion?"

SlingBlade "The rest of us did, not you. You're a Jew, you killed our Lord."

I have only spotty memories about what happened after that. I know I left the party with her and we went back to her place together, and I'm confident that I inserted my penis into some orifice at least once, and maybe twice. I have no idea if I actually came or what the sex was like. I have a vague recollection of just wishing it would end.

I woke up the next morning with a hangover that would impress Dean Martin. It was awful. I remember lying there, not recognizing anything around me and wondering where I was and how I got there. I felt some movement next to me. It was the spy. She got up from the bed, reached over to the side wall, and turned on the light. I was immediately presented with a view of her naked body: It looked like a latex glove stuffed with oatmeal. There were two huge blotched bruises on her ass. They shuddered and jiggled as waves of motion sent her lard-packed blubber rippling. She had so much pubic hair protruding from her ass crack I thought she'd shit a wig.

All at once I pondered the metaphysical exigencies of my existence. Why I was in this room? Why I was naked? Why was I staring at this discolored bag of adipose and cellulite?

Then the smell of latex hit my nose. Then seminal fluid. Then strawberry air freshener.

I vomited.

Not the type of vomit demanded by a stomach forcefully ejecting poisonous effluvium that it thinks will cause it damage. It was a quick one; essentially the same type as two nights earlier with the Georgetown undergrad and her Three Wise Men shot. You know how people say, "I just threw up in my mouth a little"? Yeah, well, I actually did.

Except I didn't catch it all in my mouth. Some of the puke got on her sheets and pillow. Not a lot, but enough that I couldn't hide it and had to confess when she asked me if I just threw up on her bed.

Every time I think I've hit bottom, every time I think I can sink no lower, every time I think I have slammed face-first into the bedrock of depravity, I find a new low. It's like my life is a limbo contest with the devil holding the stick—how low can Tucker go?

This morning it was waking up with the most repugnant sea donkey in the universe, throwing up when I saw what I had just stuck my dick in . . . and then being shamed by her for it.

Feeling guilty about throwing up in her apartment, as I left, I asked for her number. She rolled her eyes, gave me a "no one is buying your shit" look, but still wrote her number on a piece of paper for me before I left.

As soon as I was outside, I crumpled up the paper and threw it away.

Ungrateful bitch.

The Fallout

Over the next few days, we all exchanged emails recapping everything, filling in El Bingeroso and GoldenBoy on what they missed. OF COURSE, everyone ruthlessly busted my balls for hooking up with Shrek the Spying Sea Monster. But then, into that mix, PWJ dropped this:

> From: PWJ
> To: Hate, Tucker Max, GoldenBoy, El Bingeroso, Credit; Jojo, SlingBlade
> Subject: I have to come clean
>
> OK, I've been letting Credit and Max take all the heat for the party events, but there is something I haven't told anyone, and I have to come clean.
>
> You see, there was a SECOND Catholic schoolgirl at the party . . .

Tucker's schoolgirl spy was pear shaped, unattractive in every way, and a complete disaster. Nothing could fix her. This other one had a pretty face. She could be very cute. However, she would have to drop a good 60 pounds first. She was an attractive bowling ball.

Nonetheless, I am talking to this well-endowed chick in this awesome Native American outfit (another story altogether) and this Catholic schoolgirl comes up to us and just sits there listening to me with this shit-eating "I love you" grin on her face. Hanging on every word. She goes to the bathroom. So I figure, what the hell. Acting purely on instinct and hormones at this point, I follow her upstairs, pull her into my bedroom, and begin to hook up with her. She is into it but makes me promise to just kiss. After about 5 minutes, I start feeling her up. She says, "I thought we would just kiss." I pulled my hand out, rolled over, and said, "Hmmm . . . OK, I'm done kissing. It's time for you to go."

She gathered her stuff, at the door turned and said in one of the most pitiful voices I've ever heard, "You know, I thought you were a nice guy. But you're just like all your friends." She left. I chuckled for five seconds, and passed out.

Anyway, fast-forward to next morning. Bad. My sister is driving me to the airport. Tells me how glad she is I didn't hook up with the WoodNymph, because every time she hooks up with a guy, she goes psycho and all she'll talk about for the next two months is that guy, and my sister would never want to have to deal with that with her own brother. I sink into my seat.

Then the kicker. She starts talking about the Catholic School Girl (not Tucker's, mine) and how she's had the worst two years. Was engaged, fiancé was supposed to fly in from Germany, never showed up, never called, just completely ditched on the wedding. Then she found out she had cancer. It receded, but she just found out two months ago that it was back, and that party was the first time she went out since she found out.

At this point I'm ready to shoot myself. In my defense, at least it was a two-girl night. I'm rationalizing now.

The good news is that, as of now, my sister is still talking to me. Well, she is at least talking to me enough to tell me that Tucker is banned from her house and her life forever.

From: SlingBlade
To: Hate, Tucker Max, GoldenBoy, El Bingeroso, Credit, Jojo, PWJ
Subject: re: I have to come clean

Oh, boy, PWJ is going to hell on a heat seeker. I remember that second girl coming downstairs looking PISSED.

And from what I can recall, the girl I hooked up with was not unattractive, definitely above average for general population and thusly a veritable goddess in that party. Although she did have kind of bad skin. And I submit for bonus points two items:

a) college cheerleader
b) shaved

And I ended up hooking up with that girl while Jojo was passed out two feet away. Which may have been a mistake as she has called me twice since Saturday to discuss her emotional problems. I feel like Tucker. I am currently trying to avoid any and all contact with her, an act complicated by my lack of caller ID, answering machine, and the refusal of Hate to tell girls that call that I'm not home. Cancer, thy name is Jolene.

From: Tucker
To: Hate, PWJ, GoldenBoy, El Bingeroso, Credit, Jojo, SlingBlade
Subject: re: I have to come clean

PWJ, you hooked up with a girl who had cancer? How did you know? What, did you feel her breasts and there was a lump?

And wait a minute—PWJ dogs a girl with cancer, and I am the one banned from his sister's house? I will never understand why people get so upset at things I don't even remember saying.

Too many of you see this party as a disaster. I disagree. Consider what that party would have been like without the six of us:

Number of bottles of liquor brought by us: 15+
Number brought by others: 0 (seriously)
Number of mixers brought by us: 5
By others: 1 (a bottle of Sprite, which I had to look around for)
Number of shots passed out to girls by us: at least 50
By others: None that I saw, and I parked by the liquor table
Number of hookups by us with girls we weren't dating: 6
Number of hookups by others with girls that they weren't dating: 0
Number of fights started by us: 3
Number started by others: 0
Girls that left the party b/c of us: 2 confirmed, many others suspected
By others: 0
Number of people pissed off by us: 25, at least
By others: 1, maybe
Funny comments by us (including party MVP, Mr. Peepers): 1,345
By others: 12

Number of times cops called because of me yelling in the front yard: 1
By others: 0

Gentlemen, that is a record of our greatness. We are the champions, my friends.

From: PWJ
To: Hate, Tucker Max, GoldenBoy, El Bingeroso, Credit, Jojo, SlingBlade
Subject: I have to come clean

To clarify: I had no idea the girl had a disease of any type at the time of the hookup. And she wasn't in chemo or anything like that. Still, I am pretty sure I'm going to hell now.

Also, I forgot about this: In the morning when I woke up and went to the bathroom, this was scrawled on the mirror of my sister's bathroom, in lipstick:

"Lawyers suck."

The Tucker Max Experience

Occurred—April 2005

A month after I finished *IHTSBIH*, but before it came out in stores, I got this email [edited for relevance]:

> From: The Dallas Heart Ball
> To: Tucker Max
> Date: Tue, Apr 12, 2005
> Subject: We want you to be a bachelor at our auction in Dallas
>
> Tucker,
>
> I have been following your site for a while after a guy I worked with forwarded me the link. I'd like to extend an invitation for you to come to Dallas for one of the best charity events of the year.
>
> Here's the pitch: I am on the board of the Dallas Heart Ball. We are an all-volunteer organization, and all of our net profits go to the Dallas Heart Ball Fund for Pediatric Cardiology Research at UT Southwestern and Children's Medical Center here in Dallas. One of our premier events for the last two years has been our Bachelor/Bachelorette Auction (we are the only organization that has bachelorettes). We learned last year that having local celebrities helps us raise more money.
>
> We would like to have you as a celebrity bachelor at our event. Basically, each bachelor/ette is responsible for getting

together a date package. As for the date packages, the sky is the limit. Some include trips out of town, some are skydiving, and some are to sporting events. If you would like, we could have someone help you put a package together, but you probably have better resources than we do to solicit a "dream date" with Tucker Max.

We would love to have you appear as a bachelor. From reading your message board and blog, I get the sense that there are plenty of women out there who would purchase a date with Tucker Max. I think it would be fun to see just how much they are willing to pay.

I look forward to hearing from you and hope you decide to participate in this event.

[Name Redacted]

I think I laughed for a good hour at this. They want me to come up with my own date and then have women pay for it? Oh my. I couldn't get my response out fast enough:

From: Tucker Max
To: The Dallas Heart Ball
Date: Tue, Apr 12, 2005
Subject: Re: We want you to be a bachelor at our auction in Dallas

I am totally in. But I just hope you know what you are asking for.

She assured me that she understood. That always makes me laugh. People think they know, but they don't know. Like Mike Tyson says, "Everyone has a plan until they get punched in the mouth."

My date proposal to them:

From: Tucker Max
To: The Dallas Heart Ball
Date: Wed, Apr 13, 2005
Subject: For the "Tucker Max" Date, how about this . . .

The Tucker Max Experience

You will fly to Chicago for two days of sightseeing, partying, and drinking with me, Tucker Max. The details:

—We'll set a mutually convenient weekend for you to come up to Chicago.

—I will call at least once to reschedule because something better came along and I traded up. So make sure to keep at least three weekends free.

—We will talk a few times before you come to Chicago. If I haven't met you yet, I will demand pictures of you, taken from multiple angles. This is not so I can more easily identify you at the airport. It is to determine if you are hot enough to hear from me prior to your arrival.

—When you get to the airport, make sure to bring a credit card, because it is highly probable that I either forgot to buy your plane ticket or made a mistake in the reservation.

—You will fly in on a Saturday morning, and since I was out drinking the night before, there is no chance I'm picking you up. Besides, O'Hare is really fucking far away.

—This is OK though, because the El train runs right to my house and is easy to use. Don't pay attention to the scary-looking homeless guy on the train, he only wants your spare change, not your spare kidney. This isn't Detroit.

—I will answer the door in a white T-shirt with at least one hot sauce stain on it, gym shorts, messy hair, unshaven, reeking of pit sweat, stale alcohol, and fresh sex.

—Depending on how early you get to my place, there may be a girl still there. She should be getting dressed to leave by that point. If not, just ignore her. She'll be gone soon—this is YOUR special day, not hers.

—I will ask you what you want to do. If it's something I don't feel like doing, I will pretend you didn't say anything and then ask you again what you want to do. I will repeat this until your suggestion is something that sounds good to me, or until you get frustrated and ask me what I want to do. (FYI, if your suggestion includes anything that pleasures me while requiring no work on my part—e.g., fellatio—I can guarantee I will like it.)

—If there is anything about you that annoys me, I will tell you so. You will leave Chicago knowing everything that is wrong with you. If you try to defend yourself by criticizing me back, I will quickly find your deepest insecurity and viciously attack it for a solid 45 minutes. I call this "foreplay."

—I constantly have my hands in my pants. I'm not jacking off or even playing with myself; sometimes I just get afraid I've lost my penis somewhere, and I like to make sure it's still there. Just a heads-up.

—After I ignore your suggestions on what to do for a few hours, I'll be hungry for lunch. I will ask you what you want, but regardless of what you say, we will go to my favorite place in Chicago: Harold's Chicken Shack.

—Being that you're the type of person who goes to charity balls, you might be shocked by the "urban" location and decor of Harold's. Don't worry: The bulletproof glass is there to protect the cashier—she's the one who gets robbed, not you.

—I will snort and grunt as I shovel the food into my mouth with my bare hands. I'll get grease and hot sauce all over my face and my already stained shirt. I will offer you a chicken bone I've picked clean, "Want some?" The look on your face will be funny to me. I will repeat this for as many times as I find it funny.

—After this glorious ghetto feast, I will take a two-hour nap on the sofa. Be careful, I fart a lot after I eat fried foods.

—I don't care what you do during that time, but no, I am not going to cuddle with you. Unless it is postcoital cuddling.

—After I wake up, I'll feel bad that you flew all this way and didn't even get to see any of the famous Chicago sights, so I'll ask you what you want to do.

—I'll pretend to pay attention to what you are saying, while I go to the fridge. I'll get a few beers, pound them, then ask you again what you want to do.

—Depending on how many beers I've had, I may repeatedly point to my crotch and nod approvingly. This is what I call "a hint."

—If you haven't given up at this point and just surrendered to my will, bravo. I'll remind you that this is your special day, and we're going to do what you want to do.

—Regardless of your request, we will head to an early all-you-can-drink with my friends. You may ask if I am going to change or shower before we go out. I'll tell you that I will, but just walk straight out the door. I'm so funny!

—When we get to the bar, I will "forget" my money and you will have to pay for both of us. Fair warning: Unless I am already drunk and I really like you, don't expect me to thank you for it. My presence should be thanks enough.

—At the bar, I'll introduce you to my friends and I might get your first drink for you (to make sure the drinks actually are on your tab), but after that I will wander around talking to other girls to see if I can trade up.

—Some of my friends will be nice to you and try to help you forget that I am ignoring you in favor of other women. At least a few of my friends will try to hook up with you (the hotter you are, the more they will hit on you, so if none do, that means you're ugly). Don't believe the awful lies they tell you. You know the REAL me.

—A dozen or so vodka clubs into the night, and after I've already pissed off most of the other girls in the bar, if there are no better prospects, I will come back and talk to you to see if you want to hook up with me.

—If not, we'll go to another place, with more and different girls.

—On to the next, rinse and repeat.

—And the next.

—By the time we get to the fourth or fifth bar, I will be completely shit-housed, will have stains on top of stains on my shirt, there may or may not be several whores trailing us, vying for my attention, and at least one of my friends will have told you that you are too good for me and should love him, because he is such a wonderful person. (FYI: He's a hater and a liar.)

—Hopefully by this point I've succeeded in breaking you down to the point where you just give in—exasperated surrender sex is the best! I'll give you a night so memorable, it'll help you reach a place addiction specialists refer to as "the bottom."

—If you think you love me, then I'm sorry your dad was so mean to you. I'll show you that I care by shooting my compassion juice into you and then cuddling with you as it leaks out onto my sheets, because after all, it is YOUR night.

—If you hate me so much that it's obvious you aren't going to fuck me, I will do something to cause you either to storm off in anger or go home with one of my friends. Then I can go fuck one of the various sluts orbiting me without feeling bad about ruining YOUR day. You get angry revenge sex, and my friend gets laid. Everybody wins!

—We will wake up the next morning just in time for you to rush to the El and catch your flight. Since you took the train in and already know the way, I won't bother getting out of bed.

—When you get home, you will regret ever meeting me. If we had sex, you will rush to the free clinic to get tested. The results will come back negative, and you'll think to yourself, "At least the fact that he passed out a minute into sex has some benefit."

—Any and/or all of this is changeable, revocable, etc., at my will or discretion. (Insert legalese where I waive all responsibility for my actions despite what I do. I would type it out, but I didn't go to class in law school.)

—If you made it to this point, you probably think I am a funny writer. I am. And you're probably also thinking I have to be kidding. I'm not.

—Seriously.

Can't wait to meet you!

I am sure you can guess how this turned out, but I'll give you the executive summary anyway: The Dallas Heart Ball freaked out, and I was immediately uninvited.

I am really not sure what they expected, but like I said: They think they know, but they have no idea.

I'd hate to see the work I put into this wasted, so let me end with a side note: This date proposal is still on the table for any charity that would like to put it to use. Email me and we'll talk: tuckermax@gmail.com.

The Tucker Max Sexual To-Do List

One day during our first year of law school, my friends and I were sitting around drunk, comparing notes on all the unusual places we'd had sex. Some of them had pretty cool ones; I can't remember any of them, because I never pay attention to anyone but myself. I do remember that my best place ever—Barcelona Museum of Modern Art, on an exhibit—didn't rate very highly with the group.

Fortunately, I don't really care about that crap. At least not yet. Maybe after I get married and stop fucking lots of different women, then all the various places I fuck my wife will be fun to me, like it was to my engaged friends. You know, since it'll be the only variety left.

What really mattered to me was all the different *types* of women I'd fucked. In college, I thought I was pretty cool because I'd hooked up with all the major races: white, black, Asian, Middle Eastern, Indian (casino AND dot), etc. But I was quickly put to shame by GoldenBoy, who had fucked a Canadian female bodybuilder who could bench press more than he could. Wow. That's cool. Not many people can say that.

And that was just the beginning. As we went around the group, PWJ trumped me (a famous politician's daughter, in her dad's bed), Jojo trumped me (a famous female athlete), even misanthrope SlingBlade trumped me (a friend's mom). Almost everyone had some sort of cool hookup I couldn't match. This was complete fucking bullshit!

Considering that I am better than all of them, I could not let this stand. I vowed to create an epic Sexual To-Do List, one that would include every possible type of cool hookup I could think of. Then I would go out and complete it. I would never lose a dick-measuring contest again! All men may be idiots, but I will be their king!

I ended up with a huge list and an awesome collection of stories relating to it. Here is the final and completed Tucker Max Sexual To-Do List:

—hot female midget
—amputee
—twins
—virgin
—within thirty minutes of meeting her
—without knowing her name
—mother and daughter
—married woman
—mile high club
—professional model
—famous woman
—religious girl on her parents' bed
—girl with fake breasts
—Hooters girl
—military officer
—one of my teachers/professors/TA
—cop
—federal agent (two actually, DEA and FBI)
—friend's mom
—mom's friend
—paraplegic/confined to a wheelchair but still has vaginal sensation
—female professional athlete
—escort (without paying)
—carnie
—threesome (mff)
—three girls (mfff)
—four or more, all girls (mffff+)
—two different girls in 12 hours, not together or in related incidents
—three different girls in 24 hours, not together or in related incidents
—girl that weighs more than me

—girl that weighs less than 100 pounds
—MILF
—GILF
—Miss America contestant
—Miss USA contestant
—Rhodes scholar
—Marshall scholar
—real-life CIA or NSA agent (I got only an NSA agent; I would re-open the list for a hot CIA analyst)
—stripper I picked up that night at a strip club w/o paying
—daughter of someone big/important
—plus-sized model
—porn star
—giant (6'6")
—girl who doesn't speak any English
—paroled felon
—pregnant
—goth/emo chick
—girl with colostomy bag
—a funny tattoo on/around vagina
—tongue ring
—clit ring
—deaf girl
—girl with a glass eye
—midget threesome

Ethnicities/Nationalities

—English
—Irish
—Scottish
—German
—French
—Spanish
—Mexican
—Honduran
—Nicaraguan

—Colombian

—Venezuelan

—Brazilian

—Argentinean

—Swiss

—Dutch

—Swedish

—Finnish

—Russian

—Belarussian

—Lithuanian

—Italian

—Japanese

—Chinese (mainland)

—Chinese (Taiwanese; she stopped fucking me after I nicknamed her PRC)

—Chinese (Hmong)

—Korean (South only)

—Vietnamese

—Montagnard

—Cambodian

—Thai

—Laotian

—American Indian (Miccosukee)

—American Indian (Seminole—an actual Seminole, not just an FSU slut)

—Indian (Gujarati)

—Indian (Hindu)

—Indian (Punjabi)

—Indian (Sikh)

—Indian (Tamil)

—Indian (Bengali)

—Iranian (Pashtun)

—Iranian (Persian)

—Saudi

—Afghani

—Palestinian (I asked her, "Where is that country on the map?" She got MAD.)

—Turkish

—Eritrean

—Israeli (real Israeli, not some Jappy American girl—though I've fucked plenty of those too)

—Egyptian

Why?

You may be asking yourself, "What is wrong with this guy? Why have a Sexual To-Do List"? If you're asking that question, you clearly don't know anything about me, and I'm not exactly sure why you're reading this book at all. Maybe you picked it up by accident, so in the spirit of tolerance, I'll explain.

Compiling a Sexual To-Do List started out about bragging rights. I couldn't be the center of attention with my friends that day in the law school, and I hated it, so I refused to let it happen again. Now when I'm at a bar with my friends and we start comparing hookups, I have a full clip, one in the chamber, and the safety set to full auto. When someone asks, "Who's fucked twins?" or "Who's fucked a deaf girl?" I can be the one who proudly raises his hand and says, "Both." It's the ultimate win in male one-upmanship.

And it pays out dividends forever. 20 years from now, when I'm retired from the game and married with five kids, and PWJ calls to brag that his daughter was named a Rhodes scholar, I can say, "I fucked one of those." See what I mean?

If you're a man who has friends, you understand bragging rights. If you're a woman scoffing at how stupid men are to care about something so pointless, think about how it differs from competing over shoes, handbags, and diamonds. Exactly.

Most of what we do—men and women—is ultimately about some sort of status seeking. If you care only about meaningful things and not the silly status competitions most people get into, then you have my congratulations, because you're a bodhisattva. Say hi to the Dalai Lama for me and tell him I follow him on Twitter.

This may not be a completely satisfactory answer, because honestly, it's not the whole answer. There's also the element of conquest. Like when the reporter asked George Mallory why he attempted Mount Everest (30 years before Edmund Hillary succeeded). His response: "Because it's there." Same thing I answered when a reporter asked me why I wanted to fuck a midget: "Because she's down there." It's just a natural thing for a guy, when he sees something that others think is unattainable, to attain it, just for the sake of being able to say he's done it.

One of my favorite documentaries, *Man on Wire*, addresses this issue perfectly. It's about Philippe Petit, the guy who rigged a tightrope between the World Trade Center towers, then spent 45 minutes walking back and forth. As soon as he got down, the press asked him why he would do such a thing. He looked at them confused, as if he couldn't even understand the need to ask the question:

"There is no why. When I see three oranges, I juggle. When I see two towers, I walk."

I would add humbly, "And when I see a midget, I fuck."

Current Status of the List

At this point, I've retired the list and closed it to new entries because, come on—at what point does novelty turn into absurdity? Like a curve forever approaching its asymptote but never touching it, I could potentially add to the list forever. To sleep with every possible type of girl, you have to sleep with every girl. I like women, and I like having sex with them, but that's just not reasonable. I want to do things besides fuck—like write about fucking.

Besides, if the point of all of this is conquest and bragging rights, and I have both of those in spades, why keep going? There's always another mountain to climb. I'm stopping at a reasonable point, taking a moment to be proud of my accomplishments, and then moving on the next challenge. Like having a healthy, loving, committed relationship.

Beyond that, I was stretching the limits of what even I was willing to do. Everything worthwhile that was left was disconcerting to me. For example, I met a cute blind girl who seemed into me, but I couldn't do it. She had those milky, dead, cataract eyes, and they moved independently of each other, like a gecko's. She was drunk and kept feeling my face, and . . . I don't want to accuse a cripple of being inappropriate, but I swear she spent extra time on my eyes, like she was trying to determine if they were the right size to fit in her head. FREAKED ME OUT. I'm passing.

For a time, I did seriously consider conjoined twins. The problem is that there are only like 10 sets of female conjoined twins in the world, and they are all horribly deformed. (Seriously, I researched it.) If I have sex with a girl only because I want to extend the list, that crosses the line from funny-yet-enjoyable to creepy-and-pathological. Most of the fun in the list is not in the collection but in the journey: finding someone you want to hook up with who is also on the list, the experiences you and your friends have along the way, and the hilarious memories you accrue. That, and being able to brag that I fucked an amputee, of course.

Some of the things on the list are kinda pedestrian, things you and your friends have probably all done. Some others are pretty cool but still definitely attainable. And some are just straight-up amazing. Put them all together and it's like a straight flush of bragging rights. You may have the high card, but I have the better hand.

Shit, just take my three favorites: an amputee, a pair of twins, and a midget. By itself—without looking at anything else on the list—that is a legendary trifecta. How many other people can say they have done that?

Seriously, raise your hand if you even KNOW someone who has done that. I'm sure I'm not the only guy on earth who has done it, but I bet you could fit all of us into a Prius.

These are the stories of those three.

The Amputee Story

Occurred—September 2005

As a general rule, I try never to hook up with a girl solely because she is a type on my list. Even if I meet a girl who is, say, a paraplegic, I would need a "real" reason to have sex with her, something like, "She's hot," or "I like her as a person," or "She's the only girl at the bar willing to fuck me."

The amputee started off as an exception, as just a "type." A girl I knew worked with a girl who had a leg amputation. She knew about my Sexual To-Do List, and she offered to set me up with the amputee.

Tucker "I don't know. What if I don't like her? If I hook up with her only because of her amputated leg, that would be gross. She's already physically gross; I don't think I can handle being both emotionally and physically repulsed."
Friend "Tucker, trust me on this. I know you and I know her. Not only is she hot, she is very much your type, and you are hers. You two will love each other. I'd set you up even if she had all her limbs."
Tucker "You are the best gimp pimp ever."

I email her and quickly realize that my friend was right: Not only were her pics pretty hot—a legit four star—she seemed cool. And she was clearly naughty. No doubt this one was down to fuck.

We met up and she was even better looking in person. Then she told me the story of how she lost her leg in a car accident and made a joke about it:

Tucker "So you're cool with jokes about your leg?"
Peggy "Yeah, of course. It's no big deal."
Tucker "Sweet. I'm gonna run with this."

Had she not been missing a leg, it would have just been a normal night out with a fun girl and nothing to write about. But the amputation combined with her sense of humor made for some good exchanges:

Tucker "What do you want for dinner? A foot-long maybe?"
Peggy "I'm gonna ask the waiter, he'll give me a leg up."
Tucker "NICE! You're better at this than I am."
Peggy "More practice."
Tucker "I hope he recommends a beer with lots of hops."

Tucker "The normal adult body has 206 bones. How many do you have?"
Peggy "Well, I'm missing a tibia and fibula. Plus, how many bones are in the foot?"
Tucker "Not sure. You've stumped me."

Tucker "Seriously, though, if you were a hooker, would you have to charge less because you are missing parts, or more, because some guys will be into that?"
Peggy "Good question. I'm definitely out of the foot fetish game, I know that."
Tucker "Well, you could do it, but you could only charge half."

Tucker "So what's it like to play Twister with you?"
Peggy "I prefer Monopoly. I'm always the shoe."

Tucker "Your favorite movie has to be *My Left Foot*. What about your favorite song? 'Jump Around' by House of Pain?"
Peggy "'Runnin', by Tupac."

Tucker "This is weird for me. I've fucked hundreds of women with amputated self-esteem, but none with amputated limbs."

Peggy "How about one with both?"
Tucker "I think I love you."

After dinner we went back to the hotel and I watched her take off her prosthetic. It was less exciting than I'd hoped. In my dreams, I envisioned something like the scene in the original *Star Wars* when Darth Vader is woken from his sleep and puts on his mask. Unfortunately, there was no cool whooshing noise or release of carbon gas. She just slid it off and dropped it to the floor with a dull thud. The only thing that could have been more disappointing would have been if she had both her legs.

What was cool was her stump. It was ticklish, and she giggled and squirmed when I rubbed it. That was awesome, but the kicker was how she could also wiggle her stump. It was spooky. She essentially did the same thing as when she wiggled her toes, but since there were no toes anymore, it just moved the muscles that are still there—and those do wiggle. It creeped me out to the point where I had to make her stop so that I could keep the erection I'd gotten from playing with her prosthetic.

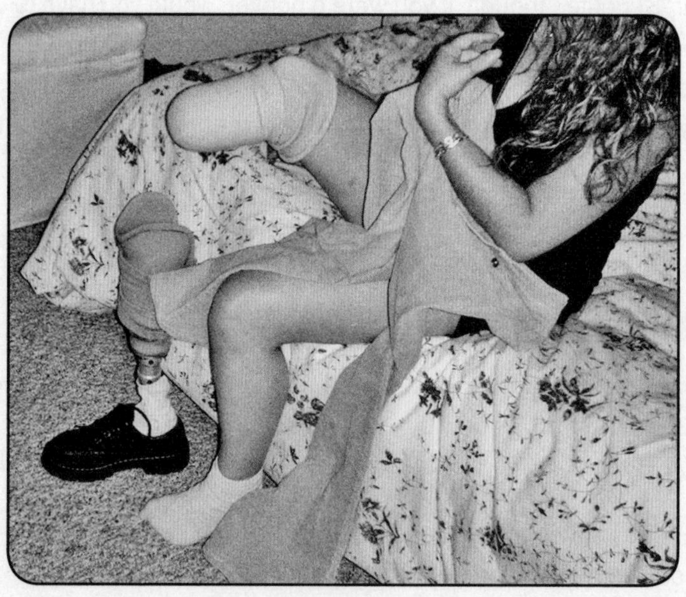

Then we had sex. I kinda hate to say this, but it was pretty normal sex. Don't get me wrong—it was great, and we hooked up two or three times, but there was nothing all that unusual about it.

Here's the thing: As you can see from the pics, her amputation is below the knee. How often do you really deal with a girl's shins or feet during sex? Not much. Even when I had her legs over my shoulders, the little stub was like a hook and that secured her to me, no prob.

As we were leaving, I told her about the Sexual To-Do List and how she now had a place on it. She actually thought it was pretty funny.

Peggy "So, now that you've checked amputee off your list, am I going to see you again?"
Tucker "Yeah, maybe. You'd be pretty cool even if you had all your appendages."
Peggy "Then you better call me again, or I'll be hopping mad with you."
Tucker "Don't get jumpy. You barely have a leg to stand on with me."

My only lasting regret is that, when I fucked her from behind, I didn't spank her with the prosthetic leg or at least find some way to use it as some sort of hilarious prop. Oh well, I'll probably get a chance to fuck another hot amputee. There are forgotten landmines all over the world, and my first book was translated into dozens of languages. Wish me luck!

The Aborted Twins

Occurred—February 2005

I've definitely hooked up with two pairs of identical twins, and possibly three. The third pair, I'm not so sure they were twins. They might have just been two girls who looked a lot alike and were lying to me. I was kinda drunk that night. If we're counting fraternal twins, I think it might be more. I don't know, I've lost track of details like that. Awesome people fuck lots of twins. Creepers take a census.

Even though I've fucked multiple pairs, I don't really have any great hooking-up-with-twins stories. What can I tell you? Real life doesn't always cooperate with my need for material.

But I do have a pretty funny story about a pair of twins I was *supposed* to fuck. It all started with this email:

> "Hi Tucker!
>
> We're 19 year old TWIN girls from [redacted]. We just started reading your website and we can't stop cuz you're so freaking hilarious (even though you have asshole tendencies). We think if you hung out with us, you'd have a good time cuz we're funny and gross . . . just like you! (not gross like unhygenic or physically disgusting), but we have a weird sense of humor we think would mesh well with yours! By the way . . . you have beautiful blue eyes :-) For your viewing pleasure, we have enclosed three pictures, we know we're flat . . . no need to bring

that up . . . OK well please write us back just to let us know you read and considered this email. Thank you so much!

Love, [redacted] and [redacted] (your new favorite twins)"

A lot of things suck about being infamous, but getting emails from hot 19 year old twins wanting to fuck you is pretty awesome.

In the abstract, at least. But then they showed up. These girls were giggly, nervous, immature teenagers. With Sleeping Beauty sleeping bags and Finding Nemo pillows. And too much makeup on. And braces. And blue tongues and teeth because they mixed the rotgut vodka they drank on the drive here with some fountain drink from 7-Eleven so they could get it down. And they didn't have fake IDs so I couldn't even take them out to a bar. You should have seen the judgmental faces on D-Rock and Bunny (my roommates at the time).

Whatever, fuck those two, they're just jealous because I'm going to fuck twins, right?

Tucker "All right, so do I get you one at a time, or both at once?"
Twin 1 "Uh . . . well . . ."
Twin 2 "We thought you would just pick one of us."
Twin 1 "You said I got to sleep with him!"
Twin 2 "It's up to him, let him pick!"
Twin 1 "You're going to do something to make him pick you, I know it, you always do this!"

This is the dark side of twins they don't show you in those Doublemint commercials.

I decide we'll head out for drinks, to see if this can be worked out. Because of the ID situation, we are forced to go to an apartment party being thrown by a friend of D-Rock. This guy went to the University of Chicago with us. I only vaguely remembered him as an annoying dork in college, but he was smart enough to get a job in finance that made him more money than he could spend on original anime cels and Philippine sex vacations, so with the extra money, he bought a really nice apartment in Wrigleyville and had people over all the time, hoping he could develop coolness by proxy.

Well, of course, he and his friends nearly choked when I walked into his party with twins on my arms. They remembered me as an asshole from undergrad, well before I was famous for it, and of course they hated me for it then. Seeing the twins enraged them.

For the rest of the night, the host and his coterie of nerd friends gawked at me and acted appalled to each other. Leave it up to hipster nerds to pretend to hate something they actually want.

Unbeknownst to them, I was having problems of my own. I was trying to convince the twins that the best situation was not me picking one to sleep with, but me fucking both of them. They were vehemently against anything that even resembled a threesome, which was fine. Yes I'm from Kentucky, but only some of us rednecks are incestuous.

This meant I had to figure out a way to fuck them both, but separately. They weren't opposed in principle to me fucking both of them; the problem was that neither wanted to be second. Essentially, if I fucked one, the other wouldn't fuck me for the rest of the weekend. It became this infuriating, circular dance whose steps were defined by whore logic and sibling rivalry. But like Solomon, I find a way to split the baby:

Tucker "But why does it matter who's first and who's second?"
Twin 1 "It's just weird."
Twin 2 "It's more special if it's only one of us."
Tucker "How about this compromise? I'll fuck one of you in the vagina and then the other one in the ass. That way, you'll both be the first of what you get . . . and thus it'll be special for both of you."
Twin 1 "I don't know."
Twin 2 "Maybe."
Tucker "I'll even shower between you two. To make it *really* special."

Because I was drunk and being loud, everyone around me heard this exchange. You should have seen the nerds' faces as they listened in. I thought they were going to shit Haterade all over the polished wood floors.

But just as I was making real headway with the "vaginal and anal can make you both special" argument, Twin 1 started to feel woozy. Apparently two pints of Popov vodka mixed with blue sugar water will do that. She ran to the bathroom to vomit, with the host chasing after her, whining, "Get it in the toilet! In the toilet!" Nice, dude—without your helpful screeching, she wouldn't know where to put her vomit.

When she came out of the bathroom, the dude followed her with a bucket, like a nervous maid. All that money, all that stuff, and no freedom to just have fun.

Now I was presented with a conundrum. With this anal on one, vaginal on another plan, I could possibly pull off the greatest twins threesome ever, but I had to figure out a way to sober up Twin 1 first.

I took her outside. It was February in Chicago, so it was fucking COLD.

Tucker "OK, if you want to be the first one to fuck me, you have to prove it by sobering up."
Twin 1 "OK. How do I sober up?"
Tucker "Do some sprints up and down the street. As fast as you can, down to the white house, then back. Do it four times, then we'll see how sober you are."

I'm not saying that this makes me cool or anything, but I will say it does strange things to a man to watch a 19 year old girl sprint up and down Waveland Avenue in the bitter winter cold, just so you'll fuck her in the pussy, before you fuck her twin in the ass.

As she was doing her Carl Lewis impersonation, some random dudes walked down the street, saw her, and stopped, completely baffled.

Random "Why is she sprinting up and down the street?"
Tucker "She drank too much."
Random "It's only too much if you can't handle it."

The sprinting actually worked. She sobered up enough that I thought she was ready to have sex, so I collected everyone and we headed home. The twins drove to the party in their car, but they were both way too drunk to drive now and so was I, so Bunny and I took their car, and D-Rock drove the twins in my car. As Bunny and I got in their car, I could not help but brag:

Tucker "Seriously, Bunny, how amazing is this? I might be the coolest dude on earth."

She rolled her eyes, turned on the car, and we were assaulted by the tape deck blaring out calypso music:

> "Up on the shore they work all day, out in the sun they slave away
> While we devotin' full time to floatin', UNDER THE SEA!"

If you don't recognize those lyrics, it's either because you don't have children or you're Amish. Either way, consider yourself lucky. That is "Under the Sea." The title song from *The Little Mermaid.* Playing, at full blast, on the twins' car stereo.

Bunny "Tucker . . ."
Tucker "Shut up."
Bunny "Hehhehehehehehehehehehheh!"
Tucker "Whatever. Sebastian is underrated anyway."
Bunny "HAHAHAHAHAHAHAHAHAHH!"
Tucker "Fuck you! That song won an Oscar!" [Fuck you too, it really did.]

We got back to my place, and they started arguing like Persian rug merchants. It appeared they rejected the whole "vaginal for one and anal for the other" idea on the ride home and reverted to arguing about who would be the one to fuck me.

Twin 1 "If you fuck him, I'm leaving!"
Twin 2 "Shut up, you're too drunk to even walk to his bedroom!"
Twin 1 "You said I got to fuck him!"
Twin 2 "You're too drunk! You can't even get off the sofa!"
Twin 1 "I worked two shifts for you! You always do this, you slut!"

You know how when you get super-excited about something and then don't get it, it makes you ten times more disappointed than if you'd never had any expectations in the first place? If I'd expected to be with just one twin, I'd have been happy with that night. But the apparent loss of the legendary twin threesome, on top of everything else, was too much for me.

Tucker "You two figure this out. I'll be in my room waiting for whoever shows up."

About ten minutes later, Twin 2 came to my room, told me Twin 1 was passed out, and fucked the shit out of me. And the next day, Twin 1 got up early and made Twin 2 leave with her, without letting me fuck her in the butt.

At least, I think it was Twin 2. It wasn't both of them, so who really cares which one it was?

The Midget Story

Occurred—July 2006

We all have dreams. Martin Luther King dreamt of racial harmony. Larry Hagman dreamt of Jeannie. I dreamt of fucking a hot female midget.

A hot female midget. Those four words had been sitting on the top of the Tucker Max Sexual To-Do List for going on eight years. As I checked more and more types of women off the list, that one remained, always there, staring at me, mocking my feeble efforts and castigating my failures. It was the one arena I'd always yearned to conquer and the one that had consistently eluded me. The last meaningful box to check off my list. It had become my white whale, and in my monomaniacal pursuit, I had become Ahab. Yet, as relentless as I was, each time it skirted my harpoon.

Then, in July 2006, I finally did it. This story is about how, by risking everything and by never giving up, I accomplished my dream:

I was living in NYC at the time. I was at the gym when I got this text message from my buddy Nils. He likes to play with my emotions, so I never take his text messages seriously:

Nils: "There is a midget convention at the hilton in milwaukee here with my girlfriend and soylent is here too"
Tucker: "Fuck you"
Nils: "Im dead serious"
Tucker: "I hate you"
Nils: "Soylent has a free roundtrip ticket"
Tucker: "STOP TEASING ME"

He called me a few minutes later, when I was at home, wiping off the sweat and preparing to cook dinner.

Nils "Did you get my message? I am in Milwaukee with my girlfriend . . . and there is a midget convention in town this weekend."
Tucker "I got your fucking message. Come on man, stop playing."
Nils "Tucker, I am DEAD serious. They are everywhere. It's like the circus and *The Wizard of Oz* are in town at the same time. I swear on our friendship there are hundreds of midgets here."

[*10 second pause*]

Tucker "I'm on the next flight."

It took me about 40 seconds to throw clothes into a duffel bag and another 20 seconds to sprint out the door and onto Park Avenue. I was in a cab to LaGuardia within one minute of getting the call. The TV and lights in my apartment were still on, I'd left a steak thawing in the sink, and I was still covered in gym sweat.

In the cab, I was so excited I nearly hyperventilated. I called all my best friends and screamed incoherent gibberish about sex with little people. The call to Junior was the best:

Junior "What is wrong with you? Why not just get a midget hooker and be done with it?"
Tucker "Junior, if you buy Dwight Gooden's World Series ring off eBay, that doesn't mean that you were on the '86 Mets. Some things you can only claim if you earn them. MIDGET PUSSY, HERE I COME!"
Junior "I will never understand you."

I was more excited about this than I was when my book hit the *New York Times* best-seller list. I felt like a six year old at Disneyland on the night before Christmas.

At the airport, in line for my ticket, I was forced to fly Midwest Airlines because they are the only airline that cares enough about Milwaukee to fly there. A very nice, very Midwestern couple was in front of me. The man's shirt had a picture of cheese on it.

Tucker "You guys going to Milwaukee?"
Guy "Yes sir, heading home after a vacation."
Tucker "Did you know there are midgets in Milwaukee right now?"

The man and his wife were silent and confused.

Tucker "HUNDREDS OF THEM!"

They turned around and mumbled something about crazy New Yorkers. Whatever, they've never fucked a midget, they don't matter.

The flight was nearly intolerable, because my mind was spinning with questions: What are their daily lives like? Do they get to live in those cool handicapped apartments with the really low door handles and counters? Since their arms are too short to reach their crotches, how do they wipe? Or masturbate?

What is the etiquette for dealing with them? Are you allowed to hold them like a football? Or drape them over your shoulder like a fire hose? When you hug them, can you hold them tight like a teddy bear and promise to pet them and love them? When she's riding me, can I spin her like a top?

I was in Milwaukee by 10pm. My buddy Soylent picked me up, and we were at the Hilton hotel bar by 11pm. Upon seeing my first gaggle of midgets, I almost shit myself.

There were six of them, sitting at a table, drinking just like normal people, their tiny little legs barely hanging over the seats, tiny little feet dangling like a toddler's. Their Miller Lite bottles looked massive as they gripped them with both their tiny little hands. Their humongous brow ridges were raised in excitement on their enormous foreheads, as they laughed at tiny little jokes.

Tucker "You know CPR, right? I think my heart might explode."
Soylent "You are so fucking weird."

Then I saw her: my MidgetPrincess. Her blond hair and sparkling blue eyes made me think of Gwyneth Paltrow. Her missing neck and bowlegs gave me an idea what Gwyneth would look like if she were placed in a vise and squished to one-quarter size.

As she glided past my table on pigeon-toed feet, I slid low in my chair, hoping to catch her eye. She looked at me and smiled, her mashed-up teeth sparkling in the oily light of the popcorn machine. I gave her an unmistakable "I want to fuck you" look, she shot me back a quick "my spine hurts" face, and I was smitten.

I started planning out how I was going to hit on her, but much to my dismay, I found myself feeling something I had not felt in so long I didn't recognize it at first: nervousness. What the fuck? I literally couldn't remember the last time I was nervous around a girl. Is this what it's like to be an average guy? This sucks.

Every time I tried to talk to one of the midgets I would start giggling and sweating; it was fucking ridiculous and comical. I felt like a middle schooler who'd snuck into his sister's college party. Eventually, Soylent—who thinks he's better than me because he isn't obsessed with fucking a midget—had to take over and get us in with them.

I think the midgets took a liking to Soylent because he is barely taller than they are and he looks exactly like Gimli the dwarf from the *Lord of the Rings* movies. Within minutes we were sitting with the little people. Midget-Princess was at the table, and even though I'd only had like five beers, the room was spinning around her. I would talk, but I couldn't hear the words coming out of my mouth. She would answer back, and it sounded like a chorus of tiny little angels. Is this what love is like? If so, I might have to try it.

Then it happened:

Soylent "So, what's up tonight at the Chocolate Factory? Any cool parties?"
MaleMidget "Oh, dude, you should come with us upstairs. It's the last night of the LP [Little Person] convention, there is a big dance on the fifth floor."
Tucker "Don't play with me. If you are lying about this, I don't think I could handle it."
MaleMidget [*looking at me like I'm a weirdo*] "No dude. It should be fun. Everyone is up there. Let's go."

I ask you to put yourself in the following situation and see what your reaction would be:

Go to a hotel. Hit the button for the elevator. Take note of the step stool sitting underneath the button panel. There is a back scratcher tethered to the stool. On the wall above the stool is a note: PLEASE DO NOT REMOVE STOOL. Ride the elevator up to the fifth floor. Walk out into the hallway, and do a double take at the FLEET of Rascal scooters in the ballroom lobby. (Rascals are those red motorized scooters that you always see old people on in the grocery store.) You might first think you stumbled into a geriatric convention, but you study the people on the Rascals and realize something:

Their feet are dangling. They are all midgets! MIDGETS ON RASCALS!!!

Reeling from this discovery, you head into the ballroom and see approximately FOUR HUNDRED MIDGETS!!! ALL OF THEM ARE DANCING TO BABY HUEY!!! AND THEY ARE POPPING AND LOCKING!

I repeat: HUNDREDS OF MIDGETS ARE POPPING AND LOCKING!!!

What would you do? WHAT WOULD YOU DO???

I got a massive erection.

As much as I would love to tell you a really cool story about how I spent the next hour hitting on all the hot midgets, dancing with them, doing tiny little body shots off tiny little bodies, and tossing midgets all around the hotel . . . I can't, because nothing like that happened.

Basically, I just sat there, vacant as a lobotomy patient, staring at the midgets, in utter disbelief at the scene unfolding before me—it was complete midget overload. Six midgets at a table had me nearly catatonic; you can only imagine what 400 dancing midgets did. And when I saw the two midgets slow dancing, but the midget guy was so short that the midget girl had to kneel to dance with him, I was done.

I am honestly not sure how the next part progressed, but I do know for damn sure I had nothing to do with it. One moment I was sitting at a table in the ballroom, staring in utter disbelief at the midget dance party in front of me. The next moment I was part of a group walking toward the elevator.

That group was me, Nils, Soylent, our female friend Jessie . . . and three midgets, one female and two male.

Tucker [*whispering*] "Jessie, there are three midgets with us."
Jessie [*normal voice*] "I know, I invited them. I think the girl will fuck you."
Tucker [*still whispering*] "If she does, I will name all my illegitimate daughters after you."

The elevator ride was awesome.

Soylent [*to one of the male midgets with us*] "So, you like midget girls or normal girls?"
Midget "Fuck that midget shit, man. I want me a BIG girl!" [*Pointing at Jess*] "Soylent, you think you could set me up with some pussy?!"
Soylent "Goddamn man, what do you think, I'm running a midget convention whorehouse special? I'm not fucking her, you are welcome to knock yourself out trying, fucker!"
Tucker "Hey man, can you talk to dolphins and pilot whales with that huge forehead of yours?"
DolphinMidget "Fuck you, asshole! Did you come here with Jessie, because I'm gonna fuck her in front of you!"
Tucker "EEK EEK EEK! That's dolphin for 'I'm sorry.' But you already knew that."
DolphinMidget "Hey, you guys wanna smoke some rock? I got a connection in Milwaukee, this taxi driver. I'm gonna call him in a minute."

Did a midget just ask me if I wanna smoke some crack with him? I had to pinch myself to see if I was in a dream. Not only are there midgets, there are midget crackheads too? How many times in one night can I think to myself, "This is too good to be true?"

At the hotel bar, Jessie started to go to work on my MidgetPrincess. Jessie was pimping me so hard, she was doing everything but smacking me up for having short money. Being pimped by a girl to another girl is pretty much the optimal situation for a guy, so I did the best thing I could do: shut the fuck up, smiled at MidgetPrincess when she looked at me, bought everyone beer, and let it all play out. When you have a girl running game for you, the more you speak, the greater the chance you'll fuck it up. Be quiet and let the girl do the work. Women trust women, not men, so the less you interfere—the *less* game you run—the better. Sounds counterintuitive, illogical, and borderline retarded? Welcome to women, enjoy your stay.

At one point, DolphinMidget accosts Jessie when she is in the women's bathroom.

DolphinMidget "Hey, baby . . . wanna get down?"
Jessie "Uhhh, no."
DolphinMidget "IT'S 'CAUSE YOU HATE MIDGETS, ISN'T IT?!"

Though she did not fuck him, Jessie found out the answer to a question we all had. She came back from the bathroom giggling.

Jessie "I just saw him pee! He pulled his junk out of his pants, and laid across the toilet sideways. It was awesome!"

When I got beers for all of us, I discovered something mildly amusing about Milwaukee. If you are ever there, order a Budweiser. Seriously, people FLIP OUT at you. I was confused at first, until it was explained to me: The city of Milwaukee is basically owned by Miller Brewing Company, and of course their big rival is Bud, presumably because they are located in St. Louis. Hey, Milwaukeeans, I'm going to let you in on a little secret: Bud, MGD, Bud Light, Miller Lite—it's all shitty beer. No one cares except fat-assed cow town hicks like you. Get over it and focus on something important, like why you're out of breath when you go from the La-Z-Boy to the kitchen.

At closing time, the whole crew—three midgets included—came back with us to Soylent's place to party. As we crossed the street, several cars zoomed past, so I reached down to hold the hand of MidgetPrincess—you know, because I'm a gentleman and shit.

She reached up to grab my hand, but hers was too small to grasp mine . . . so instead she wrapped her entire palm and Jimmy Dean sausage fingers around just my pinky.

I'm going to pause here so the visual can sink in. Me crossing the street with a hot midget. Holding my pinky. With her whole hand.

A few minutes later in the elevator, MidgetPrincess grabbed my butt.

MidgetPrincess "Damn, you got a fine ass."
Tucker "I do Pilates."
MidgetPrincess "Do you really? I bet you are good in bed."

There isn't a better opening than that. Did I come back with a smooth line? Did I woo and charm her, sealing the deal with a suave and debonair retort?

Tucker "I wanna make a mess in your mouth."

That's what I said. Don't ask me why. I don't know. Thank God she thought it was funny, because if she had been offended and left, I am pretty sure I would have slit my wrists with the closest sharp edge I could find (and for the record, I have never done Pilates, I'm not really even sure what they are).

We got into Soylent's apartment, she pulled me into his bedroom, and we started fucking. See, this is why you need good friends. In fact, this should be one of the measures of how good a friendship is: Will your buddy let you fuck a midget in his bed? If the answer is yes, then you know that dude is solid.

Clothes off, I slid right in. Her pussy was not very tight, in fact, it basically felt normal. First question answered.

One of my favorite positions is me on top with the girl's legs over my shoulders. I like that position because it gives my dick a more direct line of entry and, if I position my hips right, I hit the girl's G-spot in the process. For the most part, I am all about myself in bed, but if everyone can win, why not go with that? Plus, when her legs are over your shoulders, you control everything going on, and I'm a big fan of dominance.

After a few minutes of missionary, I moved to throw her legs over my shoulders. Normally when I do this, the girl's knees are over my shoulders and her lower legs are either in the air or resting on my back, depending on how I hit it. It went different with MidgetPrincess. I grabbed her legs, pushed them up on my shoulders, but instead of having her knees next to my ears, her feet were next to my cheeks and a few of her toes went into my mouth. Yes her legs were completely straight.

This was a bit disturbing, to say the least. About ten seconds later, she made me stop because I was hurting her. Even though her pussy was a normal width, it was much shallower than the average pussy, and with her legs on my chest (and her toes in my mouth), the head of my dick was smashing into her cervix like a pneumatic hammer. I won't lie, I was kinda disappointed, although I should've been prepared for it. I was trying to go scuba diving in a puddle, when all I really needed was a snorkel. Second question answered.

Only one final question. I got on bottom and had her ride me. Despite my best drunken attempts, I was unable to spin her like a top on my penis. It might have worked if my dick was longer, but alas, I am an average white guy.

She passed out when we were done, and I joined the party that was still going. Flush with excitement and pride, I triumphantly threw my hand in the air and yelled across the apartment:

Tucker "RAISE YOUR HAND IF YOU'VE EVER FUCKED A MIDGET!"

The other two midgets raised their hands.

Tucker "FUCK YOU BOTH!"

POSTSCRIPT: The Odds and Ends

—Later that night, after the excitement from my tiny little conquest finally died down, DolphinMidget came up to me and Soylent.

DolphinMidget "Hey man, can I borrow twenty bucks? That taxi driver I called is out front."
Tucker [*to Soylent*] "Is a crackhead midget hitting us up for a $20? So he can smoke some rock?"
DolphinMidget "I really need a hit, and I lost my wallet, man. Please."
Tucker "Oh my God. He is. He really is."
Soylent "You live a blessed life."

I don't think I gave DolphinMidget any money, but the next morning I was missing like $60 from my wallet. I am not going to accuse him of theft, because my wallet never left my pants and I can't imagine midgets are very good pickpockets, you know, with their stubby sausage fingers and all. But then again, you never know. Maybe he used his massive forehead to magic the money out of my wallet and into his tiny little crack pipe.

I figured out later why DolphinMidget was so intent on smoking crack: Apparently, it is quite painful to be a midget. Lots of them have various degenerative joint, bone, and organ problems, and sometimes the only way they can deal with the pain is to resort to illegal drugs. Who knew?

—When we were at the hotel bar after the dance, there was another hot midget in a backless red top. She was sitting by herself on one of those really tall bar stools that are basically full chairs with extra-long legs, and out of nowhere, she fell off. That was funny enough by itself, but not nearly as funny as what happened next: She decided to get back up on the stool by herself. Do you have any idea what it looks like when a drunk midget tries to climb into a chair that is literally twice her size? I'll tell you what it looks like: It looks EXACTLY like an orangutan in a slutty club top. It was awesome. Thank god she wasn't Persian, otherwise I would have had to go in for a closer look to make sure it wasn't an actual orangutan.

—Random quote from the night:

Jessie "Some of these midget dudes are ripped!"
Tucker "No, you don't understand. They have regular-sized muscles and tiny little arm bones, so they just look ripped."
Nils "They're actually crumpled."

Everybody Fails

I get a lot of email from guys, especially younger guys, telling me how amazing and perfect I am, and how they worship me because they see me as a god of drinking and sex. And not just a few emails—tens of thousands of them, all day, every day.

This has never made sense to me. My stories started as emails to my friends, and the point of them was never to impress or brag, but to entertain. No one is a hero to his friends, least of all me. The stories should not make people worship me; they should make people laugh—with me and, sometimes, at me. Though there are other things going on here—deeper meanings behind the laughs—humor and entertainment are the basic points of my writing. Not bragging or hero worship.

Don't get me wrong. I fully believe I'm fucking awesome, but not for the reasons that so many of these young guys seem to think. I've done many impressive things in my life, but going out with friends, getting drunk, acting like an idiot, and having tons of sex aren't impressive by themselves. And it definitely doesn't make me a god—it just makes me a pretty normal guy.

And just like every other normal guy, I fuck up. A lot. I feel like I wrote about many of my numerous mistakes in the last book (the post-op story, shitting myself in the hotel lobby, the girl playing me over the STD test, being so drunk I danced with myself in a mirror, etc.), but this time I am going to make it even more explicit. These stories are some of my favorite examples of me not just failing, but failing in lame and pitiful ways.

EVERYTHING GOES WRONG

Occurred—June 2006

My friend and I were out one night, and as per my usual routine, I was piss drunk. We were crassly objectifying various girls from the sidelines, when one in particular struck my fancy. My friend was unenthusiastic about her appearance, and let me know:

Friend "No. That girl is hideous."
Tucker "Whatever. She's good enough for the dick."
Friend "Your dick needs glasses."

Undeterred, I approached her:

Tucker "You are so hot that if you were dead, I'd still fuck your corpse for a month."

Her eyes widen in shock, and she leaves without a word. I thought it was funny.

Tucker "You're not better'n me!"

It was apparent I was too shit-faced to succeed with anything that was alive, so I went home alone. I started scrolling through my phone looking for booty calls and came across a girl I used to hook up with, but hadn't talked to in about a month. I called and woke her up:

Tucker "Come over. I want to see you."
Girl "Tucker, I'm not going to come over to sleep with you."
Tucker "Well, just come over . . . so we can talk. I want to talk to you . . . you know, hear about your day."

Girl "You want to hear about my day? At 3am? Right."
Tucker [*long pause*] "You aren't hot enough to have this much self-respect."

Sometimes shit like that works. Not this time.

Tucker "Hello? Hello!?"

I still ended my night like a true winner:

By drunkenly passing out in the middle of a halfhearted attempt at masturbation.

Nothing really crystallizes how pitiful your night went like waking up at your computer chair, mouse in one hand, dick in the other, with www.fuckmyhugetits.com staring back at you.

The Oversell

Occurred—November 2005

Back in my Chicago days, I convinced my buddy D-Rock to go to some fucking atrocious Lincoln Park bar full of Trixies, because I heard hot girls went there. D-Rock rewarded my choice by hatefully running up my tab. After he was sufficiently shit-housed, combative D-Rock came out:

D-Rock "MAX! Those four girls at that table are eyeing us."
Tucker "No dude, I don't think they are."
D-Rock "THEY ARE! Let's go fuck them."
Tucker "I think we need to talk to them first."
D-Rock "Correct. That's where you come in. Do the talking. Make them like you. Then introduce me. Then sex."

When D-Rock gets into this sort of state—when he's at the cognitive level of an angry toddler—there are only two courses of action:

1. Just stop arguing and do what he says, because once he's engaged with an idea, he focuses like a pit bull on a pot roast, or

2. Tell him you're going to the bathroom, then leave.

I almost picked #2, but if I had, I'm pretty sure this story would have ended up like the last time I did that: with him stumbling into my place at 4am, falling through a glass coffee table, and tracking a pint of blood all across my apartment as he looked for a Band-Aid. #1 it was.

The one ugly girl in the group got up and went to the bar to get a drink. I walked over next to her and started a conversation. She seemed interested, the conversation was going great, and she invited me and D-Rock over to her table. We were literally a second away from going over, I was just waiting for the bartender's attention to get a drink.

Tucker "This is so comical. I love how male bartenders always ignore dudes. Maybe I should go to gay bars, then I'd get served."

As any good salesman knows, once you get the sale, you stop selling. This is because everything you say once the customer has agreed to the sale doesn't make any more sales, but does risk losing the sale you already have. A lesson I should have applied. Instead I kept talking, and this came out:

Tucker "I almost wish I was gay, I feel like my life would be a lot easier. Women are crazy. That, and pussy has a troubling power over me. I'll do anything for it."

Her face transformed from the encouraging "I'm totally into this guy" look to the "Oh no, I attracted another dorky weirdo" look. It was obvious I was losing it. I racked my brain trying to think of a way to recover from that stupid fucking statement, and ended up here:

Tucker "Actually, I wish I was attracted to dogs. Then I wouldn't have to deal with men or women, because let's face it, people suck. Plus dogs are so obedient."

I don't blame her for leaving in disgust. I'd have left too.

D-Rock "You're an idiot. We were in."

The funniest part is that SHE WAS UGLY! How sweet is that irony? I flubbed an easy layup with an ugly girl. What a moron.

Hello, Nurse

Occurred—February 2002

When I was living in Florida, I got into a bar fight one night. That story may sound good, but it's not; it's just as lame as every drunk bar fight with guidos. What happened the next day at the clinic, however, is worth writing about.

It's always been something of a dream of mine to pick up a doctor or a nurse, in the office, during an exam, and hook up with her right there on the exam table. Sort of like real-life porn, except without having to fuck a used-up porn star with her "handler" watching from behind the camera. I was waiting in the exam room to get my hand looked at, and lo and behold, in walks a hot girl:

Tucker "Hello, nurse."
Intern "I'm not a nurse. I'm a fourth-year med student interning here."
Tucker "Oh, sorry. Well, nurse, intern, whatever you are, hot should be in the title."
[*Intern looks at me with a raised "are you kidding?" eyebrow*]

Tucker "What, does ruthlessly hitting on you violate some doctor-patient code?"
Intern "No. It's just kinda lame."
Tucker "Well, excuse me, Miss I'm-Hot-and-I-Know-It, I was just trying to give you a compliment."
Intern [*smiles reluctantly*] "OK, well, thank you. So, you are here because you think you broke your hand?"
Tucker "Yeah, I think."
Intern "Where did you break it?"
Tucker "On some guy's face."
Intern [*she can't help but laugh*] "Let me guess: You're in a fraternity?"
Tucker "Why does everyone always assume that?"
Intern "I wonder."

She then took out a Y fork (basically just a medical tuning fork), hit it on her thigh, and put it on my swollen hand.

Intern "Tell me if this hurts."
Tucker "OWW! Yes! So, what do doctors look for in a patient?"
Intern "One who is mature enough not to get into drunk fights at frat parties."
Tucker "Nice. In case it matters, I'm not in a frat, nor was I ever. This happened at a bar."
Intern "Glad to hear you've matured since college."
Tucker "So, how am I doing?"
Intern "Well, you have at least one and possibly two broken metacarpals."
Tucker "No, I mean with you. Like, us."
Intern "Us? Huh. I've seen terminal cancer patients with a better chance than you."
Tucker "All right, all right, but have you seen terminal cancer patients as hot as me?"

She stopped and looked at me as if she just could not believe I said that, like it was almost beyond her ability to comprehend.

Intern "I'm sending you down to get some x-rays."
Tucker "You're sending me away? No further examination? No sponge bath?"
Intern "No. You'll be just fine."
Tucker "You took chemistry to get into med school. We should go out sometime."
Intern "How about we make an appointment a month from now?"
Tucker "A month? Why that long? You have a boyfriend to dump?"
Intern "No. That's when your cast will come off."

I went back in a month, expecting her to be there, and I would get a chance to seal the deal. She wasn't. Some male nurse took my cast off. And he mocked me ruthlessly for how badly I did with the intern during my last visit.

Nurse "She specifically took today off when she saw you were on the calendar."
Tucker "Fuck you. I'll recover from this and fuck a hotter girl; you're always going to be a male nurse."
Nurse "Yeah, but I hooked up with her."

I gave up. He won.

My 21st Birthday

Occurred—September 1997

Everyone has those drinking nights that are complete disasters—I've made a living writing about mine. Perhaps one of my worst was my 21st birthday.

Growing up, I always hated my birthday. I can make up some bullshit reason why, but it wouldn't be true. The reality is that I grew up in a broken home with an unstable mom, an abusive, alcoholic grandmother, and an absentee father. Birthdays for me were not about celebration and enjoyment of the day of my birth; they were about facing these painful realities head on. Who the fuck wants to do that? Not me. I avoided them and refused to have parties.

But once I left home and surrounded myself with good friends I picked, instead of crazy family I was assigned, I began doing birthday stuff again. I was in my third (and final) year of college when my 21st birthday came along, and my friends offered to throw me a small party.

The planning was led by two friends from my old dorm, Mark and Francis. My college friends don't have the funny nicknames that my law school friends do, because the University of Chicago was so boring and socially retarded we didn't do enough crazy shit for cool nicknames to develop organically. Don't get me wrong, my friends were awesome guys, but there's a reason my school's unofficial motto is "Where Fun Goes to Die."

The plan was to do my birthday shots at a bar and then head out to a party afterward. We got to Woodlawn Tap at about 7pm. Mark bought 2 pitchers for the table and a shot for me and him. Our birthday tradition, as is standard for my generation, is for everyone out with the birthday boy to buy 2 shots, one for themselves and one for the birthday boy. This pattern continues until the birthday boy has done one shot for each year of his life. Normally, the 21 shots are spread out over the course of many hours, beginning early and ending very late, thus hopefully avoiding alcohol poisoning.

Not this time.

My friends had convinced me they were taking me out for my birthday because they loved me. This was a lie. My friends decided that they were going to get me shit-housed, fucked-in-half, retard drunk, and they would do it as quickly as possible because—as I was graduating in just three years instead of the usual four—they wanted to take advantage of their last opportunity to get back at me for all the shit I'd done to them over the course of our friendship. Like the time I took everything out of Mark's room and set it up in the courtyard of our dorm, and then invited a bum to sleep in his bed. Or the time I stapled a pork chop to the bottom of Francis's desk, and it stank so badly he was forced to sleep in the commons area for a week. And so on.

As soon as Mark and I finish our first shot, Francis has the next one waiting for me. Then another friend is right there with the next shot, followed immediately by another. I have not agreed to this plan, or even been informed of its existence, so after the fourth shot, I slam my beer chaser on the table and scream:

Tucker "HEY, GODDAMMIT! There will be a 5 minute wait between shots. And no fucking whiskey. Tequila or vodka only."

Being such great friends, everyone respects my wishes. For about 5 minutes. Then the shots start coming quickly again. 3 minutes between shots. 2 minutes. 1 minute. Next thing I know, I have 10 shot glasses in front of me, and it's only 8:15. I beg for a 20 minute break and receive a table full of condescension.

At this stage in my drinking career, I was not experienced enough to realize that the only way for me to salvage the night would be to run into the street and get hit by a car. Ten shots in an hour meant I was already doomed. At the very least I could have tried to force myself to vomit, ridding myself of the 15 ounces of hard liquor now metastasizing in my otherwise empty stomach. Not me. I remained in my chair and held up my part of the conversation by giving inebriated opinions in a volume appropriate for a helipad.

About 10 minutes later, someone places another shot in front of me. Vodka. I do it. Mister Stomach is not amused. Five minutes later, someone else places another vodka in front of me. I slam that one, too.

That's it. The corner has been turned. I can no longer discern faces from furniture without squinting and concentrating. I blithely wave off the next shot, but the ensuing boom of castigation from the bloodthirsty savages I call "friends" somehow pushes the liquid down my throat.

This shot sends my body into fight or flight. My throat desperately tries to close up and reject it, but I keep my mouth shut and force it down. I try to get up to walk around, but my body does not respond. The environment around me has become a vague, shifting mass of irregular shapes and amorphous forms, accentuated by voices I seem to recognize. My only thoughts involve hurting those around me, but I am too afraid of letting go of the table to take a swing at them. I hear someone say something about a shot.

Tucker "Guys, please, seriously, please, I am begging you with my life, please, please, no more alcohol."

Everyone has a good laugh at my expense, and another shot is placed in front of me.

Tucker "Guys, I can't do this. Honestly, guys, my life is on the line here."

The shot is held up to my face. The tequila smell is too much. I am repulsed and squirm away like I'm being threatened with waterboarding, fall out of my chair and onto the floor, the shot spilling onto my face and clothes. I look up pitifully at my friends.

Here's the other thing you have to know about me: When I was 21, I was like the Benjamin Button of alcohol consumption. I was a regressive drunk—the more I drank, the younger I acted. A few drinks in and I'd be making poop jokes. When I got really drunk, I'd drool on myself and baby-talk to girls. By the end of the night, I'd be curled up in the fetal position, sucking my thumb, covered in my own piss and shit. I didn't do this on purpose, but I was a fucking amateur in college, and that was how I dealt with alcohol at the time. Yeah, yeah, laugh it up shitheel. You ain't better'n me.

The next thing I know my arm is around Francis's shoulder and he is dragging me to the bathroom. Woodlawn Tap is a very old building and has only one bathroom. It is about four feet square with one sink, one frosted glass window about six feet from the floor, a wall-mounted soap dispenser, a door that doesn't lock, and one lone toilet, the kind you find in a home bathroom, with the water tank in the rear. He put me in front of the toilet.

Francis "All right, go ahead and vomit."
Tucker [*sounding like a drunk baby*] "Francis . . . I haz ta pee-pee."
Francis "OK, then pee."
Tucker "Buu . . . bu I can't . . . I can't . . . can you undo my shurts fur me?"
Francis "You can't be serious."
Tucker "Pleeeze? I havta pee bad."
Francis "Oh great Holy Jesus."

Francis holds his torso and face as far away from my midsection as possible while he undoes my belt and the button on my shorts, which immediately fall to the floor.

Francis "OH MAN, you're not wearing any underwear!"
Tucker "I dun like it . . . it mates me feel constrict-ted."
Francis "Jeeesus."

He turns me to face the toilet. I just stand there.

Francis "Are you going to pee?"
Tucker "Yur makin' me nerbous."

A few seconds later the flow begins. I am holding myself up by pushing both hands against the wall behind the toilet, and my penis is caught in the lower lip of my shirt. As a result, my urine first collects in the lower half of my shirt, before overflowing onto the floor. I don't notice. Francis does.

Francis "OH MAN, what are you doing? Oh, Tucker . . ."
Tucker [*I turn and smile at Francis*] "It feelz wurm."
Francis "OHHHH . . . I'm not picking your shorts up."

I finish peeing. As I lean down to pick up my shorts, my feet slip in urine and I fall on my ass, landing in the puddle of my piss on the floor. Francis groans as he helps me up. I manage to get my shorts zipped. My stomach is still upset with me.

Tucker "Francis, I doan . . . I doan . . . feel good."
Francis "OK . . . then throw up. The toilet is right there. Go ahead, get it out."

I start swaying. I can feel the vomit coming. Even though I know it's coming, and it knows it's coming, it seems to just hang there in my throat, teasing me, waiting, letting me contemplate just how stupid I am, my body punishing me just that little bit extra.

Then, as if it were shot out of a cannon, the vomit explodes from my mouth.

BLAHHHH!! BLAAAAAHHHHHHH!!

The force propels my upper body away from the toilet, and I vomit in the sink.

BLAAAAAAAAAAAAAAAAAAAAHHHHHHHHHHHHHHHHHHHHHHH!!!

The force of the second diaphragm contraction is so strong it pushes my body and head away from the sink toward the far wall. Lost in agony and bile, I stumble over to the toilet, catch myself on the tank in the rear, pull off the lid, drop it on the floor, and vomit in the tank behind the porcelain bowl.

Francis "What, what . . . what the HELL are you doing? Vomit in the bowl . . . IN THE BOWL!"

I can't hear what he's saying, so I turn my heads toward Francis. My innocent look of confusion quickly turns to wrenching pain, as the fourth wave of vomit forces its way up my throat. I project this stream of vomit toward Francis, missing him only because he was sober and agile enough to dodge it, letting it splash instead all over the inside of the bathroom door.

Francis "JESUS CHRIST!!! WHAT ARE YOU DOING!?!"

Faint and staggered by such violent heaving, I stumble back toward the sink and grab the soap dispenser for stability. It is not designed to support such weight and promptly rips off the wall, falling to the ground. I catch myself on the sink and then vomit on the soap container on the floor.

By the time I was finished, I had heaved and convulsed too many times to count. The toilet tank had vomit in it. The window, six feet high in the air, had vomit on it. Even the outside of the toilet bowl had vomit sloshed on it. I managed to get vomit in the sink, on all four walls and the door, yet somehow I had spared the actual toilet bowl. Every container and surface in the bathroom had vomit in or on it, EXCEPT the one designed for that purpose.

To this day, I don't know how I did it. Francis is no help, because he refuses to talk about the incident. It was like that scene in *Pulp Fiction* where the guy busts out of the bathroom and unloads point-blank on Jules and Verne but misses every shot. Divine providence, I guess.

Somehow tolerating both the urine and vomit my body was covered in, Francis pulled me out of the bathroom and managed to walk us to the table where everyone was sitting.

Francis "Guys, weneedtoleaveRIGHTNOW!"

Francis's urgency was less a result of my condition and more fear of the Woodlawn Tap bartenders. They are old-school hard-ass Chicagoans. These are not the type of men who call the police. Had they discovered my mess while we were still there, they would have most likely made us clean it up, beat us savagely with sawed-off baseball bats, taken all the money in our wallets, thrown us into the street, then eaten some brats while toasting Coach Ditka.

Apparently, the panic in Francis's voice was enough, and before I really understood what was going on, we were all out in the street.

It was 9:15, barely two hours into the night. And only 15 shots.

Francis and Mark took me back to my apartment. Everyone else headed off to the party. As we were walking, three girls came upon us. Their night was just beginning, and they were in good spirits. I, on the other hand, had my arms draped around the necks of my two friends, barely able to muster the strength to walk, my head hung in defeat, body dripping with exhaustion, drunk sweat, vomit, and piss.

Girl "Hey guys, what's wrong with him? Is he OK?"

The girl seemed to be genuinely concerned about my welfare.

Mark "He's fine, he's just really drunk. It's his birthday."
Girl "Oh, hey, happy birthday!"

I slowly raised my head, focused my eyes, and sneered:

Tucker "FUCK YOU, WHORE!!!"

Francis and Mark whisked me away from the traumatized girls. When we reached my apartment, the three of them deposited me in my bathtub and turned on the water to clean off some of the vomit and urine. Then they fucking left me there to decide how to best arrange my room so that I could safely pass out. (This is perhaps the best illustration of what it means to go to the University of Chicago. While being one of the most intellectually rigorous schools in the world, it still took THREE of the best and brightest putting their heads together to figure out how to prevent their friend from aspirating his own vomit. And you wonder why I graduated in three years.)

I was very thirsty. Lying in the bathtub, looking up at the faucet, I thought of a great idea: I could just put my mouth up to the nozzle. It was like drinking from a fire hose. Water was going in, but that doesn't mean it was staying in. I was too drunk to notice that I was getting completely soaked by water that was shooting out of my nose. Mark noticed.

Mark "Dude! That's a good way to get brain damage."
Tucker "Whaaaat? . . . could you get me sum food, peas. Der's brownies in da kitchen."

Mark walked off and Francis moved me over to my bed, laying me on my stomach. I felt snot coming out of my nose.

Tucker "Francis, will you peas bow my nose?"
Francis "Oh, Jesus."

Francis got a tissue and held it up to my nose as I blew. I felt much better. Then Mark came in my room and placed the phone up to my ear.

Mark "Here Tucker, it's your mother. She wants to wish you a happy birthday."
Tucker "WHAT THE FUCK . . . FUCKIN' FUCK MOTHERFUCK!"

I grabbed the phone out of Mark's hand and threw it across the room. The phone shattered against the wall. Mark's hysterical laughter was my last clear memory.

The next morning I woke up so dehydrated I couldn't even blink my eyes. Francis and Mark had placed me on my bed, with my head hanging over the side, a trash can below it. The side of my bed below my mouth was streaked with a black paste. Apparently I ate a brownie, then threw up. The trash can was filled with a watery brown paste, about two inches deep, apparently the gallon or so of water I drank at the end of the night, mixed with what remained of the brownie.

I slept all day long, my only waking hours occupied with drinking water and listening to the countless messages my mother left on my machine, wondering why I called her, cursed, and then hung up.

I eventually got much better at drinking, but the first time I did it legally, I failed.

FUCKED-UP PILLOW TALK, PART 2

Occurred—various 2006–2010

I love women, I love alcohol, and I love combining the two. If God invented anything better than drunk sex with a hot girl, he kept it to himself.

The vast majority of the time, it turns out great. But not always. Sometimes it's fucked up. I don't know what it is about sex that provides such a fertile ground for humor, but it seems like a lot of my hookups contain some sort of hilarity. Does this have anything to do with my reckless sexual behavior, combined with the fact that a lot of the women who fuck me are screwed up in one way or another?

Maybe, but we're going to skip over that reflection; the less I think about it, the easier it is for me to pretend it's not a problem. I've collected some of my favorite little exchanges that aren't part of any larger stories:

—With some random girl who was really annoying:

Girl "Why don't you last longer during sex? Ten minutes is not long enough for me."
Tucker "I don't understand. I lasted long enough for me to cum. Why would I go any longer?"
Girl "I want to cum too. What about me?"
Tucker "Who?"
Girl "Me."
Tucker "Who are we talking about here?"
Girl "ME!"

Tucker "Who?"
Girl "I HATE YOU!"
Tucker "Who hates me?"

—We stopped for food on the way home to hook up, but she didn't like my suggestion:

Girl "NO!"
Tucker "Come on, the company is owned by religious freaks. It'll be delicious *and* ironic."
Girl "Tucker, I will not fellate you as you eat Chick-fil-A!"

—After a seriously drunk night out, I did not wake up with the girl I remember leaving the bar with:

Tucker "What the fuck?"
Girl "What's wrong?"
Tucker "I didn't think I had standards, but now I'm thinking that maybe I do. At least the next day, when I'm sober."

—I generally prefer vaginal sex over anal sex for many reasons, the main one being that it's way, way better. There have been a few girls who are exceptions:

Tucker "I want to fuck you in the ass again."
Girl "You and the anal sex. What is it with you?"
Tucker "It's not me, it's you. You are the only girl I'm like this with. Your ass is way better than your vagina."
Girl "I wonder why."
Tucker "Probably because you're such a huge whore, your pussy has the consistency of chewed hamburger. Your ass has less miles on it."

This didn't even piss her off. She just agreed and bent over. Gotta love honest self-assessment.

—From a girl who fucked me within minutes of meeting me:

Girl "So now that we've fucked, I'm thinking maybe we can get to know each other better."

—With a girl who met me through my website:

Girl "I thought you'd be different in bed."
Tucker "Different? How?"
Girl "I don't know. I like to get punched and slapped and stuff. I thought you'd humiliate me more."
Tucker "Fucking-a. Some people think I'm horrible to women, while the women who *want* to be treated like shit think I don't treat them bad enough. What the fuck? I can't win."

—This girl was not only very young looking, she walked right into this old joke:

Tucker "Turn over, I want to have anal sex."
Girl "Isn't that a bit presumptuous?"
Tucker "That's an awful big word for a middle schooler to be using."

—In bed with one of my regular fuck buddies:

Girl "You won't believe who is now your biggest fan: my 15 year old cousin. He brought your book home from high school and annoyingly quotes it all day long."
Tucker "Did you tell him I shoot huge loads in you every week?"
Girl "NO! He needs to learn to respect women!"
Tucker "And you think lying to him is the way to teach him?"

—In the middle of sex, almost making me unable to finish:

Girl "OH GOD I WANT YOUR SPUNK IN MY CUNT!!!"

Seriously, who says that?

—From a girl who was less than attractive:

Her "You aren't going to make me crawl out the window like that fat girl in your book, are you?"
Tucker "No, I live alone. There's no one for you to embarrass me with."
Her "Ugh!"
Tucker "If my friends were here, though, you'd be out the window like a chamber pot."

—From an engaged girl:

Girl "God, I never cum like that with my fiancé. Sometimes I wonder why I'm even marrying him. When can I see you again?"
Tucker "Thanks, just leave the money on the dresser on your way out."

—Probably not the best way to play it:

Tucker "You're a squirter? Awesome, I want to see it right now."
Girl "OK, but you have to make me cum before I can squirt."
Tucker "You're barking up the wrong tree, honey."

—I've never been happier I was wearing a condom than at this moment:

Girl "Can you hurry up and finish? My dealer turns off his cell phone at 2am and I want to score again."

I now ask girls if they are drug addicts before I fuck them, and if they say yes, I don't fuck them at all. No sex is worth the adrenaline dump I had after she said that.

—With a girl I'd been fucking for a while but wasn't going anywhere with:

Girl "I want you to date me!"
Tucker "Well, I want to ride a unicorn over a rainbow, but neither of those things is going to happen."

—With a girl I was fucking in Florida. I told her I wanted her to pay for my vacation to Key West (and go with me):

Girl "I'd rather go somewhere else. Why Key West?"
Tucker "Because there are a lot of whores there who will suck my dick and then spit the splooge in your face."
Girl "WHAT!?!"

—From a random right after mediocre sex:

Her "That kinda sucked."
Tucker "Yeah, I totally agree. I'm not very attracted to you, so it took major concentration for me to even finish."

Because of that statement, she fucked at least 20 guys the next week. You're all welcome.

—One of my regular fuck buddies came over, but this time brought me a mix CD. She made me put it in the stereo, and the first song to come on was the 50 Cent song "Magic Stick." As she started to pull my pants off:

Girl "This song makes me think of you."

She was 23 years old and still making mix CDs. I was so creeped out that I almost asked her to leave, but she had brought a full slab of ribs over with her and gave great head.

—After we were finished fucking:

Tucker "That was pretty good. You ready for another round?"
Girl "Jesus has better things in store for me, I just know it."
Tucker "What?"
Girl "Nothing. Let's go again."

That was really funny when it happened, but the more I think about it, the more depressing it gets.

—This girl asked me if I wanted to go to dinner with her and her mom:

Tucker "Does your mom have big tits too?"
Girl "No, asshole! She had breast cancer!"
Tucker "Did she get big implants?"
Girl "SHUT UP."
Tucker "I'll go with you to dinner and meet her, but you have to tell your mom to put her prosthetic knockers on. I don't want to get all freaked out and lose my appetite."

—From a girl who wanted to come fuck me at 2am but needed a ride:

Girl "I need you to pick me up, otherwise I can't come over."
Tucker "I'll buzz you into my building. That's the maximum effort I am willing to expend on us having sex."

—This was after sex, with a girl who graduated from the University of South Florida:

Girl "Do you like sushi?"
Tucker "I'm not eating you out."
Girl "I don't get it."

—This girl recognized me at a bar and was all about it. After we fucked, she dropped this:

Girl "You know, I normally charge for this. A lot."
Tucker "You're an escort?"
Girl "Yep. But this is not sex work; being with you is like a vacation."
Tucker "You're telling me I'm Disneyland for hookers?"

—I woke up next to a girl I truly did not remember leaving the bar with. Or even meeting:

Tucker "Who are you?"
Random "Uh, you should know me: We had sex."
Tucker "No, we didn't."
Random "Yes, we did!"
Tucker "You slept with me? You must be a whore!"

—At a book signing, this one girl wanted to fuck me and was about as subtle as a head kick. She came over to my hotel, fucked me, and approximately one second after I finished, she rolled over and texted this to her boyfriend:

Girl "I have cum in my pussy. It's not yours."

—This one girl was a ridiculous screamer during sex, and it annoyed me:

Tucker "You think you could not yell at the top of your lungs next time?"
Girl "A lot of guys are into that."
Tucker "I think my name is 'Tucker,' not 'A Lot of Guys.' "

—A single mom I was fucking:

MILF "I want you so bad. I want your cum inside me . . ."
Tucker "Isn't this how you got your first kid?"

—A random I brought home from a bar:

Girl "You don't remember my name? Now we can't have sex, I can only suck your dick."
Tucker "Start sucking, and I'll try to remember."

—I was kinda seeing this one girl for a few weeks. Definitely not exclusive, and we had not even come close to having any sort of relationship talk, but more than a booty call. Like a fuck buddy. I was sore from working out the day before, so I asked for a massage.

Girl "Where did you get these scratches all over your back?"
Tucker "Uh, playing basketball?"
Girl "What kind of basketball do you play that leaves scratches like that?"
Tucker "The kind where my penis goes inside the girls on the other team?"

—After a really good fuck:

Girl "My vagina wants to give you a high five."

—I just got done fucking this girl, and I had fought back my terrible gas the whole time during sex, but I couldn't hold it anymore when we were done. So I Dutch-ovened her (farted under the covers, then pulled them over her head so she was stuck with it):

Girl "Tucker, let me out, this is awful!"
Tucker "No, you have to stay in there until you guess what I had for dinner!"

—A girl who ended up fucking me because I told her she had a big noco:

Girl "It's funny, when you said I needed a nose job . . . I have been thinking about getting one. But I don't know . . . I think it'll hurt."
Tucker "It'll hurt less than being alone."
Girl "I won't be alone!"
Tucker "You're right; your nose will keep you company."

—A girl who had read my book and fucked me ten minutes after meeting me:

Girl "You aren't at all what I expected. I thought you would be more suave and debonair."

She said it to me as we were lying in bed, with my cum in her hair. I guess the suave guys keep the cum on her face.

—After hooking up with a very crunchy girl:

Girl "Let's play Frisbee golf today!"
Tucker "If you are serious, get out."
Girl "What's wrong with Frisbee golf? I think it's cool."
Tucker "Delete my number from your phone and never contact me again."

—I was fucking a girl who lived in the same apartment building as her brother. One morning he saw us in the hallway leaving her place, said hi to her, then went into his apartment:

Girl "Sorry, he's not very social to guys I bring around."
Tucker "I wouldn't want to meet some guy who was using my sister as a cum dumpster either."
Girl "I'm not a cum dumpster!"
Tucker "I didn't say you were. Clearly, you're a beautiful and unique flower. But I am *using you* as a cum dumpster."

—This girl was supposed to get to my place at 9pm but didn't show up until midnight. As "punishment," I had her fellate me in the foyer of my place. Only afterward did she explain her tardiness:

"I'm so sorry. I would've been here sooner, but my cousin died at seven, and you know how family can be."

—Not really pillow talk, but a series of texts with a girl I was fucking:

Tucker: "I'm going to pull your hair as I fuck you doggy style"
Girl: "can we do it people style tonight? I want to look you in the eyes"
Tucker: "This isn't going to work out"

—From a girl who gave me head in a car parked behind a bar:

Girl "That was easy. Do you know how hard it is to give a black guy a blowjob?"

—Right after I really cracked a girl hard in the shitter:

Her "When do I get to fuck you in the ass?"
Tucker "Yeah, right! How about right after America elects a black president?"

This was in 2006. At that point, I only knew Barack Obama as the really nice law school professor I used to play basketball against every afternoon in undergrad. If she ever calls me again, I'm obviously not picking up.

—As I was getting started with a girl, I leaned in to kiss her:

Girl "Let's not kiss."
Tucker "Why not?"
Girl "I haven't showered since the last guy."

I was very cool with this. I'll take an honest whore over a lying prude every single time. I'll make her shower, but still . . . honesty is good.

—Right before a girl went down on me. And yes, she was serious:

Girl "I usually don't do this, you know, because I'm a vegan."

—Same situation, different girl:

Girl "Seriously, don't cum in my mouth. I only let my boyfriend do that."

—I was fucking this girl I wasn't really into, but I was drunk and weak, so I did it anyway. The morning after:

Girl "Did you know you talk in your sleep?"
Tucker "Yeah. Lots of girls have told me that."
Girl "Oh, that's just wonderful. Do you even know what you said last night?"
Tucker "No. I was sleeping."
Girl "You rolled over, mumbled something, and then clearly said, 'This girl came over last night and we had sex and it was a bad idea,' and then passed back out."
Tucker "HAHAHAHAHA. AWESOME! I'm even funny in my sleep!"

—After another fuck session with a regular booty call:

Girl "Every time I get done seeing you, I say to myself, 'I'm never going to talk to him again,' yet somehow, I always do it."
Tucker "Maybe it's because I'm so awesome."
Girl "No, that's not it at all."
Tucker "Why?"
Girl "I guess I just hate myself."

THE TUCKERFEST STORY

Occurred—March 2003

In the summer of 2002, I left Boca Raton and moved to Chicago to pursue my calling as a writer. I started off the same way everyone else does; by trying to get published. I took my five best stories at the time—all of which are now in *I Hope They Serve Beer In Hell*—and sent copies to every single agent, publishing house, magazine, newspaper, and alt weekly I could find an address for. At least a thousand query letters and emails went out.

90% ignored me, and the other 10% rejected me. There were even a few people who took the time to write me personalized rejections, telling me how awful my writing is and how I should do *anything* but be a writer. The stories that eventually anchored a #1 best-seller and spawned a new literary genre got precisely ZERO interest from the very people whose only job is to discover new talent. And publishers wonder why they're going bankrupt.

That sort of rejection would discourage most people. Not me. I'm a narcissist and a genius, and I knew what I had on my hands. If no publisher wanted my stories, I'd just put them on the internet (it may seem obvious now that putting them on the web makes sense, but in 2002 putting commercial writing on the *internet* for *free* was essentially unheard of). I launched TuckerMax.com on September 9, 2002. I remember the exact day because I'd spent the previous month so focused on all the necessary tasks to get the site up—learning about HTML, Photoshop, hosting, etc.—that I had completely forgotten that the one-year anniversary of 9/11 was two days away.

The gods love courage and defiance, and I had both. Within six months my site became a phenomenon; it was getting tens of thousands of visitors a day. I was one of the very first "internet personalities." MTV did a documentary about internet dating that starred me, I got a Hollywood agent to pitch my stories as a TV show, and of course, the book publishers—though last to the party, as usual—decided that they should offer me book deals.

In the movies this sort of thing happens overnight, but in real life, it's slow in developing. TV shows, movie deals, books—these things take a lot of time. But I was getting immediate attention on the internet, and at the beginning, that was the thing I loved the most: the newfound fame.

I'll be frank: Like most people when they get their first taste of success, I was an arrogant fuck about it. I thought my shit did not stink. I was getting a lot of attention, and though it was almost all limited to a small group of hard-core fans, within that niche I was a legit star. And that attention and adoration was very intoxicating to someone like me who, after being rejected by the mainstream media companies, had, in less than six months of full-time writing, attracted real fans.

A lot of my fans congregated on the message board community that I set up on my site. SlingBlade loved to go on various message boards of the sports teams he hated and talk shit to them, and he suggested I put one up so we could do the same thing to random people. I did, and lo and behold, the thing took off. Almost from the beginning, hundreds of my fans came every day, but instead of talking shit, it became like a real internet community.

It's kinda hard to explain the dynamic of the early Tucker Max Message Board. Some of my real friends hung out there—PWJ, SlingBlade, Jojo, TheCousin—and we used the place not only to talk to each other but to meet my fans too. The more time we spent there, the more of a community it became, all based around my writing. I probably spent anywhere from three to five hours a day on there, just hanging out, bullshitting with people, and making jokes. This was 2002, and social media was completely new, and it was exciting to interact with people I didn't know, but who loved and respected me because of my writing.

Two of the earliest members of the message board were semi-pro wrestlers, Rosh and TripleSH. Rosh was a 20 year old virgin from rural Pennsylvania who vacillated between alcoholism and religious fundamentalism. TripleSH was a third-rate pseudointellectual from New Jersey who seemed like a nice guy. They asked me to be the celebrity judge at the bikini contest at one of their wrestling shows. I agreed, for two reasons:

1. Even though they weren't paying me, I was still so new to the "fame" thing that I was really excited to get invited to be a "celebrity judge" of anything, especially hot girls in bikinis.

2. I expected to spend a few hours at this thing, and then the rest of the weekend in NYC partying with my real-life friends.

Of course, I sent a flurry of emails to my law school friends bragging about my new fame. They called me an idiot for going to New Jersey at all, and they had the gall to mock me for being such a crappy celebrity that I could be considered famous only at a semi-pro wrestling event. Fuck them, they were just jealous that they weren't famous like me. Haterz!

About two months before I was supposed to go to New Jersey, I was out of town without computer access for a weekend. Rosh and TripleSH picked this time to start a thread announcing to the message board community that I was coming to New Jersey, and that everyone on the Tucker Max Message Board was invited to come party with us. They named the event TuckerFest, and by the time I got back into town, the thread was three pages long with people discussing their travel plans. Several people had booked plane tickets already, from California, Mississippi, Ohio, Florida—it was totally out of control. Before I knew it, something like 30 people I didn't know at all were coming to New Jersey to throw me a party.

What's so funny about this is in retrospect is that, at the time, I didn't really see anything unusual about it. I mean, why shouldn't all these people spend all this money and time to party with me? I'm fucking awesome! It never occurred to me to ask what it said about them that they were so eager to do this, or why their lives were so desperately empty that they wanted to glom on to some random dude with nothing but a few funny stories on a crappy website. But such is narcissism. Those sorts of questions just don't occur to you.

Though this was going to be the first time I'd ever really met any of my "fans," I thought I knew what was coming. In my naïveté, I honestly thought everyone coming would basically be like me and my friends. That's the way these people on my message board had portrayed themselves on the internet, so of course that's the way they would be in real life. Because people are just like their internet personas, right? Besides, come on, why would nerds and tools want to party with me, knowing how mercilessly I abuse people I can't stand? These people have read my stories, they know what I'm like. Knowing that, if they still want to hang out with me, they must be pretty cool . . . right?

Silly, naïve Tucker. I was utterly unprepared for the epic shitstorm that was coming. The events of that tragically comic weekend would become the touchstone for changes in my website, my life, and the lives of everyone even tangentially involved, including the proprietors of an RV rental company in Aurora, Illinois, the staff and guests of the Teaneck Marriott, numerous residents of New York City, and the cops of Harlem's 32nd Precinct.

Part 1: The Plan

A few of the people who were planning to attend TuckerFest lived in and around Chicago, and they wanted to hang out before the event in March. I was still so new to the whole fame thing that going out and meeting random fans seemed like a perfectly good idea to me.

The first guy who wanted to hang out was named Stydie. He lived in Chicago, and I first encountered him when he sent me this email, in January 2003:

> "Tucker . . . I don't remember what color envy is (green or purple . . . fuck it who cares) but I might as well be looking at the world through envy-tinted glasses right now.
>
> I think you should know that the six hours I've been at work today have been spent on your site. I'm amazed. Impressed. If you really are fucking real you are living the life that so many of us peons can only dream of. I only wish I had the balls and sheer audacity that you possess to put these bitches in their place. The fact that you have been able to absolutely demoralize and walk all over so many of these uppity whores is very inspirational.
>
> I mean Christ . . . you're the hero of the common man . . . the people's champion. You are realizing lack of regard for rules and society that a normal schmuck could only imagine in his wildest dreams. I myself used to have this attitude in college, but the weight of the amazing amount of bullshit in the world has since crushed my spirit.
>
> While "no remorse!" used to be our battle cry . . . it's now something dejected and pathetic like "get me another blue label on the rocks so I can pass out quicker and forget about the mind-numbing social landscape that is Lincoln Park." You have reached out and grabbed life by the balls, and for that you deserve every ounce of self-gratifying attention that you undoubtedly receive as a result of this site. Tucker Max, my hat is lifted to you. Reading the accounts of your exploits helped me remember that there's really no point in being nice or accommodating because unless you are a complete asshole, the world will take advantage of you."

Looking at it now, you and I see the same thing: a desperate cry for help. But this was one of the first emails I'd ever gotten like this, and I thought it was so cool that this guy not only thought my stuff was funny, but was also inspired by it. Instead of doing what I would do now with the hundreds of emails I get like this every day—politely thank them or just ignore them—I decided to take pity and help the kid, so I invited him out with me.

He showed up to my place 40 minutes early. I was still eating dinner. He had a full-length black trench coat on and looked 15. For a split second, I thought the ghost of Eric Harris had left Columbine to haunt me.

He spent the first ten minutes stammering over small talk. Dude couldn't have been more nervous if I'd shoved an 8 ball of black-tar heroin up his ass and sent him through customs. All of a sudden, his eyes lit up, and in the most excited, high-pitched voice I've ever heard out of grown man:

Stydie "So how drunk are you?!?"
Tucker "Not drunk at all."
Stydie "Why not?"
Tucker "It's 7:30. I'm still eating dinner. We aren't due at the bar until 10."
Stydie "So what? You're Tucker Max! You should be hammered right now!"

Out of his coat he pulled a half-full bottle of Jagermeister and three warm Bud Lights. I assumed he was kidding, so I kinda stared at him—waiting for the punch line.

Stydie "Come on man, you're Tucker Max. I'm calling you out, I've already been drinking!"

Dude's serious. I guess *he* is the punch line.

This was the first time I'd ever met someone who knew me only from my stories, and for a second, I was just honestly confused. I didn't yet understand why I shouldn't hang out with this type of young, retarded male fan—but Stydie was generously providing my first lesson.

Tucker "You want to . . . outdrink me . . . with your warm trench coat alcohol?"
Stydie "Yeah, man, come on, let's see what you got! I was in a fraternity in college, I can throw 'em back!"

I had some moonshine in my freezer (I'm from Kentucky), so I poured us three shots apiece and then made him go beer for beer with me for two hours. At 10:30, we got into a cab to go to the bar. The idiot was so drunk, he started nodding off on the way there. He woke up long enough to get a beer at the bar, which he spilled on his shirt, right before he puked all over himself in the bathroom.

Tucker "I thought you were going to outdrink me, you fucking pussy! Look at yourself. No wonder you've given up on life, you're a fucking failure at it!"

Despite the fact that he really did suck in every possible way, he had that mix of overeager enthusiasm and uncoordinated energy that you just can't stay mad at, like Scrappy-Doo. And even though he was a complete dork, he had that one thing you can't teach: desire. The dude wanted to learn, so I ended up kinda taking him under my wing and trying to teach him all the things he clearly needed to know. Like how to stay awake past 10:30pm.

Stydie was actually much more active on the message board than I was at the time, and he became friends with two guys who lived in Indiana and were always posting funny shit: TheGinger and Soylent. About a month before TuckerFest, he invited them up to Chicago to come out with us. As much of a loser nerd as Stydie could be, these two were not. They were actually really fucking cool guys, dudes I might be friends with in real life.

TheGinger was a short, portly guy, and a contradiction in every way: a huge computer nerd who could drink like a motherfucker. Socially anxious, but fun as hell to go out with. Supersmart, but always doing dumb, self-destructive things. Afraid of breaking the rules, but willing to do crazy things. Had no confidence in himself, but drunk he had more balls than anyone. If you have ever known the cool computer nerd type, the ones who simultaneously fit into and break all the stereotypes, then you know what I'm talking about.

Soylent was a former recon Marine. The man looked like a bowling ball of compressed muscle and restrained violence with a head glued on top. His quiet and intimidating intensity when sober was matched only by his raucous gregariousness when drunk. The first night I hung out with him, he played the perfect wingman and jumped on the grenade for me. What I would learn later on was that he did this because actually LIKED grenades; dude wasn't so much a chubby chaser, he was just a relentless pussy hound. He didn't care what girl he fucked, as long as she was warm and wet. Typical fucking Marine, gotta love 'em.

We hung out a few more times, and those three expressed interest in going to TuckerFest. There were a few problems, though. The first was that, even though I was a good enough writer to have fans, and they were all traveling to meet me, I still wasn't making any money from my site (this was before internet advertising had any traction), so that meant I was too poor to travel to NYC for an event . . . which was being thrown for me . . . because of my fame. Ironic, I know.

They came up with the perfect solution: They would rent an RV and we'd all drive to NYC together. Are you kidding? Free trip to NYC? I began to think maybe this having-fans-thing might work out after all.

Part 2: The Education of Stydie

The day of the trip arrived, and Stydie drove to the rental place in Aurora, Illinois, to meet TheGinger and Soylent. Stydie was super-excited, driving at least 95mph most of the way, and at one point an old lady—doing a healthy 75mph herself—made the ghastly mistake of staying in the left lane as Stydie flew up behind her. He pulled up on her right side, screaming curses at her as he flipped her off, and then cut her off in an attempt to run her into the median. And she was OLD.

Tucker "DUDE! I'm not even this excited to drink with me, and I'm in love with myself. Relax!"

By the grace of the drinking gods, we arrived at Westmark RV Rental alive and without a vehicular homicide indictment. We went through the rental procedure and were signing the papers (everything in TheGinger's name, of course, God forbid I take responsibility for my actions), when I made what was probably the best decision of the weekend.

Clerk "Would you like insurance? It's $25.99 per day for full coverage."
TheGinger "No, that's too much."
Tucker "Are you fucking stupid? Have you ever driven a rental car before?"
TheGinger "Yeah."
Tucker "How did you treat it?"
TheGinger "Oh . . ."
Tucker "That RV is 10,000 pounds of speeding metal and twisted death. This thing is like three rental cars in one. THINK! WE HAVE A FULL KEG WITH US! Do you really think this is going to end well?"

Did I mention the keg? Stydie brought a full keg of beer, put it in the RV shower, and we hooked the tap up to the showerhead. I was holding a red Solo cup of beer that had been filled out of said shower at the precise moment we had that conversation.

TheGinger "We want coverage. We want your BEST coverage. Walk-away insurance, please."

By the time we got everything squared away, Soylent showed up. His car was so loaded with stuff it looked like he'd been looting a Walmart. Not satisfied with just a keg, Soylent had brought at least ten cases of beer and enough bottles of assorted liquor to stock a bar. Only four people, but enough alcohol for an Irish wake. THAT is how you start a party.

As we started packing everything away, Stydie spilled his first beer.

Stydie "Shit, sorry."
Tucker "Everyone makes mistakes. Don't do it again, dumbass."
TheGinger "Oh man, we have to clean this up, I had to leave a cleaning deposit!"

We finished packing, and Stydie spilled his second beer.

Stydie "Crap, sorry."
Tucker "You are a spastic fucking moron."
TheGinger "Stydie, the cleaning deposit was like $250!!"

The RV pulled out of the parking lot, and as we got on to the highway on-ramp, Stydie spilled his third beer.

Stydie "Fuck. Sorry guys."
Tucker "YOU IDIOT! FROM NOW ON, YOU CAN ONLY FILL YOUR BEER HALFWAY UP. DO YOU UNDERSTAND??"
TheGinger "Stydie, help me clean this up good, the lady was very clear about what it takes to get the deposit back!!"

An hour later, driving smoothly along the highway, Stydie was telling us how he is—this is a real quote—the "Prince of Cleveland" and explaining how it's one of the awesomest cities in America. As he wildly gesticulated to make a point, he knocked his beer out of his own hand, sloshing it all over the RV.

Stydie "Oh no."
Tucker "WHAT THE FUCK! DO YOU HAVE PALSY OR ARE YOU JUST FUCKING RETARDED??"
TheGinger "I'M GOING TO LOSE MY CLEANING DEPOSIT!!"
Soylent "Get off at the next exit. I'll solve this problem."

Five minutes later, Soylent came jogging out of a convenience store with a travel mug.

Soylent "This is a sippy cup. Use it."
Tucker "Awesome! You MUST drink from that sippy cup for the rest of the trip. At bars, hotel rooms, everywhere."
Stydie "Guys, come on . . ."
TheGinger "ARE YOU GOING TO PAY FOR MY CLEANING DEPOSIT??"
Tucker "More importantly, until you can drink beer like a man, we're going to call you Sippy and treat you like a baby. Now sip your beer."
Sippy [*hangs head in shame*] "Fine."

An hour later, driving smoothly along the highway, he dropped the sippy cup, the lid popped off, and beer spilled everywhere.

Sippy "Oh my God! I'm so sorry! I don't know how this happened!"

TheGinger began weeping openly. I was too angry to speak. I didn't punch Sippy in the mouth, but only because I was driving.

Soylent "At this point, I'm kinda impressed. It takes talent to suck this much."

Soylent went into his bag, pulled out a lanyard he had with him, and a huge knife. He poked a hole in the sippy cup lid, tied the lanyard through it, and put it around Sippy's neck. He was, for the rest of the weekend, referred to as SippyCup and did all drinking from a travel mug hanging from his neck. It took only five dropped beers, two equipment upgrades, and a redheaded computer nerd reduced to tears, but Sippy didn't spill again.

As night fell, we were on track to be in Cleveland around 10, giving us a solid three to four hours of drinking time at the bars. Soylent was driving and I was in the passenger seat with the map, when Sippy—two hours removed from his last spill and brimming with confidence—snatched the map from me and threw it in the back of the RV:

Sippy "Dude, I've got it from here. I grew up in Columbus and used to party in Cleveland all the time. I know this town backward and forward. I AM THE FUCKING PRINCE OF CLEVELAND!"

Want to guess what happened next?

He proceeded to take us on a three-hour tour of the Cleveland suburbs. Had he been skippering the S.S. *Minnow* with Gilligan as his first mate, SippyCup could not have gotten us more lost. And we couldn't even use the map, because dumbass Sippy had thrown it in the beer he spilled, and it shredded to pieces.

We FINALLY pulled up to the bar at 1am, just as they made last call. Did I mention that Cleveland is a 1am drinking town? Fuck you, Prince of Cleveland, and fuck your shitty city.

Tucker "I seriously want to fight you right now."
Sippy "I'm so sorry, guys. I want to fight myself."
Soylent "Sippy, I think if the drunk you fought the sober you, they'd both lose."

Part 3: The Case Western Dorks

We'd decided to stop in Cleveland for two reasons: It's the obvious stopping point between Chicago and NYC, and there was a board member there, PigPen, who we were giving a ride to.

PigPen met us at the bar with two friends, undergrads at Case Western Reserve University. The two undergrads, TweedleDoofus and TweedleDork could not believe our RV setup. Case Western is legendary for being a nerd school, on par with my alma mater. These guys, though they were probably studs in their Calc 320 class, were not used to being around people who had lives that didn't involve doing regressions.

TDork "Holy shit, look at this thing. You guys are so cool!"

Tucker "No dude, it's not us, it's you. We're not that cool; you're just that much of a fucking nerd."

They went on and on, gushing about how cool the RV was, how awesome we must be just being on this road trip, etc. The highlight was when Sippy confidently gave them drinking advice . . . as he slurped beer from the sippy cup tied around his neck.

We only had 5 people in an RV that could fit 7, and we could use two more people paying for shit, so TheGinger invited them to come with us. They gave each other a shocked, wide-eyed look, like they couldn't believe we'd allow them to hang out with us, almost like the first time you take training wheels off a kid's bike and he rides without falling down. I poured two more shots for each.

TDoofus "I'm not sure. I promised my girlfriend I'd drive her somewhere tomorrow."

Tucker "Girlfriend? You're only 21, you're not going to marry her."

TDoofus "Yeah, but I really like her. She's even not an engineer. I want to go . . . but I think I need to ask her."

Tucker "ASK HER??? You gonna ask her to hold your dick for you when you piss too? Grow a fucking sack. I thought PigPen told me his friends were men! I don't see any tits on you, so if you're a man, WHY AREN'T YOU ACTING LIKE ONE?"

TDoofus "You don't think I need to ask her?"

Tucker "Let me give you the maxim I guide my life with, the one that's led me to greatness: 'Ask forgiveness, not permission.'"

TweedleDoofus paused. I could almost see testosterone rushing through him for the first time in his life. I handed him a beer.

Tucker "The Dark Side is a lot more fun. Join us."

He turned to TweedleDork:

TDoofus "Dude, let's do it! This is so crazy!"

Their only request was that we stop at their frat so they could pick up some clothes for the trip. They're in a frat? I had to see it. And mock it ruthlessly.

We stormed that frat house like Saxons raiding the English coast, screaming and banging into things. When we hit their TV room, girls began huddling next to guys and screaming. I was expecting we'd be welcomed as long-lost brothers. Instead, we were hushed by a handful of sober nerds because "some guys have midterms tomorrow."

Soylent "I think the Tweedles are the cool guys in this frat."
Tucker "Wow. Time to teach them what cool means."

I went off to cause trouble, Sippy and the two nerds packed their bags, and Soylent went to go find supplies. Even though he'd bought out a Walmart, he'd forgotten a few things. He broke into their janitor's closet and came back to the RV with garbage bags, toilet paper, a bottle of bleach, and a mop handle. Not a full mop, just the handle.

Tucker "Dude, why do we need a mop handle?"
Soylent [*in all seriousness*] "In case we have to kill someone quietly."
Tucker "Doesn't hitting someone with a mop handle make a lot of noise?"
Soylent "I'm not going to hit them with it. If the need arises, I take this," [*He whips a seriously scary knife from his pocket*] "and tie it to one end of the handle, cover it with a condom, and stab them with it."
Tucker "Why tie a knife to the end of a mop? And a condom??"
Soylent "Do you understand how modern forensics works?"
Tucker "HOLY SHIT!"

Aren't military guys fun? We all pile back in the RV.

Sippy "Well, I guess we should find a hotel room."
Tucker "Dude, it's 2am. We got here too late to pick up any girls at bars. Fuck getting a hotel room, we're rolling to NYC."
TheGinger "We can't drive through the night! That's insane."
Tucker "It won't hurt your deposit if we drive through the night."

Soylent "Pretend your parents are fighting and go hide in the back. I'll handle it from here."

Soylent chugged two Red Bulls and pulled us out of Cleveland. Everyone stayed up drinking for the first hour, having fun and bullshitting. Then TweedleDork got a phone call. He looked kinda mortified, hung up, and then summoned the courage to ask a question:

TDork "Yeah, uh . . . I don't want to make any accusations . . . but did one of you, umm . . . take a shit on a table in the frat cafeteria?"

TheGinger spit out his beer, he was laughing so hard. Without even breaking stride, I calmly assured them:

Tucker "I can't imagine any of us would do something like that."

The Tweedles kinda looked at me weird and laughed nervously. It's not a lie if you believe it.

Everyone hit a wall at 3am, especially TweedleDoofus. He passed out. Mid-sentence. We were laughing at him and mocking him . . . until he started vomiting everywhere. It was this awful mixture of energy drink, beer, tequila, and Cheetos. We took his sweatshirt off him and used it to wipe most of it up, but it didn't get rid of the stench. The whole RV smelled like nerd death.

Everyone else went to bed. I wanted to sleep, but by the time I was tired, Soylent had been behind the wheel for about 14 hours (he had the shift coming into Cleveland also), and I couldn't leave him by himself. Friends don't let friends drive an RV alone all night while wired on Red Bull, so I drank one and rode shotgun with him.

Around 9, everyone woke up and we stopped for breakfast. Afterward, Sippy took the wheel so Soylent and I could sleep for the rest of the drive. I climbed into the space above the driver's cab and went right out.

I woke up about three hours later. It was hard to sleep with DMX blasting on the radio and the RV shaking like Michael J. Fox. I looked over the edge of the bed and witnessed a scene I will never forget.

Soylent was sitting directly behind Sippy, hands gripping the back of his seat so tight his knuckles were chalk white and his fingers nearly tearing into the fabric. Every muscle in his body was fully flexed, veins popping out of strange places in his neck and head, nostrils flared to their limits, eyes wide with the type of fear and terror you see on the face of someone staring at their own mortality.

Tucker "Dude, have you gotten any sleep?"
[*Soylent, not taking his eyes off the road, barely shakes his head*]
Tucker "Why not?"
Soylent [*in a rapid-fire, terrified, raspy voice, as he looked up at me with the most pitiful, frightened look I have ever seen on an adult man*] "SIPPY'SOUTOFCONTROL! HESGOING100BANGINGHISHEADAND LOOKINGATWRECKSNOTWATCHINGTHEROAD! WE'REALLGONNA FUCKINGDIE!!!"

I lowered my head over the ledge and looked out the front windshield to see the RV swerve around a tractor trailer, missing the bumper by no more than two feet. Sippy was bobbing his head back and forth to the music as if nothing happened, then threw both hands off the steering wheel into the air to "raise the roof." The speedometer was shaking at around the 90mph mark. He looked back at me, in the complete opposite direction of the road, and screamed with the music:

Sippy "WHERE MY HOOD, WHERE MY HOOD, WHERE MY HOOD AT!!!"
Soylent "YOUREGONNAHITTHATCAR!!!!! WATCHTHEROAD!!!! AAAAHHHHH!!!!"

Despite being so close to a fiery death, I could not stop laughing. Soylent is an ex-Marine—who's been in real combat, with people shooting at him—and here he was in a state of panicked fear, put there by the driving of a 22 year old entry-level consultant.

TweedleDork and TweedleDoofus were not far from Soylent's state of mind. Obviously unaccustomed to the effects of large quantities of the drink and still severely intoxicated, they looked like the frightened refugees you see on CNN after some natural disaster in a third-world country.

TweedleDoofus had vomit matted in his hair, TweedleDork still had sleep lines on his forehead, and both kept staring at each other with a "what the fuck have we done?" look in their eyes. I got Soylent a drink to calm him down and offered them both a drink. TweedleDork looked at me like I told him to felch a rhino, and TweedleDoofus gagged and nearly threw up again.

We drank more beer—it's amazing how much more you drink when you get your beer from the shower—and Soylent eventually calmed down. Though not before Sippy pulled the RV onto the shoulder to get past some road construction, running over two dozen orange cones in the process.

TweedleDoofus was jarred out of his PTSD when his cell phone rang. The conversation was so good, I made Sippy turn down the gangster rap:

TweedleDoofus "Hey baby . . . Uh, well, it's hard to explain. I'm in an RV driving to New Jersey . . . No really, I . . . I . . . I don't know. Is there any other way you can get a ride? I'm really sorry. What about April? Can she give you a ride?"

TweedleDork explained that today was the funeral for TweedleDoofus's girlfriend's grandmother. It was in Akron, and he was supposed to drive her.

Tucker "Wait, THAT is what you had to do for your girlfriend? You had to drive her to her grandmother's FUNERAL? HAHAHAHAHAHAHA. You're fucked! Why did you come with us last night? You let me talk you out of THAT? Dude, how stupid are you?"

He gave me the angriest look a nerd can give someone he is afraid of, and walked into the bedroom in the back. TweedleDork turned away from us and spent the rest of the drive blankly staring out the window, rocking back and forth in the captain's chair.

We arrived in NJ a few hours later and checked into the hotel. After putting our stuff in the room we immediately went out to eat. TweedleDoofus and TweedleDork stayed in the room. When we got back, we found this note on the bed, along with a $20 bill:

> "Guys,
>
> Sorry, but we have to go back to Cleveland. I know we were supposed to stay the whole weekend, but this wasn't what we expected, and we really have things to get done at home. We'll take a taxi to the bus station, and get a bus home. Here is $20, I hope this covers our share."

There isn't much to tell about that night. I ignored all my fans and went into the city with my real friends, got hammered, talked a ton of shit to all kinds of posers, threw peanuts at hipsters, daring them to confront me—none did, of course—and blew a sure thing with a very good-looking girl by insulting her panty hose. Whatever—let's get to the good part.

Part 4: The Harlem RV Story

Saturday morning I woke up refreshed and ready for a big day. There were two "events" my fans had planned for that weekend: Saturday night was the party at a bar in Hoboken that they insisted on calling TuckerFest. On Sunday, I was to celebrity-judge the semi-pro wrestling bikini event, and they were all going to attend.

Jojo and Credit lived in Manhattan, so on Saturday morning, I decided to drive the RV into the city, watch the Kentucky basketball game at Jojo's apartment, pick them up, and then drive back out to TuckerFest that night.

Around 10am, I collected Nils, TheGinger, and Sippy, and we went to pick them up. Already in the RV were Soylent, PigPen, and three of the most wretched fucking people I have ever met. Their internet names were Xgatax, Ambersnax, and Rockwolf.

Xgatax: I'm not sure I can convey in words how annoying this girl was. Sickeningly obese, covered in acne, at least three chins, with the loud, obnoxious fat-girl voice that seems to carry for miles and never stops, she smoked, and had the stupidest sense of humor since . . . EVER. Don't believe me? Think I'm exaggerating? Look at this picture and tell me you can't see that description:

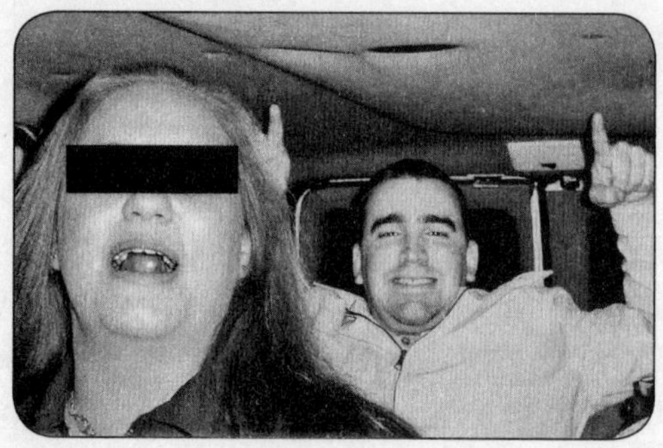

Ambersnax: When I first looked at her, I had to move from directly in front of her so I could see her whole face at once—her nose is THAT big. She not only breathed and smelled with that thing, I think she took fluids and food through it too. I'm confident I could have fit my dick in it. I can't even describe what the rest of her face or body was like; her nose overshadows my memory. The one thing I do remember was her voice. Ambersnax's awful cackling voice pierced my spirit. If the US Army played recordings of Ambersnax excitedly telling jokes to the detainees at Gitmo, they would all break within the day. Imagine Fran Drescher, but without the class or sophistication.

Rockwolf: When I met him, he had on Doc Martens, a cheap black leather jacket, greasy slicked-back hair, and jeans with holes in them. His facial hair looked like he messily ate a Popsicle and then rolled around on the floor of a barbershop. This guy was such a tool, I had a hard time even believing it at first. I honestly thought he was kidding. About everything. He wasn't.

After watching Xgatax's cackling sending shock waves through her blubber, and listening to Ambersnax's nasally shrill screeching, I had an immediate and visceral hatred of them both. These two were the very archetypes of people I hate most, and I was determined to break them emotionally. I owed it to the world.

I took a few deep breaths, broadly outlined in my head the attack strategy that would wreck them in the most brutal fashion possible, while providing the most amusement to myself and my friends, when it dawned on me: These aren't just annoying whores who are bothering me at some bar, who I can insult, laugh at, and discard.

These are my fans.

I'd already met three of my fans from my site—Sippy, TheGinger, Soylent—and despite their quirks, they were solid enough guys. I thought all my fans would be like that, maybe a bit off in some way or another, but at least normal and fun enough to hang out with.

These three were disasters in every way possible. I know it seems like I am savaging them, but trust me—they were worse in person. The girls especially; they were the type who make you wish for Revelations to start. There was nothing redeemable about either of them . . . *except that they were my fans.*

I didn't know what to do. This wasn't like any situation I'd ever been in. I couldn't be around these three morons. I'd fucking kill them or myself. But they loved my writing, they were part of the message board community on my site, and they came here to meet me. In any other situation, I would verbally maul people this annoying, but in this case, I just couldn't. Still, I HAD to get them away from me.

Tucker "All right, we are going into the city. You two are in your pajamas and need to get dressed. Go, hurry up."
Amber "OK, we'll be fast."
Xgatax "Don't leave without us?"
Tucker [*blank stare*] "Go."
TheGinger "Plus, we need more towels, so bring a bunch back with you."

I tried to convince Rockwolf he needed to change, but he was fully clothed (in the same shit he wore the night before, he made a point of telling us). The dude was clearly a tool, but he wasn't in the same league as the two girls, so I just let it go. As soon as the girls were in the hotel, I got behind the wheel.

Tucker "Someone get me a beer. We're leaving."

We weren't there to see it, but someone told us they came running out of the hotel ten minutes later, their arms full of towels they'd taken off a maid's cart. It would almost have been worth it to stay and see that.

Soylent took the passenger seat, and I floored it. As I pulled out of the parking lot, I was still getting accustomed to the fact that a 40 ft. Winnebago does not have the same turning radius as a domestic sedan. I ran the RV over a huge curb, sending it up onto two wheels, screeching the tires, dumping half the liquor bar onto the floor and shattering three bottles. The RV slammed back down, and everyone in the back had a panicked look on their face. I turned to them and smiled.

Tucker "What are you pussies afraid of? We have walkaway insurance. Get me another beer."

There was a lot of traffic on the way into the city, so even though I was driving, I did what I always do to pass the time: I drank. I had no intention of drinking very much, but when we hit the George Washington Bridge, I was already on beer five. Even I realized this was not good. In order to slow myself down, I had to find something else to occupy my attention, so I started rifling through Sippy's CD case. The titles of his mix CDs confused me.

Tucker "'Stydie's Christmas Mix'? What the fuck is on there, Perry Como? 'Stydie's Easter Mix,' 'Stydie's Summer Mix'? Sippy, what the fuck is this shit? Oh, look at this gem: 'It Is Most Definitely On.' You wrote that . . . in marker . . . on the CD."
Sippy "I title them based on—"
Tucker "You have a CD called 'Stydie's Rockin' Out Music.' Stop speaking. Nothing you can say will save you now. You have lost at life."

He meekly bowed his head and drank from his sippy cup. Out of sheer curiosity, I popped in "Stydie's Christmas Mix." What came on? Ludacris's "My Business." Then DMX's "Ain't No Sunshine." Then R. Kelly's "Remix to Ignition."

Tucker "Sippy, what the fuck? The Yuletide rolls around, and Ludacris comes to mind? Time to exchange presents, and you think about DMX! Little cousins coming over for Christmas? PUT ON SOME R. KELLY???"
Sippy "No, I name the discs based on—"
Tucker "QUIET ON THE BRIDGE! Torpedo room?"
Soylent [*in the passenger seat*] "Torpedo room here, Captain."
Tucker "Open outer bay doors."
Soylent [*rolls down window*] "Outer bay doors are open."
Tucker [*ejecting Stydie's Christmas Mix CD*] "FIRE!"

I flung the CD out Soylent's window, watched it skip off the windshield of another car, and everyone cheered with the type of over-excitement only boredom can cause.

Soylent "Direct hit, Captain!"
Tucker "I AM THE GREATEST MAN ALIVE!!!"

This little game helped me tolerate the GWB traffic. The highlight was getting one of the CDs into someone's open window. I think it was "Spring Jams."

Most of his pitiful CD collection was gone when I came across "Gonna Get Her Back." I put the CD in and the whole thing was hard punk, hate-the-world music.

Tucker "Sippy, how the hell is this shit going to help you get a girl back?"
Sippy "Well, uhhh, umm, it's not 'get her back' as in 'get back with her,' it's 'get her back' as in 'hurt her because she tore my guts out.' I made that when I drove back to Dayton after my ex-girlfriend dumped me."
Tucker "Oh wow. You really are the ghost of Eric Harris."

The George Washington Bridge brings you into the city at around 178th Street. That is the upper end of Harlem, which extends all the way down 110th Street, the top of Central Park. Jojo lived on the Upper East Side, around 93rd. Translation: We had a lot of poverty to drive through.

We took Broadway, one of the main streets through Manhattan. I quickly noticed that a lot of people were staring at us. I didn't realize why, until I caught a reflection of the RV in a storefront window.

7 white guys in an RV, all the windows open, rap music blaring, drinking beers and yelling at passersby. How many times do you think anyone, black or white, has seen that on 165th and Broadway?

Even though I had tried to slow down, I was probably on beer 10 or so by the time we got into Harlem. I felt fine—this was probably my drinking peak as a human, when I could pound 10 beers and still smoke a DUI test (I'd done it before, but that's a whole other story).

At least I *thought* I was fine. Somewhere around 150th and Broadway, we pulled up to a stoplight. Next to us was an off-duty ambulance.

Tucker "Hey everyone, watch this."

I honked my horn and leaned out the window, screaming curses at the ambulance. It took a second before the EMT in the passenger seat glanced over. He immediately did a double take, then another one, and smacked the driver as he pointed to us.

With their attention fully in hand, I started rolling my fingers and then pointing forward. If you had crazy reckless friends in high school like I did, you know what that means:

It's the universal sign for "Let's street race."

The driver's eyes got wide, and the passenger started laughing, like he couldn't believe it. I kept motioning forward, revving the engine, as Nils and Soylent caught on and leaned out the side windows.

Nils "YOU FUCKING PISSANTS, YOU WON'T RACE US! YOU COWARDS!!"
Soylent "COME ON, YOU PUSSIES! BE MEN! RACE US!!"

Both the ambulance driver and passenger were still laughing when the light turned green. I wasn't kidding. I peeled the fuck out—literally peeled out an RV on 150th and Broadway, smoking the tires—and blew past that fucking ambulance, leaving them, and all the pedestrians, staring in disbelief as we sped off.

We beat an ambulance in a drag race!!! The RV erupted in cheers. I laid on the horn in celebration.

Tucker "GET THE FUCK OUT OF MY WAY!! I AM THE GREATEST MAN ALIVE!!"

Three blocks later we stopped at a red light, still high fiving and toasting our victory, when the ambulance caught up. It stopped right next to us, the guys intentionally motioned to me, looked me in the eye . . . then threw on their lights and siren and pulled through the red light, laughing as we sat there, stopped.

Tucker "YOU MOTHERFUCKERS!!"

I was about to pull through the light—a RED light at a major intersection—when Soylent grabbed my arm.

Soylent "Tucker . . . you have a full beer in your hand."

I looked down. I did indeed have a red Solo cup, full of beer, in my hand. I had not only just drag-raced an ambulance through Harlem, in a 40 foot RV, I did it while *I was still actively drinking.*

Tucker "Perhaps I should wait for the light."

I stopped revving the engine, handed the beer to Soylent, and proceeded calmly to Jojo's apartment. It was noon. It would be my last good decision for 7 hours.

Rockwolf had been such an annoying fuck to that point, everyone was fed up. I would write about the stupid shit he said and did, but it wasn't funny annoying, like Sippy, it was "drown this loser in the toilet" annoying. It came to a head when his phone kept ringing—I think it was Ambersnax calling him—and Soylent told him to turn it off. He wouldn't, so Soylent calmly took his phone from him and threw it out his window. Rockwolf freaked. He implored me to pull over (I wouldn't) and, too afraid Soylent would strangle him with the shower hose if confronted (he would), bitched at everyone else for letting Soylent throw his phone out the window. Everyone laughed and told him to shut up.

So what did he do? He jumped out of the RV. THROUGH THE WINDOW.

This is not the General Lee. This is a 40 ft. Winnebago. It has doors that open, that are used as exits. Apparently that was too convenient for Rockwolf. He felt that leaping out of the side window—while we were still moving (albeit slowly)—was the best way to get to the street to retrieve his piece of shit phone. After crawling under a car to retrieve it, he ran down the block to catch up, where we'd gotten caught at another red light, and climbed back into the RV (through the door). He was pretty quiet after that.

Parking in New York City is almost impossible when you have a car; with an RV, you'd have an easier time finding a Yankee fan who doesn't breathe exclusively through his mouth. We circled the block about six times, until I finally just said fuck it and pulled the RV into a combo bus stop/fire hydrant space.

TheGinger "Tucker! We can't park here! It says 'No Parking ANYTIME'!"
Tucker "Fuck that. You can't tow one of these things. We're fine."

We rolled into the corner bodega and bought every single 40 oz bottle of malt liquor they had, maybe 25 in all—they were only $2.39 apiece—and took them up to Jojo's apartment. He lived in a 500 sq ft one-bedroom, which is palatial by Manhattan standards. It was on the 28th floor, and as soon as Soylent walked into the apartment, he was in love:

Soylent "Look at how high we are!"

He stuck his head out the window, saw a bunch of town houses below, and directly under our window were all of their backyards.

Soylent "Who lives there?"
Jojo "I don't know. Someone with money, obviously, those are brownstones."
Tucker "I bet they think they're better'n you."
Soylent "Those motherfuckers."

He took one of the 40's, held it out the window, then released his grip. I was watching the basketball game, only half paying attention, when all of a sudden I heard a faint smash, and Soylent and Jojo started cracking up laughing:

Soylent "DIRECT HIT!"

I got up to see, all the way down, a lawn chair askew and bent out of shape, with a huge wet circle around it.

Soylent "That is awesome!! I bet I can break that bench they have! Watch!"

After that, it got bad.

Soylent was throwing things out the window like the apartment was a ship taking on water. CD cases, cell phones, old wine bottles. Rockwolf saw where this was going and stood WAY back from the window. After Soylent duct-taped a 40oz to a pot full of water and then jettisoned them out the window together, Jojo stopped him. Thank God it was cold and no one was outside. Dude would have killed someone.

We all watched basketball and got drunker, while Soylent—with nothing to do now—got bored and decided to take such a huge shit that he not only stopped up the toilet, he nearly cleared the apartment with the smell. Nils, who was heavily into the liquor at this point, decided that he would fix the toilet. The first thing he did was take the top of the tank off and drop it on the bathroom floor, smashing it into 20 pieces.

Nils "Whoops."

Everyone started laughing. Nils, being a gentleman, peeled off three twenties from his roll, handed them to Jojo, and sat back down on the sofa. So much for his plumbing career.

Jojo "You're not even going to clean it up? You break my toilet tank and just think you can pay me and that's it?"
Nils "I gave you forty acres. You want a mule, too?"

We all laughed. Jojo just stood there staring at him. Nils peeled off another $20 and handed it to him.

As the afternoon progressed, we moved from "normal drunk" to "sorority formal drunk." Once the 40's were gone (mostly out the window), Nils broke open his bag of liquor. Did I not mention that? Nils had flown in from San Francisco and brought with him a duffel bag filled with ten bottles of top-shelf liquor. He flew them in instead of buying them in NYC, because he'd stolen them from a law firm event. Bombay Sapphire, Grey Goose, etc. He thought it would be a good idea to chug half a bottle of Jagermeister and then pour the rest on my head. I took umbrage and dumped my 40 on his head.

Jojo "MOTHERFUCKERS! I HAVE TO LIVE HERE."

By that point, there was half an inch of alcohol, beer, broken glass, and porcelain on his floor. It looked like the Double Deuce after a hard Saturday night. It was time to go.

Tucker "Aren't you coming with us to the party?"
Jojo "Nah man. I'm not riding around Harlem in an RV with a bunch of drunk-ass crazy white guys."

Back down to the RV—which was still there, just like I fucking said it would be.

Tucker "WHO HAS THE KEYS?"
TheGinger "You do, Tucker."
Tucker "Oh. Yeah. OUT OF THE WAY, THERE IS AN RV TO BE DRIVEN!"
Sippy "Dude, do you think you should be driving?"
Tucker "Do you think you deserve the sack attached to your body? No, but you have one anyway."
TheGinger "What does that mean?"
Tucker "It means I need another beer. WHERE IS MY CO-PILOT! SOYLENT, MAN THE TORPEDO ROOM! AND SOMEONE GET ME A BEER!"

[WARNING: What is about to follow is a story about me driving an RV around Harlem while severely drunk. Drinking and driving is criminally dumb. Everyone knows that. I don't have any legitimate excuse for what I did—I was stupid in my twenties, what do you want from me? Don't get me wrong, this is a very funny story, but it's funny only in retrospect, because no one got seriously hurt. That doesn't mean, of course, it was not a VERY stupid decision on my part. It was, and I was wrong. Fortunately for your sake, sometimes the stupidest decisions make for the best stories.]

As soon as I got into the RV, I slammed it into reverse and ran over something very loud. TheGinger ran to the back of the RV and looked out the window.

TheGinger "Tucker, that was a *New York Post* dispenser!"
Tucker "Dissin' Flava Flav when he's da butta on ya toast! Fuck the *New York Post*!"
TheGinger "What about my deposit?"
Tucker "Fuck your deposit too! Stop being a bitch!"

I floored it and tore off down the street.

TheGinger "OH MY GOD! It's stuck under the bumper! There are sparks everywhere! TUCKER, STOP! MY DEPOSIT!!!"
Tucker "Yeah, yeah, we're all gonna fucking die. Get me another beer, you pussy."

Casually, I check the rearview mirror. He was right: There really were sparks flying off the back of the RV.

Tucker "Check that out, it looks like the aurora borealis!"
Soylent "You really *are* drunk."
Tucker "You don't know me!"

WHAM!

New York City streets are narrow. RVs are wide. I learned this the hard way . . . by smashing the sideview mirror into a parked car. Soylent reached out the window and fixed the mirror on his side. I immediately overcorrected and clipped another car on my side.

Soylent "I think I'm going to start keeping count."
Tucker "Only faggots and pussies count. Get me another beer."

Driving through Harlem, someone decided that since they were open, it would make sense to throw a can out the window. It almost hit a pedestrian, who jumped in shock. Everyone laughed, and it started a throwing frenzy. Everything that wasn't valuable was tossed out the window: ice, napkins, pillows, pot holders—you get the idea.

As we reached the FDR Drive, everything not valuable was gone. Nils became frustrated, tore the curtain rods off, and tossed them out the window. Everyone cheered as they bounced down the freeway behind us and cars swerved to avoid them. Encouraged by this, Nils decided that the interior wood paneling would make an excellent projectile and started ripping it off the walls.

Sippy "Nils, stop! You can't throw the paneling out the window!"

Sippy pulled Nils away from the paneling. Nils looked at him with shock, then contempt, then grabbed Sippy in a bear hug and started pushing him out the window. If Sippy wasn't going to let him have any more projectiles to throw at cars, then Sippy would become the projectile. TheGinger dove and grabbed Sippy. By the feet—*because he was already half out the window*—and held on for dear life. Everyone else rushed to pull Nils off Sippy and drag him back inside the RV.

TheGinger "Nils! What are you doing?"
Nils "Throwing stuff out the window."
TheGinger "SIPPY IS NOT STUFF!!"
Nils "Oh . . . sorry Sippy."

TheGinger saved the day by opening the trash bags and handing Nils empty beer cans to throw. Everyone quickly discovered that throwing beer cans out the window was A LOT of fun. We even made a game of it. I think we called it "Who can hit the most things with beer cans?"

TheGinger—who was so drunk at this point he either forgot his neuroticism about the RV or got caught up in the moment—was hanging out the left side window and launched a Solo cup of Guinness at a car. It was a perfect shot, going right in the open T-top of a red 280Z, sloshing thick, sticky beer all over the interior.

TheGinger leaned back in the RV laughing wildly to himself, just in time to see Nils lauch a full, unopened 22oz of Heineken—he switched to full bottles because we had thrown all the empties—out the passenger side of the RV, smashing right on the hood of a Jeep Grand Cherokee, leaving a HUGE dent.

I don't know if you've ever wildly driven an RV on the FDR and thrown bottles at cars, but if you haven't, I'll tell you what happens: Most of the drivers get freaked out and try to avoid you. But some people get PISSED, and take the opposite approach. They come after you. The drivers of the 280Z and the Grand Cherokee were two of those people.

I was driving down the middle of the highway, the 280Z driver was this Hispanic guy, and he was on my left side, keeping even with me, screaming and yelling out his window, pointing at me to pull over. On the right side was the Grand Cherokee, driven by a very pissed-off black woman. She was screaming so loudly I could hear her clearly in the RV—and this is while driving like 40 mph. I am not sure what she was saying specifically, but the message was clear: She was losing her fucking mind.

From any objective perspective, we were unquestionably in the wrong. But I don't live in some bullshit world of objective reality; I live in MY reality, and in that wonderful land of free beer and unlimited hot girls, we'd done nothing wrong. Of course, I was so drunk at that point, I was convinced of my own divinity, so the idea that I would stop the RV to answer for my actions was unthinkable. I am Tucker Max! I've never done anything wrong in my life, I don't give a fuck about these plebeians, I have a party to get to where my fans are waiting to worship me and reinforce my hubris, and I'm not stopping until I get there!

We informed the drivers of my intended course of action in two ways:

1. We flipped them off. Repeatedly and enthusiastically.

2. We threw more beers at their cars.

Because the two vehicles were essentially even with the RV on both sides and were going below the pace of traffic, there was a ton of empty road in front of us. The 280Z pulled way out ahead, got in our lane, STOPPED on the FDR, and the dude got out of his car, with his hand in his jacket pocket.

Sippy "Tucker, he has a gun!"
Tucker "He's bluffing."

I hit the brakes, swerved the RV into the lane he abandoned, and went around him. As we passed, I leaned out the window and flipped him off again.

Tucker "FUUUUUUUUUCK YOUUUUUUUUUUUUUU!"

Everyone cheered. He just glared as we zoomed past, keeping his hand in his jacket.

Tucker "I TOLD YOU HE WAS BLUFFING!!!"

Still jacked up from adrenaline after smoking the red 280Z, I was high fiving Soylent and not paying attention to the road. When you have an on-ramp coming up fast, this can cause a problem.

Credit "Max, watch out, you need to get on the Cross Bronx."
Tucker "I DON'T WANT TO GO TO THE BRONX!"
Credit "No, you idiot, the Cross Bronx Expressway takes you to New Jersey."

Tucker "That doesn't make sense!"
Credit "Just get on the ramp!"
Tucker "Which ramp??"
Credit "Left, the left one!"
Tucker "WHICH WAY'S LEFT?!?!?!"

I really said that. I was that drunk.

And of course, I went right, and of course, that was not only the wrong way, it dumped us right back into Harlem, where we immediately got lost. This was 2003, before everyone had a GPS in their phone. No one had ANY fucking idea where we were or what to do.

And at that exact moment, the moment we realized we had no idea where we were, the Jeep Grand Cherokee pulled up next to us, and a very, very pissed-off black woman started going ballistic at us. Instinctively, I gunned the RV and took off . . . and that was when the hour-long car chase through Harlem began.

I am not kidding or exaggerating one bit. A Jeep Cherokee, driven by an angry black woman and with an equally pissed-off black guy in the passenger seat, spent the next hour chasing a 40ft RV with 8 white guys in it, all across Harlem. And I mean ALL OVER Harlem. I think the highest we got was 210th or so, and the lowest we got was 120th. And no matter what we did, we could NOT shake this woman. I ran a red light, she ran a red light. I swerved all over the roads and drove across grassy medians, she followed me. This bitch was on me like cheese on macaroni.

I think it was somewhere around 125th and Malcolm X, I turned the RV down a side street, and she made her move. The street was wide enough for her to speed past me, and once she did that, she pulled her SUV sideways across the road, blocking us in, and came bolting out of her car, doing the angry-black-woman dance.

AngryBlackWoman "YOU MOTHERFUCKERS! I GOT YOU NOW, BITCHES! GET THE FUCK OUTTA THERE, IMMA FUCK YOU UP!"

She started banging on the RV, screaming curses at us. The guy with her pulled her away from the RV, and I actually had to pause and laugh for a minute, it was that ridiculous.

Credit "Tucker, I've seen you make some women really mad, but I think this tops them all."
Soylent "You gotta admire her determination. I think I would've let it go at this point."

By then, I'd stopped drinking, and though I was FAR from sober, I was clearheaded enough to start thinking about what the consequences would be if the cops came. I didn't really pay attention in law school, but after a quick recount of our actions over the past few hours, I came to the only logical conclusion: We needed to get the fuck out of there, STAT.

I clearly couldn't go forward. There were some cars behind us, but it was a two-lane street, so if I could just get turned around, I could go the other way. There was a driveway to the left, giving me some room to maneuver.

Tucker "TheGinger, go to the back window of the RV and call out my space, I'm going to turn this thing around."
TheGinger "Yes! Brilliant!" [*scurries to the back window*]

I pulled into the driveway, threw it in reverse, and started going back.

TheGinger "OK, OK, getting close, close . . . STOP!!"

I heard the faint sound of metal crunching. Shit. I put it back in drive, went forward as far as I could, cranked the wheel, then went back in reverse.

TheGinger "You're really close . . . STOP!!!! TUCKER, STOP!!!"

Crunch again. Big one. TheGinger frantically sprinted to the front of the RV.

TheGinger "Tucker, you hit like four parked cars!!"
Tucker "Why didn't you tell me I was close?!?"
TheGinger "I DID!"
Tucker "Well, there's not enough room to get turned around. Sippy, get out and ask them to back their cars out, we can just reverse it back down the street."
Sippy [*in the most petrified voice I've ever heard out of a grown man*] "WHAT!?! HAVE YOU SEEN THAT WOMAN? I'M NOT GETTING OUT OF THIS RV!"

Soylent sighed, got out of the RV, and walked back to the cars. He politely asked the drivers to reverse down the street and let us out, because there was an obstruction in front of the RV. AngryBlackWoman, who was sitting in her SUV talking on her cell phone, saw him and came running down the street screaming:

AngryBlackWoman "OH, HELL NO, MOTHERFUCKER! I DONE CALLED THE COPS!! YOU AIN'T GOIN' NOWHERE!!"

She told the drivers the whole story. Soylent stood there for a second, saw the inevitable conclusion, and calmly walked back to the RV.

Soylent "They're not moving. We're stuck until the cops come. Someone get me a beer."

At that moment Rockwolf said, "I'm outta here," and for the second time that day, flung himself out the RV window and ran off. I'm totally serious. The dude sprinted past AngryBlackWoman and all the people starting to mill around, down the street, and off into the night. He did it so fast I almost didn't believe it.

I stepped out from behind the wheel and surveyed the RV. TheGinger's anxiety was back; he was sitting on the bed on the back, trembling. Credit was shaking his head in dismay. PigPen was staring straight ahead in his seat, like he just witnessed a murder. Nils was passed out and snoring.

Sippy was sitting in a chair with his head in his hands . . . crying. Tears. Out of his eyes.

Tucker "Why are you crying?"
Sippy "BECAUSE WE'RE FUCKED!"
Tucker "It's not a big deal, dude. We'll figure it out."
Sippy "Tucker, we were driving an RV around Harlem, throwing beer bottles at people and crashing into cars! We're totally fucked!"
Tucker "Stop being melodramatic. We're fine."
Sippy "What are we going to do Tucker?!? Sit in a pool of diamonds and pearls, sipping champagne out of the skulls of our enemies?!?"
Tucker "Shut up you pussy. Go lie on the bed and cry yourself to sleep. Let me think. I'll get us out of it, I always do. I'm a legend for a reason."

I took my fleece off and started drinking water and began thinking about how to handle this once the cops arrived. AngryBlackWoman came over to the RV and banged on the windows.

AngryBlackWoman "YOU CAINT JUST TAKE YO JACKET OFF, I KNOW YOU, MOTHAFUCKA! DAT WATER AIN'T GONNA HELP, YOU GOIN TA JAIL!!"

I thought of pulling the curtains to give us privacy—but couldn't, because there were no curtains left in the RV. Nils, who was STILL snoring through this whole ordeal, had thrown them out hours ago.

Tucker "OK, gentlemen, here's the deal. The cops are coming, and we're almost certainly going to be arrested, so just prepare yourself for that."
Sippy "ARRESTED?!"
Tucker "It's not a big deal. If we're smart, we should be able to get out of this without any charges. We just have to come up with a coherent story and stick to it. The only two issues the cops will care about are the damage done to the various cars, and if the driver of the RV was drunk. The car damage is covered under the insurance policy that we took out with the RV. I told you walk-away insurance was the way to go, didn't I?"

TheGinger "YOU'RE THE ONE WHO CAUSED THE DAMAGE!"

Tucker "Don't be so negative. It was smart to get the insurance, I did it, everything'll be fine. The cops could pursue some sort of assault charge, but they won't do that if we aren't dicks. There is no issue with everyone being drunk, the law is clear on that. The back section of an RV is not considered a car for the purposes of open container laws. The only problem is if the driver is drinking. And I was. A lot. Are any of you sober? Because I'm not. If you are, it'd be nice if you claimed you were driving. Come on, Credit, you've only had like three beers. You'll beat this."

Credit "No chance, Max. Unlike you, I have a job, and I'd like to keep it."

Tucker "Great. Anyone have any ideas how I can sober up real real fast?"

PigPen "I heard sucking on pennies works. Something about the copper."

Tucker "Anyone have any *good* ideas?"

Soylent "Dude . . . Rockwolf was driving."

Tucker "GODDAMN RIGHT HE WAS! And that motherfucker threw all that shit out the window too! He did everything illegal that happened! What an asshole!! That's the last piece of the story. For everything else, just tell the truth, and we're fine. So just relax and chill, I'm going to do push-ups and mountain-climbers in the back and try to sweat out some of this alcohol before the cops get here."

TheGinger frantically tried to clean the RV for some reason, but it still looked like shit when the first cop showed up 15 minutes later. There were probably 25–30 people milling around the RV by the time he knocked on the door. He had a short, military-style haircut and was visibly pissed off.

MilitaryCop "If any of you motherfuckers get out of this RV, I'm going to beat the holy living shit out of you. There is a mob out there, so STAY IN HERE until backup comes."

Two more cops got there right after him. One cop was a pissed-off Haitian and the other was a fat white guy who looked like Chris Farley. The Haitian and the military-looking cop dealt with the crowd, and the fat cop opened the door to the RV, took one step inside, and choked on the smell.

FatCop "Holy shit," [*cough, cough*] "You guys been drinking a little, huh? So, tell me what's going on here."

What did Tucker Max do? Talk shit to the cops? Tell them to get the fuck out of my face? Ride them ruthlessly? Challenge them to a drinking contest?

If you think I did ANYTHING like that, you're an idiot who has never dealt with a cop. I acted like a BITCH. Cooperated fully and couldn't have kissed this guy's ass any more if he was sitting on my face.

Here's the thing: Some cops are dicks, but the vast majority aren't. Most cops became cops because they wanted to help people and catch real criminals. Assuming you haven't committed a serious crime, if you are very, very accommodating and helpful to them, you're going to be fine 99% of the time. You just have to remember, at the scene, they are God. They can arrest you for ANYTHING they want, they can jack you around, they can ruin your entire day. Granted, if they are just jacking you around, then in the long run nothing is going to stick, and you'll get released . . . but only after hours or days spent in a holding cell. If you fuck with a cop, he WILL fuck you up, so even if you're guilty, in the short term your best play is usually to cooperate as much as possible. (FYI: If you are black, ignore everything I just wrote. You're fucked no matter what you do.)

Using this strategy, I explained the whole situation to the cop, telling the truth about everything, except inserting Rockwolf as the culprit for all the drunk driving and most of the littering.

FatCop "I'm confused. How do you guys all know each other again?"

How, in 2003, do you explain to an NYPD cop what a message board is? We just gave him the basic details, but he got confused and focused on getting us out of there.

FatCop "OK, you have insurance, that's good, we'll give that info to the victims. Are any of you sober? Can any of you drive?"

We all kind of looked around at each other. I raised my eyes at Credit, and he shook his head vigorously.

Tucker "Sippy, how about you?"
Sippy "No way! I'm wasted!"
FatCop [*to Sippy*] "Why do you have a sippy cup tied around your neck?"
Soylent "Because he's the Prince of Cleveland."
FatCop "What?"

A bunch of new cops got to the scene, and a plainclothes Hispanic guy, who acted like he owned the place, stepped into the RV, reeled from the smell, took one look at us, and called FatCop out into the street with him, while MilitaryCop came in and asked us the same questions FatCop did, and we gave the same answers. MilitaryCop saw Nils sleeping and kicked him.

MilitaryCop "Hey, wake the fuck up. This ain't no goddamn naptime."

Nils had been passed out for at least an hour, and he groggily woke up with no fucking clue what was going on. And he was pissed.

Nils "What the fuck? Leave me alone."

He rolled over and went back to sleep.

You know what happens when you directly defy a cop's order, especially a hard-ass ex-military cop? Nothing good.

MilitaryCop "Get the fuck up, NOW!"

Nils waved him away, infuriating MilitaryCop. I saw him about to explode, so I stepped in and shook Nils.

Tucker "Be cool man, these are cops."

Nils angrily stared at me and half sat up. MilitaryCop was satisfied with this and started casually searching the RV. He opened the first cabinet and stopped, in shock.

MilitaryCop "Holy shit. Captain, come in here, you gotta see this."

The Hispanic cop (he was the precinct captain) saw the multitude of bottles, his eyes went wide, and he ordered everyone outside and up against the RV. We could hear them inside, looking through everything:

MilitaryCop "My God, look at this fuckin' bar. They have fucking Johnny Walker Blue in here. I can't even *afford* this shit!"
FatCop "There's a keg in the shower!!!"
Captain "A keg in the shower?"
FatCop "Holy shit. Look at this fucking contraption! It's hooked up to the showerhead!"
MilitaryCop "And the fridge is full of beer too!"

Here we were, seven white guys, assuming the position up against the outside of an RV. There was a crowd of at least 100, kept away from us only by the 10 or so cops now on the scene. I was in the middle of the RV. Soylent was at the end, calm as a Hindu cow. Sippy was between me and him, shaking and crying, tears streaming down his face. I think he may have wet himself. TheGinger was on the other side of me, mumbling anxiously to himself. Credit was still shaking his head in dismay, PigPen was wide-eyed and terrified, and Nils was fuming at the end. I whispered down the line.

Tucker "Everyone, just be cool. Remember the story, stick to it, and we'll be fine."

Sippy sniffled through his tears. Soylent yawned and rolled his eyes at Sippy. Nils took a different strategy. He turned around and faced the cops:

Nils "Are we done? Can I fucking go now?"
MilitaryCop "Shut the fuck up and get back up against the RV!"
Tucker "Nils, shut up dude, you'll get in trouble!"
Nils "I want to know what's going on! I demand answers right now. I am a paralegal in the biggest IP law firm on the West Coast, I won't stand for this bullshit!"
MilitaryCop "I'll show you what you're going to stand for."

MiliaryCop shoulder-checked Nils up against the RV, cuffed him, and swept his leg, sending him right to his ass. The crowd went fucking ballistic, cheering and hooting.

"Fuck dat mothafucka up!!!"
"You got knocked da fuck out!!"
"Dem some drunk-ass mothafuckas!"
"Look, dat one cryin! HAHHAHA! He cryin' yo!"

A black and Puerto Rican crowd. Witnessing a white cop beat the shit out of a white dude. IN HARLEM. I'm going to go out on a limb and say this is something they'd never seen before. A few seconds later, AngryBlackWoman comes up with the Haitian cop, screaming and pointing at Nils.

AngryBlackWoman "Dat's him, dat da motherfucka who fucked up my car!!!"

The crowd laughed and egged her on as the captain walked AngryBlackWoman up and down the RV, looking at each of us.

AngryBlackWoman "Yeah, dat mothafucker was driving right der," [*pointing at me*] "and dat mothafucker be throwing shit at my car!" [*pointing at Nils*]
Captain "All right, cuff those two and get them in the car and take them back to the station. Get everyone else back in the RV. Johnson, you drive it to the station. We'll sort everything else out there."

The crowd went crazy, chanting and mocking us, led by AngryBlackWoman.

AngryBlackWoman "Yeah, dat's right, you goin' to jail mothafucka! Dat's what you get for fuckin' up *my* car!"

No question, had I not been in the process of being arrested for DUI, reckless driving, and criminal endangerment, I would have thought this whole scene was as hilarious as they did. I even started to laugh for a second at the absurdity of it, when MilitaryCop saw me, came up right in my ear, and hissed angrily:

MilitaryCop "You must be fucking crazy. Do you realize how lucky you are? If it'd been 30 degrees warmer, you'd be fucking dead. These people would have set this RV on fire and ripped you apart in the streets, you idiot."

FatCop walked me and Nils to his car, and put us in the backseat. I looked at the dashboard clock. It was 7:18pm.

Part 5: The Harlem Cops

The story breaks into two parts for a while. We were arrested in the 32nd Precinct, which is where they took the RV, everyone in it, and Nils. Since I was a DUI suspect, they had to take me to the 21st Precinct to blow, because that was the closest Breathalyzer station.

Instead of me telling you second-hand what happened to my friends when I wasn't there, the story of the 32nd Precinct will be told by TheGinger, up until it reunites with my story.

Part 5A: The 32nd Precinct (as told by TheGinger)

After Tucker and Nils were taken to their "private cars," the Hispanic captain and his partner told us to get back into the RV. The crowd was dispersing, and the cops' mood had improved quite a bit once they realized that they were not going to have to deal with a full-scale riot.

They used the RV as an improvised paddy wagon, taking us back to the precinct to figure out what to do with us. Once there, they marched us into the precinct and every cop in the joint was staring at us like we walked on all fours and had horns in the middle of our foreheads. The desk sergeant just glared at us as they took us into the squad room and told us to sit in some hard plastic chairs back in the corner.

"ID from all of you," a cop said. We handed him our IDs and he went through the whole "Indiana, Ohio, Pennsylvania . . . WHAT THE FUCK?"

routine again. We stuck to the vague and unbelievable story and the cops didn't ask any more questions about it.

I vividly remember that even though we had booze everywhere, the cops thought we were in Harlem buying drugs and the captain told the sergeant to toss the RV. At one point he said flat out, "Tell me where the drugs are and this will be much easier." We didn't have any drugs at all, but they didn't believe us. They tossed it, and then tossed it again, and found nothing. I remember them being very surprised by this.

At this point, I noticed that more and more cops were coming into the squad room. And they were calling other cops, and we of course overheard them:

Cop1 "Steve, you ain't gonna believe this shit. We got seven WHITE BOYS down here. Yeah, in the Three-two. No, I'm not fuckin' with you . . . and they're in an RV . . . fuck you too, asshole . . . and check this out, they've got a full bar. With a fuckin' keg in the shower. You gotta get your ass down here and see this shit."

The cops were coming in and starting conversations with us:

Cop2 "So, whose RV is it?"
TheGinger "It's rented. I rented it in Chicago."
Cop2 "Really? How much was it?"
TheGinger "$600 for four days."
Cop2 "Really? That's pretty cheap. I'd like to do that. Rent an RV and take the family on vacation."
TheGinger "Well, the RV is cheap, but the gas is a killer."

About this time, an older cop walked in, found ten cops talking to us and milling around, and shouted, "You motherfuckers, get out of here and get back to work." Then he motioned to us. "All right, all of you fuckers on your feet."

I thought we were fucked. I thought they were fucking with us and this was the part where they arrested us and then took one of us back to the bathroom for the ol' nightstick enema.

"We need to get a picture," said the cop.

"For . . . evidence?" I asked.

"No," he said with a smile. "We want this for our bulletin board. Nobody's going to believe this shit."

At this point, another cop walked in with a beat-up Polaroid camera and said, "I found this in the property room!"

So we all posed for the camera, gave it the thumbs-up and let them take a picture. When they were done, Soylent asked, "Hey, will you take another for us?"

"Sure," said the cop. He took another picture and handed it to Soylent. Here it is:

The older cop inquired, “Where are you assholes staying?”

“New Jersey.”

“Well, you motherfuckers take that RV, get the fuck out of New York, go back to Jersey, and don’t come back. Keep your asses on the other side of the river.”

After having the NYPD literally throw us out of New York, we all piled into the RV, and Credit took the wheel and headed down 135th Street before someone realized that Sippy hadn’t pulled in the steps of the RV. It was one of his jobs, and despite our ordeal, nobody was willing to let him slide.

He jumped into action, flinging open the door of the RV while we were moving, smacking into several of the cop cars parked along 135th Street, along with several civilian cars, before he composed himself and got the door shut. Car alarms were blaring as we all shouted at Credit, “Go, just go!”

About 30 minutes later, we arrived at the Black Bear on Washington Street in Hoboken, where the open bar and meet-and-greet for Tucker was being held. We told the crowd that the guest of honor had, indeed, been arrested in Harlem. For DUI. In an RV.

Part 5B: The 21st Precinct

FatCop was the one who took me to the other precinct. What so many people don’t understand is that cops have a HUGE amount of discretion in terms of what cases they pursue and the ones they don’t. If you didn’t do anything that bad, and if the cop thinks you are a decent person and you treat him with respect, he’s going to give you every benefit of the doubt, if for no other reason than he doesn’t want to be bothered with all the paperwork.

After we dropped Nils off at the 32nd, it was just me and FatCop in the car, and I started talking to him, looking for common ground. I found out he loves fishing and hunting, and couldn't wait to retire and move upstate to some land he owned. Awesome. I grew up in Kentucky, I can talk hunting and fishing with anyone. I never tried to sell him on my innocence, I didn't even bring up the case at all, I was trying to sell him on me as a person. If I could do that, he'd argue my case for me.

At the new precinct, FatCop sat me in the holding area with the other DUI suspects and checked me in. I was sitting next to this DRUNK-ass black guy. He had to be like 60 years old, reeked of gin, and wore a dirty green zoot suit, with sunglasses on, inside, at night. The cops knew him by name; apparently this is his average Saturday night. He glanced at me, then did a double take, like a cartoon:

Drunk "HEY SARGE! DER A WHITE GUY BACK HERE IN CUFFS!! YOU DUN FUCKED UP!! HAHAHHAHAHAHA!"
DeskCop "Shut the fuck up, Jonesy."
Drunk "You arrested?"
Tucker "Yep."
Drunk "For what?"
Tucker "DUI."
Drunk "DUI? Whatchu doin' drivin' 'round Harlem?"
Tucker "I got lost."
Drunk "Ain't dat da truth! Hahahahhahaha!"

FatCop came and sat down next to me.

FatCop "In New York, only state police can administer Breathalyzers, and the two closest are stuck at the scene of some accident. They won't be here for a while, so we just have to wait."
Tucker "OK, no problem. So, what's the biggest deer you ever bagged?"
FatCop "Oh man, one time up in the Adirondacks . . ."

For two hours, we talked hunting, fishing, trapping, guns, everything. I just asked him questions about the things he seemed to want to talk about, reinforced his opinions on those issues, avoided any conflict, and always acted interested in what said, without being overly obsequious about it. It was the perfect friendship seduction.

When the state police showed up two hours later, FatCop went into the hall to talk to them. There were four DUI suspects in the room, two of which got there after I did. But strangely, they tested those two first. Then they tested the old gin-drunk black guy, leaving me for last.

FatCop "Wow. He blew a .31. That's the highest one they've had in a few years."

A .31? Remembering the night I took a Breathalyzer a few years ago, I felt shamed. I only got to a .23 before I blacked out.

In the Breathalyzer room, the state police informed me that everything would be filmed and then they administered all the standard DUI tests—touching my finger to my nose, walking a straight line, etc. I aced them all.

Tucker "You think I can get a copy of the video? You know, for my fans."
StateCop "No."

Then came the moment of truth: I blew a 0.07! YES! I BEAT THE DUI!!

Considering it was about 10pm, and I'd stopped drinking about the time we started the chase, around 6pm, and had time to work myself into a serious sweat before the cops came . . . I was real, real lucky the state police had been delayed. Blowing at 8pm, I would have certainly blown over a .08, the limit in New York. I'd be horsefucked. But even though 0.07 is below the limit, I wasn't out of the woods yet.

FatCop "Well, we can still charge you, given the circumstances. You say you weren't the one driving?"
Tucker "No man, it was that other guy, the one who ran off, Rockwolf."
FatCop "OK. Let's head back to the 32nd, see what the captain says."

We got back to the 32nd Precinct, FatCop brought me to the front desk, and sitting there was a sergeant who was the perfect stereotype of a New York City cop: late forties, red hair, grizzled voice, big meaty jowls, and huge forearms.

FatCop "He blew a 0.07."
DeskCop "That's the RV driver?"
FatCop "Yep."
DeskCop "Well, here's the fucking party! Son, let me tell you something: I've been on the force for 23 years, 21 of them in Harlem, and I ain't never seen any shit like this before. Seven drunk white guys in an RV, with a full bar and a keg in the shower? In Harlem? I wouldn't have believed it if I hadn't seen it. That's the craziest shit I ever even heard of."

I'm going to put that on my tombstone. As they took me back to the holding cell, I was beaming like a kid who just hit a game-winning home run in Little League. Legitimately one of the proudest moments of my life.

There were two small holding cells. One with two black guys passed out, and one with Nils sitting on the bench, looking pissed. As soon as I got in there, Nils looked at me with the most pitiful, hangdog expression ever.

Nils "They said I threw a bottle at a car. Is that true?"

He was completely sincere. I thought to myself, damn, he is REALLY playing his part up. The cops can't even hear us in here. Oh, well, I'll go along.

Tucker "No, of course not."
Nils "Then WHO threw the bottle?"
Tucker "Rockwolf. He did it, *remember*?"
Nils "No! I don't remember anything, I was passed out, and they don't believe me. They think I threw a bottle at some car."

He grabbed the bars and started shaking them.

Nils "HEY! I TOLD YOU I DIDN'T THROW ANY FUCKING BOTTLES!"

He kept this up for at least ten minutes, hitting the bars, yelling and carrying on like a crazy person. He was really going overboard trying to sell his story. I sat there and agreed with him, trying to get him to calm down. Eventually a cop came back there, some plainclothes I hadn't seen before. He went over the story with Nils:

Cop "OK, so this Rockwolf guy, who ran off as soon as you stopped, he was the one driving AND the one throwing things out the window?"
Nils "YES! You fucking finally get it, congratulations."
Cop "And what were you doing?"
Nils "I was fucking passed out. Like I was when you assholes found me!"
Tucker "Nils, chill out dude, he's just trying to help us."
Nils "Fuck this fucking BULLSHIT! I didn't fucking do anything, I am sick of this!"
Cop "So Rockwolf was doing everything—driving drunk and throwing bottles out of his window—and you guys just chilled out and let him?"
Tucker "Yeah man . . . he's a bad dude. We should never have hung out with him."
Cop "Yeah, he sounds like it. What does he look like?"
Tucker "About my height, my build, brown hair, brown eyes . . . pretty normal looking. Except he's a tool."
Nils "THIS IS BULLSHIT! I DIDN'T THROW ANY FUCKING BOTTLES!"
Cop "OK, maybe he was driving. But, you're a big dude. You ain't normal. Why did that lady point YOU out as being the one that threw it? You don't look like the guy he just described."
Nils "I don't know . . . how the fuck am I supposed to answer for some crazy black woman? We all look alike to them, I guess."
Cop "Uh-huh. OK. Just calm down, we'll get this sorted out soon."

Maybe twenty minutes later, some other cop came in with a huge fat black guy who fucking stank. Badly. They put him in our cell, and he immediately lay down on the floor and passed out. This went over with Nils about as well as a fart in church.

Nils "What the fuck? This guy fucking smells like shit! Get him the fuck out of here!"
Tucker "Dude, just chill. This is not the right way to deal with cops."
Nils "Fuck these assholes! I DIDN'T THROW THE FUCKING BOTTLE AND NOW THEY WANT ME TO SIT IN FAT ALBERT'S STINK?? FUCK THAT!!"

I could keep writing everything Nils yelled IN ALL CAPS, but you get the point. He was a drunk, belligerent fucking asshole. For an hour. The only thing that eventually shut him up was when the plainclothes came back in, pretended to believe Nils's story this time, and bought him a 7UP and a bag of Fritos from the vending machine. Nils was like a happy kindergartner after that, thinking he'd won the hearts-and-minds battle. Idiot.

I'd gotten to the 32nd sometime after 10pm, and at midnight, FatCop came and took me out to the front area. The captain was out there with the Irish Desk Sergeant, and the Haitian Cop.

Captain "So you weren't driving?"

Good cops are like good poker players—they are good at reading people. I wasn't about to try to bullshit this cop, but I had OBVIOUSLY been driving the RV. The way to deceive someone like that is to remember the old adage: It's not a lie if you believe it. When he looked into my eyes, for that second, I really believed in my soul that I hadn't driven that RV.

Tucker "No sir, I was not."
Captain "OK . . . go sit over there."

I was across the room but I could hear them talking:

Captain "What do you think?"
HaitianCop "I think he was drinking and driving."
FatCop "He passed the field tests and only blew a 0.07. He could be lying, but I talked to him for a while, he seems like an OK guy."

DeskCop "We tossed the RV good, like I told you, there was nothing there but alcohol. I don't think they're criminals, just really fucking stupid."

The captain thought it over, told the Haitian Cop something, and then walked off. Ten minutes later, FatCop came over with a piece of paper and walked me to the front door.

FatCop "OK man, we're not charging you. Take care."
Tucker "What about Nils? The other guy with me?"
FatCop "Oh, no no no. He's going to the Tombs."

I thanked him profusely, shook his hand, and walked out of the 32nd Precinct a free man. It was 12:04am. I tried to hail a cab to take me to my friends, so I could start drinking again—you know, to celebrate this astounding victory.

Do you have ANY IDEA how hard it is to find a cab at midnight in Harlem? You'd have an easier time finding pussy in a monastery. After ten minutes I started walking south. A mile later I'm at the corner of Malcolm X and Martin Luther King . . . there are SO MANY jokes I could make here, but *The Autobiography of Malcolm X* is one of the most profoundly moving and influential books I've ever read. So I'll skip the jokes and tell you exactly what happened. I had to literally get in the light under a streetlamp and stand in the middle of the street, waving cash in my hand, to get a taxi to stop.

I eventually got Credit on the phone, and he said that everyone left TuckerFest in New Jersey hours ago, and he brought the only cool people from the event to a bar in Greenwich Village. Twenty minutes later I walked in to a massive round of applause. Even though only 10 people there knew me, half the bar erupted, because my friends had told everyone the RV story. TheGinger, Credit, and Sippy filled me in on the details from what happened in the 32nd Precinct, I told everyone my DUI story and what happened with Nils, and of course everyone saw me for the hero I was, a modern Jesus risen from the dead to drink again. The guys bought me endless rounds of shots, the girls fawned over me, I drank and partied until 2am, and then went home with a cute girl who worked for *Playboy.*

Let's sum up the day, just for perspective:

Beginning at 10am, I poured a constant stream of alcohol down my throat, got behind the wheel of an RV, drag-raced an ambulance, destroyed an apartment building, crashed into dozens of vehicles, hurled bottles and cans at random cars, got in a multi-vehicle chase, terrorized the most dangerous part of New York City for hours, started a riot, got arrested, sobered up enough to beat every charge within five hours, went back out, got drunk again, and finished the night by fucking a *Playboy* girl at 3am. And at 3:30. I finally passed out after fucking her one more time, at around 4am.

Just one day in my life, and only one possible conclusion from it:

I AM THE GREATEST MAN ALIVE!

Part 6: The Dorks Strike Back

You have no idea how much I wish the story ended there.

As I rode a cab back to the Teaneck Marriott Sunday morning, Sippy called and told me where everyone was hanging out. I walked into that hotel room still riding the highest of highs . . . only to immediately come crashing down.

The previous night at the NYC bar, Credit and PlayboyGirl told me about the TuckerFest party in Hoboken, and how awful it was, how it was packed with nerds and losers, and how it was good I didn't make it there. I don't know if I didn't listen or didn't believe them. Maybe I was just too enamored with myself and what I had pulled off that day to care, but right there in front of me in that hotel room was seriously the sorriest collection of dorks I've ever met in my life. I was in shock.

I have tried to push the memory of those people out of my mind, but some things you can't unsee. Like the kid with a lazy eye wearing a Members Only jacket with mustard stains on it. Or the girl who was probably only 23 but already dressed like a crazy cat lady. And I'll never forget the college kid who had flown there from Columbus, Ohio. He was a virgin. The fucking kid was going to COLLEGE at OHIO STATE and he had NOT BEEN ABLE TO FIND ANYONE TO HAVE SEX WITH HIM! There were others, but the PTSD has blocked the memories out.

I couldn't handle it, and went down to the RV. I figured if the intolerable nerds were in the hotel room, then the cool people must be in the RV, right?

I heard them before I saw them, and it got worse after I opened the door. Before I could identify the new odor that immediately stuck to my lungs, I saw PigPen next to Ambersnax, smiling and holding her hand, Soylent at the table next to Xgatax, looking bored, and TheGinger with his face frozen in terror. Like he'd just seen an alligator drag a baby into a lake.

Tucker "What the fuck is going on here? TheGinger, what's wrong?"
TheGinger [voice shaking] "Go look in the garbage can. The one the keg is in. Then go look at the bed."

As the two trolls insecurely overlaughed to each other, I peered into the plastic Hefty can. Floating in the water surrounding the keg like dead bodies were at least ten used condoms. On the bed, there was so much blood it looked like Roman Polanski's house after the Manson family was done with it.

THAT'S what that smell was: Nasty period sex.

Tucker "Are you fucking kidding me? Who did that?"
TheGinger "PIGPEN AND AMBERSNAX!!"

The troll cackling reached unprecedented levels, and PigPen and Ambersnax gave each other a little hug. I wanted to puke. You know that nasty, old nudist couple that goes to swingers clubs and is always too eager to be there? The ones that clearly weren't ever cool in their lives but opted for the sexual deviance scene because it was the only one that accepted them? I don't really know them, because I don't go to disgusting places like that, but I imagine that PigPen and Ambersnax are that couple in its youth.

TheGinger "And Xgatax gave Soylent a blowjob! In the same bed this morning!"

Out of frying pan, into the estrus blood. I went outside, took a deep breath, relaxed, and pushed all of it out of my mind. At least I still had my first big celebrity event to go to. That was something cool, something that could get me away from these fucking losers and put me back in my rightful place: Greatness.

After a short van ride there, we arrived at the address that Rosh had given us. At first I thought we had to have written it down wrong. What kind of wrestling event goes on at a crappy, run-down Elks Lodge in the north Jersey suburbs?

I was about to pull out . . . and then I saw Rosh, waiting for me in all his enthusiastic, spandexed virgin glory. OK fine, I guess amateur wrestling doesn't normally sell out Madison Square Garden. After all, Rosh and TripleSH had told me that this wasn't WWE, so it might have been unfair for me to expect this to be in a nice venue. But they didn't tell me anything that could prepare me for what I was about to walk into.

Before I could even get the car door open, Rosh was already yapping at me like an excited puppy dog about God knows what. As we came to the entrance, I could hear the wrestling going on in the back hall and started to head there when a girl sitting by herself at a cheap card table stopped me:

Girl "It's $5 to get in."

At first I thought she was kidding. Then I saw the sign that had "5$ entrance" taped on it. This is the gate? I just stood there, not responding, almost in awe of the audacity of this woman. To try and charge ANYONE to be there, much less the lone CELEBRITY invitee . . . I just walked past her. I think she got mad, I have no idea, Rosh handled it. I turned the corner into the main hall. I still don't know what I was expecting, but whatever it was, this was not it.

The wrestling ring looked like something you'd buy at Toys "R" Us. Inside it were two "wrestlers," guys who were built like your average Teamster. Shit, they probably were Teamsters; it's not like those fat fucks do any actual work. There were maybe a hundred people milling around, I guess you would call them spectators, except very few were paying attention. They looked like they'd gotten lost and stopped to ask directions. The quality of that crowd was about the same as an average redneck carnival. I got momentarily excited when I saw that they had a bar . . . except it served only soft drinks and water.

Sitting here thinking about, I don't think I am a good enough writer to accurately describe the awfulness of this event. I will say this: Unless I someday attend a Big Ten women's basketball game, this will go down in my personal history as the single worst sporting event I've ever attended.

While I was standing there still processing this scene, a little kid came running up to me and started talking to me like he knew me. He knew my name, why I was there, what I was supposed to be doing . . . slowly, it dawned on me:

This is TripleSH. This is the wrestler who invited me here.

He was like 5'5" and might have weighed 110 pounds. I've seen more muscle on a chicken wing. I've taken shits bigger than this dude. He was wearing spandex tights, a singlet, a terry-cloth headband . . . AND A CAPE.

He was giddy that I was there and introduced me to the promoter—some greasy sleazeball I wanted a glove to shake hands with—while bouncing around me like a little kid.

You should've seen the "bikini contest" I was there to be celebrity judge for. It was like Lucifer opened the doors to hell and unleashed the Ragnarok. I am pretty sure one of the girls had a vestigial tail. I wouldn't have fucked these girls with Rosh's dick and the Teamsters pushing.

I was completely and officially freaked the fuck out and did the only thing I could do: I retreated deep inside myself. Stood there like a statue, silent, unable to move, unable even to process the trauma I was witnessing.

The reason why I freaked out at that moment was because, at the time, I thought this would be a legit event, sort of like my celebrity coming-out party, but instead, it was a completely preposterous shit show. Of course now, looking back at my hubris, I laugh hysterically at myself. I mean—how could I be stupid enough to think that an AMATEUR WRESTLING EVENT that was held in an ELKS LODGE in nowhere NEW JERSEY would be anything other than a complete joke? That's one of the downsides of narcissism—sometimes you forget to check your internal thoughts with an external reality.

Jojo—who is not only a smart motherfucker but has known me for years—saw what was going on with me and knew exactly why I was freaking out. And of course, because he's also a cocksucker, he found it endlessly amusing.

Jojo "Max, you're famous!!"
Tucker "Dude, what the fuck is going on?"
Jojo "These are your fans, Max. This is your fame!"
Tucker "Fuck you. If these are my fans, I'm out. If this is fame, I don't want it."
Jojo "Come on Max, they love you! Embrace them! Don't give a fuck and just fuck shit up."
Tucker "Look at this, dude . . . I think I'd rather die."

So what did Jojo do? Did he try to counsel me, maybe help me work through these issues, perhaps help me probe my narcissism to understand why I was reacting this way? Fuck no. In law school, Jojo's nickname was the Instigating Negro because he constantly fucked with people. He would find your weakness or pain and then hammer that sensitive spot over and over again, causing you maximum awkwardness and him maximum enjoyment, and that night, he decided to fuck with me by acting the way that all my fans wanted me to act: like a fucking fool.

The dude went straight Koko B. Ware, running around the Elks Lodge with some girl's pink shirt tied to his head, flapping his arms and yelling at the wrestlers, trying to grab the mike from the announcer, booing the bikini girls, making fun of everybody—basically, act like a complete clown.

Which is precisely what the people who's shown up for "TuckerFest" had expected me to do in this situation. Except I didn't. Didn't mock one person, hardly even spoke, too freaked out to do anything other than stand there and stare at this abortion of an event.

Why was I like this?

This story happened in March of 2003, and as I sit here and putting the finishing touches on it, it is April 2010. It took me seven fucking years to grow up enough to be honest with myself about the nature of my reaction and admit what happened that day:

I sold out.

It might not be obvious how, so let me explain.

These people who had set up the TuckerFest event were the very definition of posers. They read my stories on the internet, saw in me everything that they weren't but wanted to be, and then tried to have what I had by pretending to be something they weren't. They weren't out to do what I do—celebrate life, drink for the enjoyment of it, and experience the happiness that comes from being around people you like—they were trying to fill the holes in their souls by sucking my essence out of me.

I couldn't consciously explain all this at that moment, but I could feel the icky residue of their self-loathing all over me. I could see it in their eyes, the way they looked at me. I was not a human being to them. I was an image. An object for them to use to cure their insecurities and negative emotions. And even worse, they expected me to dance like a monkey for them, to be the person they were too afraid to be, to do all the things they wanted to do. They wanted a marionette.

These are the worst kinds of posers, the ones I relish mocking, and I should have absolutely killed them. But I didn't. Not one single fucking insult. If I had randomly stumbled in there with Jojo and SlingBlade, I would have lit those fucking losers up. But in the moment, I did nothing at all.

How does that make me a sellout? Well, the only reason I treated these people differently is because they were my only fans at the time. I was too afraid to be myself, because I was afraid of losing the only fans I had.

I've gone through my life never caring what other people thought, doing the things I wanted to do and being the person I wanted to be. But by not lighting these fucking posers up the way I normally would have, I was tacitly admitting to myself that I DID care what they thought. Even though I hated them as people—as fans, I cared. I cared because without them, I wouldn't have fans, and without fans . . . I wasn't who I thought I was.

So I did nothing. To me, an artist sells out when what he does is not motivated by internal forces, but by external ones. Under that definition, on that specific night—I fucking sold myself out, plain and simple.

I'm sorry to get so serious in the middle of a story that is meant to be funny and entertaining, but all I can do when I write is put down what I remember and felt about the events and actions of my life. That is basically the extent of what I remember about that Sunday at the semi-pro wrestling in the Elks Lodge in New Jersey. There is no joke to make, and I'm not going to pretend it didn't happen or make up a bunch of insults and funny jokes that never occurred. That would be selling out again, in a way.

Better just to truthfully admit my flaws, so I learn my lessons and move on . . . right to the bar and get real drunk, and forget this awful incident.

Part 7: The Trip Home and the Fallout

Nothing else of note happened on Sunday, except two big things: At some point on Sunday, Rockwolf had the audacity to put up a post on the message board about what he did on Saturday, and then fill everyone in on what happened.

After he jumped out of the RV window and ran off, Rockwolf made his way back to the Teaneck Marriott, got into Nils's room with a key he stole off Nils, and ordered like $250 of room service, which was mostly two bottles of champagne, that he then took with him and went home (he lived on Long Island).

We tried to call Nils and tell him about this—and to see when we could come get him out of jail—but no one could find Nils. I don't mean that no one could reach his cell; that was obviously turned off because he was in jail. No, I mean that no one could find any evidence that he even existed. After he left the 32nd Precinct and was transferred to The Tombs for arraignment, he disappeared. All day Sunday, the NYPD claimed to have no record of any Nils Parker ever being in their system. That was not good.

Considering that Nils was a real friend, I actually cared about his welfare and spent most of Monday morning tracking down what happened. Eventually, we found out that his name had been entered incorrectly into the system, "by accident." His first and last names were reversed, hence no one had been able to locate him and that's why he wasn't arraigned until Monday afternoon. Dude spent TWO DAYS in The Tombs. Another reason not to be a dick to cops.

His uncle and I got him out of the clink, and then he called Rockwolf and threatened him. Rockwolf almost started crying on the phone and swore he'd mail him not only a check covering the cost but also an apology. And he did. Nils still has the apology letter:

Nils,

Here's the money I owe you. As for the "good explanation" you wanted, that I can't give since I have almost no memory of the nights events. You have my most sincere apologies though for what I did. I have no idea why I would have done something like that but after drinking all day with you guys, after I left you I went and drank with some old friends in Manhatten, then went back to the hotel and started drinking there. Needless to say I wasn't in full control of my decision making. But anyway I'm sure you don't care. So here's you money and your apology.

Sincerely,

With that handled, it was time for the RV crew to head back home. The drive was grinding. The keg was tapped, the beers that hadn't been launched at cars on Saturday were now empty, and we'd even emptied the bar.

The RV looked like it had been looted. Blood, feces, urine, cum, menses, beer, liquor, and grape jelly covered every surface. At least half of the interior was ripped out, ripped up, or broken. The stove no longer had anything removable on it; grills, knobs, everything had been either tossed out the window or broken for drunken enjoyment. The pillows, curtains, and curtain rods were long gone. Ever seen a picture of Detroit? That's what our RV looked like.

Surveying the damage, TheGinger was catatonic. Sippy had a thousand-yard stare. He looked like a fresh military recruit who'd been rushed into battle, seen the worst carnage imaginable, and left part of his soul on the battlefield. PigPen was so proud that he'd had sex with a real, living girl that he refused to shower or clean himself. He smelled like the panty hamper of a sorority house.

Tucker "Hey, TheGinger, remember how worried you were about the cleaning deposit? Seems like it was yesterday."
TheGinger "The cleaning deposit? At this point, I'm seriously worried they're going to make me buy the RV!"
Soylent "There's a solution to that."

Soylent pulled some matches out of his backpack.

Soylent "You bought the insurance. We can always just torch it."
Sippy "WHAT?!? Haven't we had enough police contact this weekend?"
Tucker "It would be a fitting end to the weekend."

We discussed the pros and cons of setting the RV on fire and trying to claim a total loss on it, but TheGinger was too paranoid we'd get caught. He ended up canceling his credit card before we got the RV place, and we made sure to return it after they closed, so we didn't have to be there.

Everything in my life changed after that. That weekend represented the end of an era for me. It was my last truly reckless, balls-to-the-wall, risk-everything-because-I-have-nothing-to-lose weekend. Christ, how the fuck do I top that? Burn down a city? I mean, I basically did the maximum amount of awful, illegal shit without crossing the line into a serious felony. To go any farther, I'd have to do something that even I couldn't walk away from. I did plenty of crazy shit after that, but nothing quite like the Tucker-Fest weekend. I think part of me knew that I'd pushed the limits to their absolute breaking point and it was time to ease up on the throttle. I still sometimes marvel that we all made it out of that night alive. Soylent read the first draft of this story and said:

"Reading it on paper, it almost doesn't seem real. And I was there."

It was also the first time I'd thought of myself as a "celebrity." Even though I was just a ridiculous celebrity judge of a broke-dick wrestling event in New Jersey, it was the start of my weird journey into fame, and I had no idea just what I was getting into . . .

THE POST-FAME SEX STORIES

Introduction

I wanted to write a best-selling book that made me famous, and my first book did just that. In most ways, the success I've had thus far is a dream come true. But here's what they don't tell you about achieving your dream:

Once you get it, it's never, ever what you expect it to be.

Take women for instance. Before I wrote *I Hope They Serve Beer In Hell*, I did great with women, but not really any different from any other awesome guy out there. Yeah, I had game, but I still had to go out and get girls. I couldn't just sit at home and expect them to come to me; no normal guy can, regardless of how awesome his game is.

Once the book became popular, that changed radically. Over the past five years or so, I've been with so many girls, it's hard to actually quantify. You remember that cartoon *Duck Tales*, where Scrooge McDuck goes swimming in his giant vault filled with gold coins? Since 2006 or so, it's been like that for me, except with vaginas.

So what happened? How did I go from "great game" to "a sea of vaginas"? Fame. Being famous changes EVERYTHING. Normal men line up for women, but women line up for famous men, and once I became even a little famous, they lined up for me. I took full advantage of it, and I got tons of hilarious stories from this period . . . except they weren't *exactly* the same type of stories as before.

Accordingly, I have divided this book into two sections. The first part—what you just finished reading—was very similar to my first book in style and content. The second half of this book is slightly different. It is made up of interrelated sex and hook-up stories from the period in my life after *IHTSBIH* came out (30–34), the time during which girls started coming to me by the thousands. I call them the "The Post-Fame Sex Stories."

Looking at it from the outside, you might think having all these women wanting to fuck you would be amazing. In some ways, it really is everything you imagine it to be—and more. But everything in life is a trade-off, even the greatest thing you can imagine.

Having an essentially unlimited amount of free pussy is like owning a Ferrari: It's super-exclusive and hard to get, and everyone who doesn't have one kinda wishes they did and is a little envious of those who do. But when you actually own it, though you may love certain things about it, you realize what a serious pain in the ass it is, how much it breaks down, and how expensive it is to maintain. You know about the hidden costs that those who don't own a Ferrari will never understand.

Biggie said it best: "Mo money mo problems." Pussy is no different.

The Tattoo Stories

I don't have a tattoo, nor do I ever plan on getting one. I barely know what I want for lunch, how the hell will I know what I think is cool at 25 won't utterly repulse me at 45?

I have nothing against tattoos on other people, but I'm getting pretty sick of flipping a girl over to fuck her from behind and being confronted with another piece of crappy slut art. Yes, honey, I'm sure your specific whore brand has all sorts of unique symbolism that will prove how special you are, but you need to stop turning your head to tell me about it, because I really don't care.

Despite my personal opinion of them, I have gotten used to whore brands, because they're like HPV: Most of the female population has them, but has no idea how or why they got them. What I REALLY don't get are women who put tattoos on or around their vaginas. I mean . . . WTF? I can't imagine the scenario where I'd let someone jab a needle full of ink into my penis or ball sack.

In my journey through the vaginas of this great nation, these are the four tattoos that have really made me stop and question where my life is going. Or more accurately, where my penis—that brave but naïve soldier—is being deployed.

Aren't You Lucky?

Occurred—November 2002

One of the first girls I ever fucked from my website told me she had two tattoos. One was right between her breasts, her initials in Celtic. Whatever. During foreplay, I asked her where the other one was. She hesitated, then said:

"Oh well, I might as well show it to you, you're going to see it anyway."

She pulled her pants off to reveal a long string of words right above her vagina, stretching all the way across her pelvis. Set inside alternating blue stars and pink hearts, like a slutty Lucky Charms leprechaun, were the words:

"Aren't you lucky?"

I looked at it for a second.

"That depends on how many guys have been asked that question before me, doesn't it?"

Lucky + You

Occurred—November 2007

A stripper I was fucking had this tattoo right above her pussy that said, "Lucky + You." At first I just assumed it was another of the various ways you could phrase something about being lucky to get her pussy (why do women have such issues understanding probability?), but then I thought about it: What the fuck is the + for? She explained it to me:

Girl "My pussy's nicknamed Lucky. The plus is because you and Lucky are now together."

Immediately, I was reminded of the old joke: "LOST DOG, one eye missing, mangled ear, paralyzed hind leg, crooked tail. Answers to the name Lucky."

I made double sure to wrap it with that one.

Time Flies When You're Fucking Tatted-up Whores

Occurred—October 2007

This girl had been emailing me to fuck for months, and since I wasn't going to be anywhere near her city anytime soon, one day she decided just to take it upon herself to drive 18 hours. Not fly—drive. 18 hours. To fuck me.

I can understand 4 or 5, even up to 8 hours—after all, I'm awesome. But to DRIVE for TWO days, just for my dick? I wouldn't even drive that far to masturbate.

As could be easily predicted, she was a hot fucking mess. Great body with nice fake tits? Yes. Everything else a disaster? Yes. I later described her to a friend as "someone who would chase her birth control with warm Natty Light." I mean, for fuck's sake, she walked into my place wearing a thin white halter top over a leopard print bra. This is the type of girl I would expect to find passed out in the men's bathroom of a biker bar.

When I meet new people, especially girls who want to fuck, I usually like to talk to them about themselves, probe into their lives and figure out their personality. It's always interesting to see if I can get them to open up and discover the thing they try to keep hidden. Sex is only one part of the enjoyment of another person, after all. If I didn't learn about all their hidden dysfunction, how else would I know how to manipulate them?

Well, this was a rare exception. I could tell just by the crazy, desperate look in her eyes that there was nothing but pain and misery in her past. And not the funny, network sitcom–type pain that you can guiltlessly laugh about; this was the bad kind that wins the Pulitzer Prize for literature. I had no desire to open that Pandora's box of awful parenting leading to a series of abusive boyfriends and culminating in some demeaning job in the sex industry. It was bad enough to almost make me not want to fuck her. Almost.

But what would you do if an attractive woman—even one with crazy eyes—was standing in your living room, massive tits beckoning you from behind leopard-print lingerie, asking you to "beat up my pussy"? If you're a guy and ultimately respond with anything other than "fuck her," you're either happily married, gay, or a liar. You should probably make her shower first, but the point stands.

As she came out of the shower, I pulled her into the living room and pushed her down on the sofa. I was right about to fire it in her, when I saw some dirt or something on her thighs. I stopped to investigate; small black spots around a woman's crotch are not something you can just file under "worry about later."

I looked at them, got confused, then went in for a closer look. I couldn't believe my eyes. It was kinda dark in my place, so I turned on every single light. Yeah, there is no question what it was.

It wasn't dirt or sores. The dark spots were permanent ink. Four little tattoos on her inner thighs. They were flies, buzzing around her vagina. And then two longer tattoos, maggots, made to look like they were crawling out of her vagina.

I literally gagged when I realized what they were.

Tucker "Are those flies . . . and maggots?"
Girl "Yeah."
Tucker "Why the hell are those there?"
Girl "I don't know. I thought it was appropriate at the time."

Appropriate?!? Flies and maggots congregate in two places: stinking piles of excrement and fetid, rotting corpses. Which, exactly, did she think her pussy most closely resembled?

I didn't want to know the answer to that question. This was too much emotional dysfunction for even me to deal with. Before that exact moment, the list of things that would have stopped me from fucking a conscious, willing woman who was lying naked and freshly cleaned on my sofa was four items long:

1. She has open sores or infections
2. She is actively shitting herself
3. She is actively pissing herself
4. She is actively puking on herself

That was the whole list. Well, not anymore. Thanks to Polly Rottenpuss, you can add one more thing to it:

5. Tattoos of flies and/or maggots around the vagina

Next-Level Shit

Occurred—December 2005

The month before I moved to NYC, I decided to spend some time in the area looking for an apartment. It's about a 13 hour drive from Chicago to NYC, and since there were some cute girls from Pittsburgh who had been emailing me, I decided to stop and hook up with a few of them.

There was one girl in particular who I wanted to hang out with, Jess. She had good pics, wrote intelligent emails, made it very clear she wanted to fuck the shit out of me, and was a big drinker. But it was something else that really clinched it for me. A week or so earlier she posted this on my message board under a thread about road head:

> "One of my very best friends, a guy I dated for about 4 hours in high school, found out his girlfriend was cheating on him, with

a 17 year old baby daddy named Daeqwon. I cannot explain in writing how livid we both were to learn this. I also cannot explain in writing how vengeful and twisted he and I both are.

Instead of immediately dumping her and letting me tear her to pieces, he took her out on a huge date. Kind of like Tucker's butt sex story—he buttered this bitch up. Dropped $250 on dinner and took her to the fucking ballet. All because he knew that a little romance and a little Dom would get her to open wide and give him a slob job on the ride home. And slob she did—he later said it was some of the best head of his life.

His life, not hers.

Before their date (immediately before) I ran over to his apartment really quickly—and let him fuck me. In the butt. Seriously, we are strictly friends, totally platonic. He didn't come. Just a few in-and-outs to make sure his wang was nice and tasty. After he put it in my ass for a few minutes, he very carefully stuck his dick back in his boxers, saying he didn't want to let anything rub off.

Two hours later he let his raging whore of a (now ex-) girlfriend suck on his penis for about 20 minutes. He claims at one point, she almost stopped, because he was laughing so hard he swerved off the road.

See you in hell."

This was clearly a girl I needed to party with. Right before I got to Pittsburgh I called her to make a few things clear:

Tucker "I like to fuck before I go out drinking, so are you up for a quickie or two before we hit the bars?"
Jess "Yeah, of course, definitely."
Tucker "Excellent. And one more thing: Just because I fuck you before we

go out does not necessarily mean that I will go home with you. I'm not saying that I'll be going out with the intent of hitting on other girls, but I never know what is going to happen. If you are not cool with me fucking you early and then potentially going home with some other girl, let me know now. I don't want you to get pissed and stab me in my sleep."
Jess "Oh no. I'll even help you pick them up, maybe we can have a threesome."

This girl is going to make someone a great ex-wife someday.

I get to her place and she looks just like her pictures: cute face and a really good body. I am so happy that she sent me honest pics. I have no idea why, but some girls seem to think that when I meet them in person, I won't notice that they put on 40 pounds and 20,000 miles since their last good picture. Even better though, there is also a bonus that her pics did not show: an amazing ass. To be honest, I am more of a tit guy than an ass guy, but hers is a piece of art.

We hang out for a while, she seems like a pretty cool girl, and we fuck. It's cute: She is kinda nervous at first, but eventually she relaxes and we have pretty good sex.

Afterward, I notice a tattoo on her right hip. It is the initials R.H. with this weird design in between them. Obviously, I assume the worst.

Tucker "Who is that? Ex-boyfriend?"
Jess "No, fiancé."
Tucker "He dumped you? Hahahaha, that tattoo doesn't seem like such a good idea now, does it?"
Jess "No . . . he didn't dump me."
Tucker [*joking around*] "What, you dumped him because you caught him fucking your friend?"
Jess "No. He died. I got this after his death."
Tucker "What, he couldn't just break up with you? He was so sick of your shit he went and died?"

She actually laughed at that joke, but I did feel legitimately bad. Well, not really, but I sensed that a good person would have felt bad.

We went to a place called Fat Head's for beer and wings. The bar was filled with what is apparently the unofficial mascot of Pittsburgh: the loud, drunk blue-collar idiot. These two older guys were sitting next to us in their Greg Lloyd jerseys and Harley-Davidson bandannas, screaming at the Penguins game on TV, when we sat down.

Yinzer "So, yinz two aren't gonna argue like that last couple, are you? He spent two hours yelling at her 'cause she wouldn't fuck him, and she was pissed because he was never home."
Tucker "No, sex is not a problem in this relationship. In fact, right now she has a bunch of my cum in her. And even a little on her. You can probably smell it if you get close."

His eyes got all big and he leaned back and elbowed his buddy.

Yinzer "You hear this guy, Dale? He's talkin 'bout shooting cum at her!" [*turning to Jess*] "You don't mind him talkin' like this?"
Tucker "She's lucky I'm even here." [*Jess nods in agreement*]
Yinzer "DAMN! I wish I had your balls!"
Tucker "I wish you had a breath mint, but I guess we don't always get what we wish for."

After that, they left us alone.

The place had like 40 beers on tap and another 40 in bottles, most of which I had never heard of, but Jess confidently recommended Arrogant Bastard Ale. It was quite good. Not only is this girl bisexual, good in bed, a huge fan of mine, and cool to hang out with, but she really knows her beer.

At this point I started to get excited; when you reach in the ho grab-bag, you never know what you're going to get. Well, it looked like I had picked a winner. So of course I did what only a fool would do: I looked the gift whore in the mouth.

Tucker "I know you like girls. What about threesomes with guys? You ever do that?"
Jess "Oh yeah."
Tucker "You do know that girl, girl, guy = awesome, but guy, guy, girl = gay, gay, whore."
Jess "I know, but this was kinda different."
Tucker "How? You were in love with both and couldn't decide so you had a fuck-off?"
Jess "No . . . this threesome was more about the guys."

Oh no.

Tucker "What?"
Jess "Well, my boyfriend and this other guy and I had a threesome, and they kinda focused on each other—"
Tucker "You fuck gay guys? Are you telling me I just fucked a fag hag?"
Jess "NO! It's not really like that, you see my boyfriend—"
Tucker "You do know that virtually all AIDS cases are transmitted three ways: IV drug use, sex with prostitutes, and SEX WITH GAY MEN! If you don't fuck those risk groups, you are probably going to be fine, yet here I am, fucking a girl who screws homosexuals. This is just fucking great. Where is the closest clinic?"
Jess "NO WAIT! It wasn't like that, listen. My last boyfriend is gay now, but the first time he ever hooked up with a guy was that threesome. And it wasn't really a threesome. We were drunk and high and this kid got blacked-out drunk and passed out and my boyfriend sucked his dick."
Tucker "That was his first time with a guy? Yeah right, and you are the first girl I've ever fucked."
Jess "NO! IT WAS! I've known him since he was 6! He is gay now, but that was the first time he'd done anything with a guy. He talked about it a lot before then, but that was the first."
Tucker "Did you fuck him after he started putting random dicks in his mouth?"
Jess "NO! That's pretty much the reason we broke up!"
Tucker "Pretty much! What are the other reasons? Murder? Arson? You

mean raping a guy who was passed out wasn't enough, there had to be other reasons?"

Jess "Did I mention that the blacked-out guy was 17? And a virgin?"

Tucker "I am going to take a wild guess and say that this ex-boyfriend is the same guy who you let fuck you in the butt right before he had his cheating whore girlfriend go down on him?"

Jess "Uhhh . . . yeah . . ."

Tucker "This just keeps getting better. Please tell me that incident was before he started fucking dudes?"

Jess "YES, of course!"

Tucker "That is the first good news I have heard since this conversation started."

Jess eventually calmed me down by plying me with beer and promises that she knew her ex very well and that even though he is a big gay slut now, that really was his first time. I didn't believe her and was still going to get tested, but I felt much better.

Then she started talking about the T-shirts I sell on my site and how she wished I had one that said I FUCKED TUCKER MAX.

Tucker "Who would wear that?"

Jess "Are you kidding?!? I would wear that shirt with pride. The only problem is that lots of girls would buy it who haven't fucked you, so you'd have to have a limited edition only for girls you've actually fucked."

Tucker "Well, if you are really serious about wanting people to know you fucked me, you should get a tattoo. Get I FUCKED TUCKER MAX right above your pussy."

Jess "I would totally get that tattoo."

Tucker "Yeah, OK."

Jess "I'm completely serious. I will get it right now."

Tucker "Get out of here, there is no way you'll get that tattoo."

Jess "Let me close our tab. I'll do it right now."

This isn't happening. This girl cannot be serious. She is just bullshitting me, trying to lie her way into my heart. I am totally going to call her on this . . . after she pays the tab, of course.

Tucker "Are you drunk?"
Jess "No, not at all. I've had like three beers. I'm a fucking bartender, I drink more than this before I even go into work."
Tucker "All right, come on, stop fucking around. You and I both know you aren't going to do this. Let's go to another bar."
Jess "I am totally serious. Come on."

We start walking toward the tattoo place. No way . . . she can't be for real.

Tucker "Are you serious about this?"
Jess "Absolutely."
Tucker "Why do you want to do this?"
Jess "For me, this is like . . . it's . . . this is like for a devout Catholic if Jesus were to come down from heaven and say, 'I validate you.' "
Tucker "I don't care what anyone else says, you aren't crazy, you are prescient and way ahead of your time. Good for you."
Jess "That, and tomorrow I am going to take a picture of this and send it to my dad and say, 'Happy Fucking Birthday, Dad.' "
Tucker "No you're not."
Jess "Oh yes, I am completely serious. Then I am going to show it to the whole family on Thanksgiving."
Tucker "Why do you hate your dad?"
Jess "He married my horrible bitch stepmom and basically left me on my own."
Tucker "So let's see . . . the two men you have loved the most—your fiancé and your father—abandoned you?"
Jess "Well, yeah . . . I hadn't really thought of it like that."
Tucker "And your best male friend turned gay after dating you?"
Jess "Yeah . . ."
Tucker "I guess this tattoo is just the logical course of events. I may leave you, but the tattoo never will. Makes sense. Let's go!"

We get to the tattoo place. I have never actually been in a tattoo parlor before, at least not sober, and I cannot believe all the pictures everywhere. Every wall is covered with art, some of it really good, some of it bad. The Jesus with the lazy eye was my personal favorite. The girl working there is straight out of an anti-drug commercial about the horrors of crystal meth: missing teeth, crazy eyes, twitching and dressed like an outdated Christina Aguilera.

MethGirl "What can I do for you?"
Jess "I want a tattoo. Just four words, right below the left hipbone."
MethGirl "OK, what do you want it to say?"
Jess "I fucked Tucker Max."
MethGirl [*at least a 5 second pause*] "Are you serious?"
Jess "Yeah."
MethGirl "OK. It'll be about 30 minutes until Jeff is done with the guy ahead of you."

She walks off, and I kinda start to feel pangs of guilt. Can I really let Jess go through with this? This girl is totally fucked up, but she isn't a bad person. I'm torn about what to do. And beyond that, once she gets this thing, she and I will be inextricably linked from this point forward, for better or worse. I need some guidance, so I turn to my higher power:

What Would Tucker Do?

I decide that Tucker would at least have to see if she is sure about her decision. I can't make her do anything, but I can at least make sure she knows what she's getting into:

Tucker "You know this is permanent, right?"
Jess "Yeah, of course."
Tucker "You do realize that every dude you fuck from now on is going to see this, right?"
Jess "Yeah."
Tucker "Look Jess, I think you are making a great decision and this is clearly the coolest thing I have ever seen. But not many other people on earth would agree with me."
Jess "I know."
Tucker "Because of this tattoo, you are going to have problems with every guy you fuck from now on not named 'Tucker Max.' I love this tattoo idea,

but we aren't ever going to date or get married. That job is going to fall to someone else, and he might not like that tattoo. Do you understand that?"
Jess "Yes, of course."
Tucker "And you are still cool with it?"
Jess "Tucker, I idolize you. I mean, I relate to you, you are my fucking hero, and your writing is part of me, it is part of who I am and helps me define my existence. I want everyone to know this. I want my parents to know this, I want my kids to know this, and my future husband has to be OK with this."

I pause and actually picture that scenario: her pulling down her pants to show her children this tattoo and then trying to explain it to them in a way that would make sense to a child . . . then I have to push the thought out of my mind. Sometimes, the unresolved pain that seeks me out and surrounds me is too much to contemplate.

Tucker "OK, as long as you know. If I were anyone else on earth I would call you stupid, but personally, I think this is awesome."

At that point her phone rings. It is one of the bouncers she works with, who she tells me has a crush on her. I can hear only her side of the conversation, but the rest is easily figured out.

Jess "I am at a tattoo parlor . . . I'm getting a new tattoo . . . on my hip . . . 'I Fucked Tucker Max' . . . yes, I am totally serious . . . oh Jesus . . . yes, I am sure I want it . . . no I am not drunk . . . what? . . . did you just say that I am one of the greatest girls you've ever met? . . . make me fucking sick . . . whatever, unless you're drinking in the city with us, then I don't want to hear from you for the rest of the night . . . bye."

We pick out the correct font for my logo—Bank Gothic—and Jess goes with the tattoo artist to work on the outline. I am in the front room waiting for them to call me back so I can watch this, and there are like six teenage trailer park idiots also waiting for tattoos. These kids are straight out of the upper deck at an Eminem concert: flat-brimmed NBA logo hats, cigarettes behind their ears, frail wispy mustaches, grimy fingernails, and cheap fake gold chains. They haven't heard my conversation with Jess, but they heard what the tattoo was going to be. One of them says to me:

GhettoBastard1 "She really gun get dat shit?"
Tucker "Looks like it."
GhettoBastard1 "Hey dawg, yur name Tucker Max?"
Tucker "Yeah."
GhettoBastard1 "Damn! Dat your girl? You datin'er?"
Tucker "No man."
GhettoBastard1 "How long you known her?"
Tucker "I don't know, like three hours or so."
GhettoBastard1 "DAMN!!!! HAHHHAHAHAHA. YO DAWG, DIS GUY'S A PIMP, YO!!!!"
GhettoBastard2 "HE MUST HAVE A HUGE DICK, YO!! HAHHHAHAHA!!"

These kids are cracking up laughing and in complete disbelief. I only have an average-sized dick, so I don't think I can explain to these kids why Jess is getting this tattoo. Higher-order thinking is probably not something they excel at.

I would never have written this story had I not gotten pics of not only the final tattoo, but also of the whole process. I was there and I wouldn't even believe it without seeing the pictures. Here are two from the set (There are only two pictures because my publisher is too cheap to publish the rest. You can find them on my site, tuckermax.com.):

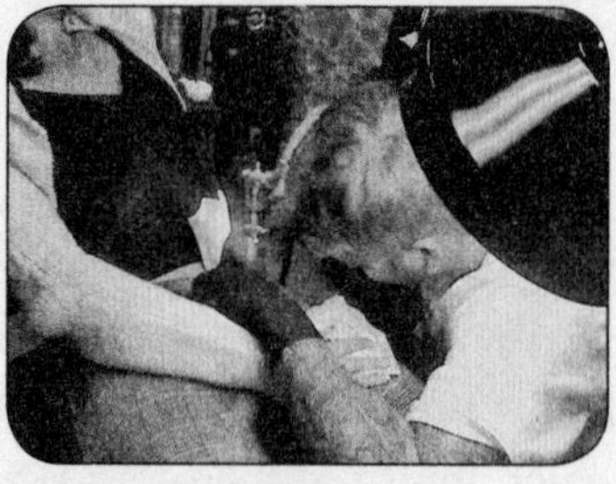

I immediately sent the pics to my buddy (and editor), Jeremie Ruby-Strauss. His only response:

"That is some next-level shit."

I Want to Cum Get a Load!

I opened my MySpace account about the same time as everyone else, right when it became popular in early 2005. I put this under the "Who I'd Like to Meet" section on the front page:

> "Just about any hot girl who wants to hook up with me, I want to meet. Email me and we'll set it up.
>
> But I'd be even more down to meet a girl who wants to do my laundry. I can find sex easily, but finding a girl who will do my wash is hard. Seriously, ladies, I am not joking about this. Bunny used to do my laundry but now that I have moved this arrangement is no longer possible. If you are down, email me and we'll figure it out. I will repay you with witty banter, hot animal sex, a swift kick to the spine, or whatever turns you on."

I kinda wrote that as a joke; the tongue-in-cheek tone should be pretty obvious. But at the same time, I was not completely kidding. I really do hate doing laundry, and if putting this up meant I could get girls to come over and do mine for me, awesome. You never know what you can get until you ask for it.

But I mean, c'mon, of course I can always pay someone to do my laundry. How else are the children of immigrants going to pay for college? The real reason I wrote this was because I knew it would get me laid. How the fuck does asking girls to do your laundry get you laid? Very simple:

Most of the girls who email me to hook up are pretty straightforward about it, but a large percentage of women lie to themselves about who they are and what they want. Ask them directly if they want to fuck me, and many will say no. But give them some bullshit white lie they can use to bridge the cognitive dissonance between what they *say* they want and what they *actually* want, and they will snatch it out of the sky like a falcon. After all, emailing me for sex is whorish and unseemly. But offering to wash my dirty clothes as a thank-you for writing such a great book, and then using it as a pretext for allowing a moment of premeditated spontaneity to just "happen," that's completely healthy and aboveboard. Riiiiiiiiiiiight. What it's also called is "whore logic."

I understood these dynamics when I put up those simple little paragraphs. But there were three things I had not accounted for:

1. It would not only work, it would work flawlessly. I did not have to do my own laundry—not even one time—from early 2005 until I took the message down in late 2008 (only because I started dating HotNurse, and she did it for me).

2. Hundreds (if not thousands) of girls would use it as an excuse to email me, and a shocking number of them would actually come over. I slept with all of them (except one). I wish I could say that it was my amazing game that won them over, but even I know that's bullshit. They wanted to fuck me from the start, they just wouldn't admit it to themselves and needed an excuse. The best evidence of this is that more than a few never even bothered to do my laundry after we had sex. Which is fucking bullshit, by the way—I fully expected them to clean my clothes. The sex was the optional part, not the laundry.

3. And, of course, lots of women lie to themselves about a lot more things than even I realized. These are my three favorite stories that involved the laundry/self-deception link.

PoopLips

Occurred—July 2007

When I was living in NYC, I got this email:

> "Tucker Max,
>
> I have to be honest. #1, I am blackout wasted right now and it is taking me all I have to write this email. #2, I have met you before, at a book signing, and I think you are great. #3, I live in NYC and I would love to hang out. OK, I will probably not fuck you (although I think you are hot . . . I am weird and think sex means something) BUT despite this, if you want I will do your laundry. Whatever, if you want to see what I look like I am on facebook. Point being, cool, sarcastic, me."

If you know anything about women, then you are smiling right now as much as I did when I got that email. If a woman mentions something—even to tell you she's not into it—it means she's at least thinking about it, which is more than half the battle.

We emailed back and forth for a few days and finally she decided the best way to do two loads of whites and two loads of colors was to meet me at a bar, dressed for a night out. It took only two hours of drinking for her to gather up enough courage to admit why she was actually out with me, and of course it had nothing to do with dirty clothes.

We go back to my place, make out at the front door for a minute or two, then drunkenly stumble in and throw our clothes everywhere. She gives me one more peck on the lips, pushes me onto the bed, shoots me this devious, almost nefarious look, and then dives toward my crotch . . .

. . . skipping past my penis . . .

. . . totally ignoring my balls . . .

. . . and starts feasting on my asshole.

I am not exaggerating when I say “feasting.” She buried herself in it like a hungry dog in a jar of peanut butter. I look down and her face is so far into my ass crack that all I see is her hair. It looks like a blond mop growing out of my taint.

Don’t misunderstand—I am not complaining. I like it when girls eat out my ass, and she was a fucking expert: She jacked me off while her tongue worked my ass like a lesbian porn star. That is not an easy thing to do, but she did it, and did it well. By the time she was done, you could have eaten off my asshole.

Of course, after I came, the reality of the scene rose up and smacked me in the face. I could think about only three things:

1. If she was so eager to do this to me, how many other guys had she done this to? More disturbing,
2. I had forgotten until that moment that I hadn’t showered since my last shit. And MOST disturbing,
3. She hadn’t even asked about #2.

The next morning, I roll her over onto her stomach and hit it from behind, because I’m afraid she’ll try to kiss me. Sorry Typhoid Mary, I’m not tasting any feces, not even my own.

When we are done, I jokingly call her PoopLips. She doesn’t understand why.

Tucker “Uhhhhhh . . . are you the same girl as last night?”
PoopLips “Please die. Of course I’m the same girl, DUH!”
Tucker “Do you not remember licking my ass like it was a Push Pop?”

PoopLips "OH MY GOD I DID NOT!"
Tucker "Of course you didn't. After all, if you don't remember it, then it didn't happen, right?"

I tease her about it a few more times, she denies it more, and I assume she is just playing around. Then I make her leave because, you know, I have to play Madden or something.

Later that week she came back over. This time she wore normal laundry-washing clothes . . . and a pearl necklace. Like a legit, real pearl necklace, not costume jewelry. She might as well have painted a bull's-eye on her face with the words AIM HERE. Not thinking her ridiculous prop was enough of a hint, it took her only about three minutes to spit out this gem:

PoopLips "No one has ever cum on me. I was a good girl in college."
Tucker "Right. Just like you've never eaten out an asshole?"
PoopLips "I didn't do that!"
Tucker "Of course you didn't. But that thing you didn't do, you'd better repeat it, if you want to see me again."

She put up about as much resistance as the French gave the Germans in 1940. She went right to work, gave me unreal head, and of course there was fantastic rim action too. This girl knew her way around a dick; she was much better at sucking dick than any French girl I've ever hooked up with. And they supposedly invented fellatio.

Tucker "So are you still going to maintain you haven't eaten out my ass?"
PoopLips "Obviously not, as I just did it. But you are the first guy I've ever done this with."
Tucker "Does that lie work on other guys?"
PoopLips "I'm telling the truth!"
Tucker "Of course you are."

It always makes me laugh when girls play the "I never do this" game. I mean, of course every girl has to have a first time, and many girls have purposely come to me to be their first (that story is coming up), but seriously, ladies: When you claim never to have done something, and then are enough of an expert to teach a Learning Annex course on it . . . I mean, come on. Just like it takes years of practice to consistently knock down an NBA three-pointer, it takes a lot of practice to be good at oral sex. Yeah, he may have all the natural talent in the world, but Kobe Bryant still shoots 500 threes a day. Whether you are lying to yourself or just to us, stop. Being a head doctor is nothing to be ashamed of.

Tucker "Well, whatever the case may be, you keep sucking dick like that, and you're going to have a husband in no time."

She feigned anger, but I could tell she was proud of her skills.

PoopLips "Whatever, you know I am very smart."
Tucker "Who said you weren't? Intelligence and fellatio skills are not mutually exclusive."
PoopLips "I know if I wanted to, I could be all successful and whatever, but all I really want is to have a family and be a stay-at-home mom."
Tucker "You going to kiss your kids with those lips?"

I promised PoopLips I would not disclose her real name, and of course I will abide by that oath. But gentlemen, for one of you, she's going to be using your toothbrush, drinking from your water bottles, and kissing your kids. She'll dress conservatively and wear pearls, and she'll swear she's never done anything like "that" with any other guy.

I'm Not That Type of Girl

Occurred—May 2007

One day I got an email from a girl who went on and on about how fascinated she was by me and by my life, and how, even though she didn't want to sleep with me at all—no, NOT HER, she didn't do things like that—she really wanted to get to know me. Since she loved doing laundry, she would be happy to do mine while she was at my place "picking my brain." Yawn. Of course she attached a picture to this email, the same email where she strenuously took pains to explain that she had no desire to have sex with me.

She gets to my place in NYC at 3pm on a Tuesday. She is dressed up like she's going to see *Phantom of the Opera* on Broadway: very fashionable blouse and skirt, full makeup, and smells great. She actually does start a load of laundry, but I watch her do it, and though she is going through the steps properly—separates colors and whites, turns the water on, pours the detergent in, waits for it to fill a little, then puts the clothes in—it's pretty clear by her deliberate motions that she's not used to this at all:

Tucker "Have you ever done laundry before?"
Girl "Well . . . no, not really."
Tucker "Then how did you know what to do? I mean, it's not brain surgery, but I doubt anyone would just get it right by luck."
Girl "I had our maid teach me the steps before I came over."

I laugh for a good five minutes and then tease her relentlessly about it. From there, it takes her only about twenty minutes to decide she wants to find out if my reputation is true, and we fuck. Afterward, we have this conversation. I wrote this thing out almost right away because it was so shocking to me at the time (though considering that she is big in the Tinsley Mortimer socialite crowd in NYC, it shouldn't have been):

Girl "So . . . would you have a threesome with me and another girl?"
Tucker "Are you kidding? Why not ask me if I want a ribeye and a beer? Of course I would."
Girl "This is exciting! I'm sure it's not your first threesome, so you more than likely know what you're doing. How does it work? I have never even kissed a girl!"
Tucker "Don't worry about that. I have that angle covered very, very well. I basically lived with a bisexual girl for a year. I've had so many threesomes I got bored with them for a while. All you have to do is show up and follow instructions, I'll handle the rest."
Girl "That is too sexy. Do you provide the girl or me?"

Tucker "I can. Depends what you want to do and what kind of girl you want. The more info you give me, the better you will like the actual event."
Girl "I want someone extremely attractive. I don't have fake tits, so it would be nice to experience a girl with some. Most important, the girl must be clean. So this means no fat girls or strippers. Or Asians. I assume you don't sleep with other types of ethnic girls anyway."

She seriously said that. I thought she was kidding at first, but then I remembered this was an Upper East Side WASPy girl, and all those types are undercover racists.

Tucker "Would you like me to dance for you too, Massa?"
Girl "I'm not saying I'm anywhere near the hottest girl around, but this is my fantasy and I want it to be an amazing night to remember the rest of my life."
Tucker "You've thought about this a lot, haven't you?"
Girl "I have always wanted to have a threesome with another girl. However, my very conservative boyfriend does not approve of my choice."
Tucker "Wait, wait—you have a boyfriend? And your boyfriend doesn't want to have sex with you AND another girl?"
Girl "Thank you! He is an abnormally conservative person. He is a pediatrician on Long Island and seems to think it's beneath him."
Tucker "Then why are you dating him? And why are you here fucking me?"
Girl "Don't get me wrong, he is a great man. Plus, I'm not the type of girl that does this, so I don't need to date someone who enjoys nightly multi-partner sex sessions. That is why I chose you. From reading your stories, I knew you had an immense appreciation for great sex. We don't have to worry about feelings getting in the way or embarrassing encounters afterward. Just amazing sex, then we can go on our way. Sound good?"
Tucker "You chose me? Haha. OK, whatever, fine with me. But you say you aren't the type of girl that does this . . . but you are doing it. So that means you are that type of girl."
Girl "No, it doesn't."
Tucker "What? If A = B, and B = C, then A = C. The transitive property is one of the foundations of logic."

Girl "But I'm not that type of girl."
Tucker "Do words have meaning to you? How can you do something and then claim you aren't the type of person who does that? If you suck a dick, that makes you a dick sucker. If you fuck me, that makes you a cheater."
Girl "No, I'm not one of 'those' types. I don't do those things."

After she left that day, I never talked to her again. That is how repulsed I was by our conversation. I will never lay claim to being some sort of moral crusader as I may not have the most conventional moral code, but I do live by a very distinct and clear set of principles—they are just different from most people's.

I literally stopped fucking her because I found her morally repugnant. I know, makes me laugh too.

Nils and the Pepperdine D-Girl

Occurred—January 2008

When writing this story, I sent Nils an email asking him which of my laundry whores he thought was the funniest or the most delusional, because there were so many and I wanted to whittle them down to the best three. Nils is a longtime friend and wrote and produced the movie adaptation of my first book with me, so he was on my couch in LA during some of this time and met many of them. He sent me a one-sentence email:

"That fucking Pepperdine D-Girl. I still get angry when I think about her."

Oh yes. I had almost totally forgotten about her. It started when she sent me a basic email about wanting to clean my clothes but did something no one else had done: She included a pic of herself . . . with a washer and dryer. Seriously.

I started writing up the story about her, but a few days later Nils sent me this follow-up about her. I laughed so hard at the length and depth he went to express his lingering disdain for her, that I scrapped what I wrote in favor of his version.

> “For the extensive catalog of your negative qualities identified and exploited by journalists and haterz for their personal gain and amusement, there has been little discussion of your two greatest qualities: loyalty and generosity. There is no greater example than the 18 months during which we finished the script and got it funded. I'd quit law school, moved in with my then-girlfriend, and you floated me cash, picked up food and bar bills, and let me crash on your couch no questions asked for as long as I needed to. When it came time to make the financing deal, you represented my interests faithfully, making sure they were in lockstep with yours and fully accounted for. It was the kind of loyalty and generosity you rarely see in this world anymore, and the kind you NEVER see in Hollywood.

It was not unconditional, however. It came with a price. That price?

Putting up with your stupid whores.

And of all the species of whore in the Tucker Maxonomy of Whoredom, the ones who fucked you under the pretense of doing your laundry were the worst. In normal relationships, laundry is a relatively intimate thing. You can learn a lot about someone by his laundry. What size he is. What colors he likes. What kind of underwear he has. How well he wipes. You can become familiar with a person rather quickly by doing his laundry . . . unless of course you are on the business end of a purely exploitative exchange of services, and you don't realize it. Like these stupid whores.

They do your laundry, fuck you, and then hang out, sometimes overnight, and it feels almost like a real relationship. Relaxing. Cozy. They don't realize that the only reasons you haven't kicked them out yet are that they haven't done anything to annoy you and it's easier to just ignore them while you watch TV or work on the computer. Plus, there's morning sex to consider.

This comfortable familiarity gets compounded exponentially when, God forbid, they become part of a weekly rotation. Then it's like they're actually a part of your life, with a special seat at the table. Like the topmost of all the bottom bitches.

That is where the Pepperdine D-Girl comes in.

The Pepperdine D-Girl has a name, but I have purposely forgotten it so when I meet people out in the world with the same name as her they are not immediately ruined for me. She came over every other Sunday for some months, but I was fortunate enough to meet her only once during one of my multiweek stretches on your couch while we finished the script.

She breezed in, not bothering to ring the doorbell, nodded to me, pretended that Murphy and Maxie [ed. note: the dogs] loved her by being overly enthusiastic to see them, and went right back into your bedroom. With a novice laundress, I imagine it would be laundry first, fucking second. Lest you get taken for a ride. Not with Pepperdine. She'd been around long enough that you knew she'd get to washing once the fucking was done. I think they call that trust. Gross.

I could hear you rooting around on top of her for a while, and that all went the way it normally does. Problems began when she'd put the first load in the washing machine and was tired of you ignoring her in the bedroom while you were on your computer. That's when she came out into the living room where I was, ostensibly to visit with the pups. She played with Murphy for a second and then stared at the TV waiting, I guess, for me to engage her in conversation.

That was not going to happen. I learned long ago not to attempt conversation with any of the girls you fuck. To do so would be to risk opening the floodgates to a tsunami of annoying. Instead, if I absolutely had to speak with them, it was best to treat it like a lie detector test. Yes and no questions. One word answers when at all possible. Eyes straight ahead.

Pepperdine blinked first.

PDG "I really like the script."
Nils "Thanks."
PDG "Tucker let me read the most recent draft."
Nils "Cool."
PDG "I'm a development executive and read tons of scripts."
Nils "Really?"

What she really means is that she is the assistant to some junior executive she's probably fucking who makes her read all the shitty scripts he gets but does not want to suffer through himself. Many studio executives started their careers in a similar position, and by that I mean, on their backs.

PDG "Yeah, most of them suck."
Nils "Yeah."
PDG "Yours is really funny."
Nils "Cool, thanks."

She tried to penetrate my whore-hardened exterior, with no luck. She sat for a while longer until the washing machine buzzed and she had to toss the wet clothes in the dryer. The dryer whirred to life as she started a second load in the washing machine. She tried your room again and I thought for sure I was rid of her, but lo and behold she reappeared in the living room a few minutes later, this time with a drink.

It was a horrifying feeling. This girl was already more comfortable than she had any right to be. Now she was going to lubricate her broken soul with alcohol and, unless you came out from your cave in the back of the house, I was going to be stuck with her for a FULL drying cycle, which can be as much as ninety minutes depending on the clothes being washed. I was praying for thin cotton blends.

About fifteen minutes into our awkward silence, Jeff came home. Jeff has about as much patience for these girls as I do, and he takes great pleasure in making sure they know that's exactly what they are: one of your whores. After putting away his stuff in his room, he came out into the living room and started to poke and prod her.

At some point, he offered as a point of fact that only daddy issues could lead a girl to agree to do a stranger's laundry as a condition of HIM being willing to have sex with HER. She took great offense to this. She did NOT have daddy issues.

Damn you, Jeff. Damn you straight to hell. He hooked me right into the conversation.

Nils "So you have a good relationship with your dad?"
PDG "I wouldn't say that."
Jeff "What would you say?"
PDG "I mean, we have our fair share of issues."

Jeff and I looked at each other to make sure we heard that right. Pepperdine doesn't have daddy issues, but she and her dad have their . . . fair share . . . of issues?

Jeff "What's the difference?"
PDG "There's a huge difference."
Nils "OK, so tell us what that difference is."
PDG "Like, he didn't rape me or molest me or anything."
Nils "You don't need to have a history of sexual assault to have a fucked-up relationship with your dad."
Jeff "What'd he do?"
PDG "He's just an asshole. He like neglected and abandoned us. He's just like totally selfish."
Nils "So you have daddy issues."
PDG "No, my dad and I just have problems is all."
Nils "And you don't think those problems have anything to do with the fact that you're doing a stranger's laundry so he'll fuck you."
Jeff "And never date you."
Nils "Ever."
PDG "No, that doesn't mean I have daddy issues."

Jeff and I nearly fell off the couch. The conversation went around in circles like this for another half hour as Jeff and I walked her through the logic of her position over and over again. We repeatedly brought her to the inexorable conclusion one must take from her actions, but she repeatedly refused to acknowledge the obvious implications. I got more and more agitated until I couldn't handle it.

Nils "Your father is selfish. He abandoned and neglected you. You are rightly mad at him for those things. You don't have a good relationship with him. Since you refuse to address them, those feelings have to go somewhere. Where do you think they go? Right to Tucker Max. Who is currently selfishly neglecting you while you do his laundry in exchange for him having sex with you. You don't think this relationship is just modeling your trauma? You don't think those are daddy issues?!?!?!"

Each time she simply refused to take that final step to the obvious conclusion. She even started to cop an attitude.

PDG "NO! YOU DON'T EVEN KNOW WHAT YOU ARE TALKING ABOUT! WHAT ABOUT *YOUR* ISSUES?"

It was somewhere around this point that I completely lost it. Her shattering stupidity, her idiotic retorts, her overly familiar attitude, and her Pepperdine D-Girl sense of entitlement mixed like the liquors of a Long Island Iced Tea, and I was quickly drunk on rage.

I started screaming at her—red in the face, voice going hoarse, spittle flying out—to get the fuck out of the living room and out of my sight. I think I even said that I couldn't wait to find out when she killed herself so I could send a note to her dad congratulating him on a job well done.

I don't remember much else. I must have blacked out from the seething anger. All I can remember after that point was Jeff laughing and you—holding back laughter yourself—coming out and bringing her back to your bedroom to save her. Tucker, it might be the most loyal, generous thing you've ever done. For me and for her."

The point of these stories is not to criticize girls who pretend to do my laundry in order to fuck me. I got my clothes and my dick cleaned, how could I not like it? Plus, let's be honest: We've ALL deluded ourselves about aspects of our lives at times, that is just part of the human condition. God knows I have all kinds of blind spots in my self-perception. But, in the end, there was a pattern that stood out clearly to me, one that I want to point out:

Ladies, be honest with yourself about who you are and have the courage to be that person. If you want to fuck, then go fuck. If you want to get drunk, get drunk. And there is nothing wrong with sucking a dick. If people try to judge you or shame you for doing safe, consensual things that make you happy, I can guarantee you they're bad people. Tell them to lick the dark part of your ass and cut them out of your life. No one has it all figured out, especially not the people who are acting like they do and judging you because of it. Pretending to be something you aren't because you're trying to please a bunch of judgmental hypocrites and shitheads is not the way to be happy. Living the life you want to live is. It really is that simple.

[Also—I'm single again. Any girl who wants to do my laundry, feel free to email me: tuckermax@gmail.com.]

The Things I Put Up with for Pussy

There are only three things men do exclusively for ourselves:

1. Play video games
2. Get drunk
3. Masturbate

Ladies, you may not realize this, understand this, or even believe this, but everything else we do is ultimately for you. Men create art, build businesses, donate to charity, invent things—really do anything noteworthy—because we want to impress women, and thus get them to have sex with us. If women didn't exist, we'd still be naked grunting apes living in caves. In a very real way, pussy is the key to human civilization. Most scientists believe sexual selection (men doing things to impress women so the women will have sex with them) is probably the reason culture exists at all, and even Darwin himself said that sexual selection is more important than natural selection. You don't have to like it, but it's a fact. If you understand it, you understand men.

Of course, pussy doesn't motivate men to do only great things. It also inspires men to do truly stupid shit. How else can you explain body spray, hair gel, tanning beds, and chest waxing? Pussy. Men will do ANYTHING—amazing or stupid—if they think it'll get women to like them.

I'm no different. All through my teens and twenties, I did all the normal stupid shit guys will do for pussy. I even wrote a book about it. Speaking of—why do you think I wrote my book in the first place? I intentionally left behind a lucrative career in law to get up every day, face impossible odds, endure all the pain, fight all the battles, and do all the grueling work a beginning writer has to do to reach eventual success. Why the fuck would I go through all that shit? PUSSY. Don't get me wrong, I love writing and I love entertaining people and I am passionate about it, but there is ZERO point to any of it without women. Nothing else could motivate me like that.

And you'd think once women started coming to me for sex, once there was such a plethora of pussy in my life that I had my pick, that I had more pussy thrown at me than I could ever fuck, I'd at least stop doing stupid things to get it.

Yeah, right. I'm still a man. But, instead of *doing* stupid shit to get pussy, I am now *putting up* with stupid shit because of the type of pussy that is coming to me. It is a subtle difference, that has a large effect on results. The next three stories are perfect examples.

Too Old for This Shit

Occurred—October 2006

When I lived in NYC, I spent a few weeks hanging out with this cute girl, Colleen. After we'd been fucking long enough to feel comfortable making demands, she begged me to come out drinking with her and all her friends. She said her friends were huge fans, wanted to drink with me, and they were convinced they could hang with me.

Initially I said no. There is nothing more tedious or annoying than some group of idiots who feel the need to compete with me in something. I don't give two flying shits if someone can drink more than me, has fucked more than me, is funnier than me, or has better stories than me. The vast majority of the time they are really fucking lame and suck at what they think they're good at, but even if it's true and they are better at something than me, I don't care, because it doesn't matter. What does matter is that I did it when and where it counted, and until they beat me there, no one else will care either. For example, Earl "The Goat" Manigault was probably the greatest basketball player of all time, but Michael Jordan is universally regarded as the best ever. This is because The Goat only did it at Rucker Park, while Michael did it where it mattered: in front of the world.

I told her all this, and that I had no desire to be paraded around as some trophy for her to show her friends. But she worked on me, and I eventually agreed to go. Why? Same reason as always:

Pussy.

Colleen is not stupid. She got me to agree by inviting only hot females, all Midwestern girls, and strongly hinted that she and one of her friends might be up for a threesome. OK, Geppetto, I'm in. And of course, she promised they weren't annoying and didn't care at all about anything other than hanging out and having a good time. Stupid me, I believed her.

As soon as we got there, it became clear this would be another "we can outdrink Tucker Max" theme night, which I hate. They were all recent college grads from schools like Kansas, Mizzou, Oklahoma, and Texas A&M, and seemed to think that four years of swallowing all the beer and cum they could fit in their stomachs prepared them to drink with me. They were pretty hot, and actually kind of fun, so after a few minutes of flirting with me, I said fuck it and took the challenge.

Stupid, silly girls. I started with a round of Brutal Hammers (vodka and red wine) and then went shot for shot with them, picking awful things like Cement Mixers, while doubling up on their beers. They bravely tried to keep up with me for a while, but my victory was wrapped with a decisive moment:

After a particularly vicious shot (Rumple Minze I think), the Oklahoma alum got up from her chair, claiming she had to go to the bathroom. She stumbled along toward the ladies' room, bouncing from wall to wall, until she tripped and began to fall. As she fell, she put her arms out to break her fall, but literally missed the floor. How do you miss the floor? I could not have answered this question before that night. As she fell, she reached her arms out like she was trying to grab something, but she was so uncoordinated from all the drink that she ended up flinging her arms around her body, putting herself in a bear hug. Luckily for her, she was able to break her fall with her face.

The sight of her forehead smashing into the hardwood floor of the bar—in addition to the loud CRACK sound it made—brought everyone rushing to her aid. Everyone except me. I went into uncontrollable spasms of laughter. I completely lost it. Even if it does make me the bad guy . . . that shit was FUNNY. I could see a honey badger wearing a top hat and monocle attacking a bus full of Chinese exchange students, and I wouldn't laugh as hard as I laughed then.

This incident was all the proof needed that I'd buried these girls like the kindergarten drinkers they were. So much for the Big 12. At least kids from the South would've tried to fight me after they lost. These pussies just got mad at me because I laughed at the traumatic head injury of a drunk slut. Whatever. When you can throw'em back like a real drinker, come back and see me. No wonder SEC schools win the BCS national title every year.

Easy victory in hand, I led some of them back to Colleen's place. I decided that my victory entitled me to a threesome and picked one of the hot, sloppy drunk friends. Apparently that was a no-go, because she had a boyfriend who "lives in Toronto."

Tucker "HAHAHHHAHAHA! You HAVE to be kidding me. You have a boyfriend in Canada? Get the FUCK out of here."
MizzouGirl "I DO!!"
Colleen "She does!!"
Tucker "Did you stop learning new lies in high school? You're going to have to come up with a better reason than that not to have a threesome."

Her phone rings at that exact moment; it's her boyfriend. She holds the phone up for me to see, and her friends seem to think this is proof that he loves her and she shouldn't cheat on him. I take the phone from her, still ringing, and answer it:

Tucker "Do you really live in Canada?"
Boyfriend "What? Who is this?"
Tucker "I didn't ask you about your problems, buddy. Focus: Do you or do you not live in Canada?"
Boyfriend "Who the fuck are you? Put MizzouGirl on the phone."
Tucker "Oh dude, sorry, she can't come to the phone. She has something in her mouth."

I hang up on him. As you can imagine, this causes all sorts of comedy. MizzouGirl just about knocks me over taking the phone back and calling him. Then she spends an hour trying to convince him that "Tucker Max was only kidding about me giving him head!" I know it's possible for girls to hang out with me and not have sex, because it happens all the time, but apparently he did not. Poor insecure Canadians. No wonder your Winter Olympics sucked so much.

At this point, I'm ready to fuck. Colleen is a screamer, and because her bedroom is right next to the living room where everyone is hanging out, she wants us to fuck in the bathroom down the hall. She whispers this to me conspiratorially, like we are doing something crazy. Bitch, please. I get up from the sofa, grab her hand, and in front of all her friends:

Tucker "Excuse me ladies, I'm going to muddle up her vagina."

I bend her over the sink, and things are going fine for a few minutes. Then I hear chaotic stumbling coming down the hallway toward us, and I assume her friends are going to bust in on us and take a picture, like it's high school or something. Fine with me; I actually start to prepare for them and shift myself so I am facing the door. That way I can smile and give a thumbs-up as I plug her from behind. You know, to optimize the picture, because there is a 100% chance they're putting it on Facebook.

But instead of the door slowly opening and a camera popping in, there is a huge crash, the door flings open, and the roommate hurls herself directly into us, separating me from Colleen's vagina. She tries to grab the sink but misses, and instead falls onto the floor, all while projectile vomiting. Everywhere.

ALL OVER THE FLOOR, ALL OVER MY LEGS, ALL OVER EVERYTHING.

Nasty, brownish puke, stinking of cheap shots, sushi, and bile.

Tucker "Are you kidding me? Yeah, you ladies can really drink. Legendary. I can't handle this crew. I surrender."
Colleen "Shut up! Help me clean this!"
Tucker "Are you fucking retarded?"

I don't even do my own laundry, and this bitch wants me to clean some OTHER person's puke?

Look, if I was some horn-dog 18 year old and just happy to be getting ass, maybe. If I was 22 years old and stupid enough to think I could still pull a threesome out of this, maybe. 26 year old Tucker Max would have played it right: He'd take a steaming dump on the roommate's bed as retribution for interrupting his coitus, and been so proud that he meted out proper justice that he'd drunk-dial his friends to tell them about it. Then he'd pull Colleen out of the bathroom by her hair after she washed herself off, fuck her until she had multiple organ failure, cum on her face, drink all her beer, and then piss it out on the puking roommate passed out in the bathtub.

But 30 year old Tucker just gave up. I used her expensive down comforter to wipe the vomit off my legs, then walked home without even saying good-bye. Nothing but a boring night destroying amateurs, ending with ruined jeans and my dick in my hand. No steaming dump, no drunk dials, no facial, and no karmic, retributive pissing.

I have put up with some stupid shit in my life for pussy, but this was too far. Even I have a line, and this bitch vomited all over it.

Why You Don't Fuck USC Girls

Occurred—March 2008

As a group, college girls are pretty stupid. They don't realize this because, compared to college guys, they seem smart and mature (sorry, guys, it's just true, the same thing applied to me at that age).

Some schools are worse than others. I could probably write a separate book about all the stupid FSU girls I've met in my life, but it would be annoying and repetitive, just like their sloppy blowjobs. I have nothing good to say about Notre Dame girls (or guys), but that's pretty common; when I was in Ireland, even the actual Irish told me they hated the Fighting Irish. But there is one school whose female population stands out to me as possibly the worst in the country:

The girls from USC, the University of Spoiled Children.

I dealt with USC girls when I lived in LA. I fucked a bunch of them because they are, as a group, pretty fucking hot, and were often an easier and better option than normal LA girls. That's not really a compliment, though. It's like saying they were the best toilet to lick.

But it was because of a USC girl that I pretty much completely stopped fucking any girls I met in LA. It started with this email:

> "Dear Tucker,
>
> I just finished reading your amazing book and read it through twice because it was so so funny. And you are hot! But I think I can totally drink more than you! I am in college and all we do is drink! I am the best of my friends and you can't hang! lol! Let's hang out so I can drink you under the table, then crawl under

there with you! Plus I go to school at USC in Los Angeles! It's perfect!"

And led to the following email exchange:

Tucker: "If you read my book, you should know that no words you can write will ever be as important as the pictures you take. Send them."

USC Girl: "Well duh i do NOT want to be like the time you fucked a fat chick on purpose . . . HA! . . . and refrain from giving you pics for a while. In fact i apologize for not including pictures in my first e-mail that is simply unacceptable. Anyways, I have attached a few for your viewing, hope you like them. and truss me im that hot in person ;)"

Tucker: "You're cute. I'll drink/hook up with you. I'm free Wednesday."

USC Girl: "TUCKER MAX! i am pausing a drinking game to respond to you right now bc i am so excited!! to be honest, i wish you could cum out tonight because although it is easter, it is my birthday and I want u to give me my gift and i am going out. and i will be drunker than u. however wednesday AND thursday work for me!! lets do this!! u better be ready i am going to bury you and then hop on!!! lol!!"

I know what you are thinking, and you're right. Even at the time, I knew it: This girl is a dumpster fire of emotional baggage. I'd be safer entering the core of a nuclear reactor than I would be entering this girl.

But I met up with her anyway.

Why, even fully realizing the high probability of disastrous failure that these emails are indicating, would I STILL willingly and recklessly place myself in the path of this whornado?

You know the answer is pussy. There is no other possible defense.

She walked into the bar, and even before I talked to her, I knew I'd made a bigger mistake than I'd calculated. She had one of those goofy perma-smiles, like the kind worn by people who watch *The 700 Club* without irony. You know, that girl who, when you're talking to her, leans in and just stares at you like you're speaking another language? Yeah, her. Even if I ignored her until it was time to go home and fuck, this girl was still going to be a handful.

I watched her ping-pong around the bar looking for me, like a giant superball made out of glitter, stupidity, and the freshman fifteen. I groaned and considered my options. She's not hot, but she's cute enough. She doesn't have a very good body, but she does have nice tits. She's way too immature and is going to be annoying as hell, but still . . . I'll be drinking, and she's definitely going to fuck. I'm already here, all the work is done . . . I guess I'll fuck her.

It's pussy, right? What did I have to lose? You know, besides my dignity and self-respect?

USCGirl "Tuuucker Maaaax! Oh my God! I'm so going to drink you under the table!

Tucker "Sweetie, the only way you could drink me under the table is if I go there to hide from you."

USCGirl "Are you drunk yet?"

Tucker "I just got here."

USCGirl "So what!?! You need to catch up!"

Tucker "Have you been drinking already?"

USCGirl "Nope, so let's do shots!"

Tucker "Shots are for frat boys and fat girls. If you really want to drink, let's get doubles instead."

USCGirl "What's a double?"

Tucker "Are you joking? A double vodka soda? You don't know what that is?"

USCGirl "No."

Tucker "You claim to be this crazy drinker, and you don't know what a double is?"
USCGirl "No, I've never heard of it!"
Tucker "You can't even figure it out from context?!?"

She goes on to tell me other gems, like how she won't eat Italian food anymore because her aunt died from choking on a bay leaf. She doesn't mean this to be funny at all, but I can't stop laughing at this. Taking this unintentional comedy as a sign that she is actually funny, she starts telling me her "Tucker Max" story that she promised was SO hilarious.

USCGirl "OK, so one time I was giving this guy a hand job."
Tucker "A hand job? When was this, high school?"
USCGirl "Well, yeah."
Tucker "You know how to give the best hand job ever? Use your mouth."
USCGirl "No wait, listen, so I was giving—"
Tucker "Here's a great story: I knew this girl once, and I told her to go get me another double vodka soda, because I needed to get drunk to fuck her. You want to guess how it ends?"
USCGirl "Ugh, fine!"

We play this game for three more doubles, and she is getting seriously shit-canned. She goes to the bathroom to punch herself in the cunt or whatever it is women do in there, and I hear a crash. Mind you, this is a pretty small bar, and the bathrooms are right next to where people sit, so everyone hears this. A woman goes into the bathroom to see what happened, and a few seconds later emerges, helping USCGirl walk out of the bathroom, explaining to me that she fell.

Tucker "Are you that drunk?"
USCGirl "No! I'm fine, I can drink way more."
Tucker "OK, I think we need to have sex now, before it's too late."
USCGirl "I know, I'm so turned on too."
Tucker "Not really what I meant, but let's go with it."

USCGirl "We are going to have so much fun!!! But wait—you aren't going to write about me, are you?"
Tucker "No way. We're just drinking and fucking. No one gives a shit about that. At this point in my life, you'd have to do something really ridiculous to get me to write about you. From what I can tell, you're just a run-of-the-mill drunk slut."
USCGirl "Cool!"

I have a long history of making wildly extravagant predictions, both about myself and the world. Many have come true, some haven't, but I'm never scared to go out on a limb. So of course, the one time I make a prediction as conservative as I am capable of, it blows up in my face. Whom the gods wish to make a fool, they first make certain.

Instead of narrating what happened next, I will give you two things written that night. The first is from Nils, who was at my house when we got back from the bar:

> "They stumbled in around 1:30am. I say "they" because it is hard not to stumble when you are trying to herd a drunk, babbling, 5'9" college girl up your stairs and through your front door. Tucker straddled her as they entered, like the parent of an infant who'd just learned how to walk and is a little too excited and overconfident with her new ability. Had he not been in that toddler-safety-net position, she would probably have taken a header through the wrought-iron screen door or taken a bite out of the front porch.
>
> I was on the couch working and got the cursory introduction "[Girl], this is Nils. Nils this is [Girl]." Big mistake. Before he could get her spinning retard wheels pointed in the right direction, she lurched over to me. "We need to have a heart-to-heart," she said as she flopped down next to me on the couch. Of course at this point she had absolutely no body control,

so she bounced off the couch cushion, tipped over, and face-planted right into my laptop. Tucker peeled her off of me and dragged her into his room, saving me from the heart-to-heart and my laptop from any more of her drool."

This is what I wrote a few hours later, at approximately 5am that morning [edited for redundancy]:

"I am so fucking pissed off right now, I don't even know what to say. This is enough to make me understand why domestic violence happens. I am not in the tell-a-Tucker-story mood, so I'll cut to the chase.

College girl emails me, wants to get drunk and fuck. Sends pics, meet her at a bar, she is fucking annoying. Stumbling drunk after three drinks. Seriously she swore she was sober when she got there—THEN SHE FELL DOWN IN THE BATHROOM! After like four drinks. When we leave the bar, she is so drunk the bums are offering her change and telling her things are going to get better.

Get back to my place, my dog is looking at me like, "Daddy, what the fuck are you doing?" My dog eats desiccated pig ears and barks at the vacuum cleaner . . . and yet she still feels entitled to judge me over this girl.

Then the girl passes out while I am taking a shit. Wonderful. I just go to sleep. Whatever, we all get drunk and act like idiots at times, I of all people understand this. I figure I'll fuck her in the morning when she is coherent again and can participate.

But that's not going to happen. It's 5am and I'm so mad I just kicked her out of my house.

Why? Let me show you what I woke up to:

Sometimes I hate my life."

Now, there are some things to consider in this picture:

- That dog with the priceless look on her face is Murph. She is not only disgusted that I made her sit next to the pee (for size comparison) but is clearly enraged that this "temporary mommy" tried to mark her territory.

- Murph is a 50 pound, hunting beagle/Australian heeler mix. She is not a small dog. The urine puddle is bigger than she is.

- I don't have a mattress pad under my sheets. That means she made a puddle that big despite the fact that most of the urine seeped directly INTO the mattress.

- The mattress is for a king-size bed. The puddle takes up HALF OF IT.

- Look at the shape of the urine stain. It's nearly symmetrical. Like a Rorschach inkblot of slutty collegiate incontinence.

- The kicker: She went to the bathroom in my house BEFORE she passed out.

- SERIOUSLY WTF! HOW DID SHE PISS THAT MUCH!!? THE HUMAN BLADDER IS ONLY SO BIG! WHERE DID IT ALL COME FROM?! YOU COULD SEE THAT PUDDLE ON GOOGLE EARTH!

The next day she sent the requisite "I've never done that before" email:

> "Dear Tucker,
>
> I am still in shock about what happened last night and I feel terribly. That is the first time that has ever happened to me and I honestly don't even know what to say. I'm so sorry."

Note that her apology email has nearly perfect grammar and spelling. I guess when you empty your bladder into someone else's bed, you pay attention to formalities. My response:

> "I know what to say: You owe me for a new mattress and sheets. I already ordered a mattress and bought sheets this morning. The total is $550. Be glad I don't have a Tempur-Pedic mattress. You can bring the check over tomorrow night, any time after 7pm."

The next day, my friends took the piss out of me:

Jeff "You should make her pay for some enzyme spray cleaner, or the next one will smell the spot and think it's OK to pee there too."
Ryan "At least you didn't have to fool this one into thinking she pissed the bed instead of you. You're improving each time, that's the key to success."
Tucker "Thanks assholes."

Nils "So you didn't fuck her last night?"
Tucker "Nope."
Nils "You know you're going fuck her when she comes over. I'd bet money on it."
Ben "No question."
Tucker "HAHHAHAHAHAHA! Dude, how funny would it be if I fucked her on the old mattress! Shit, now that you planted the idea in my head, I know I'm going to do it. SHIT!"
Nils "Yeah, without us influencing you, you'd never think of these things on your own."
Jeff "When you fuck her, flip her over on the old mattress and push her face-first in the stain, as punishment for ruining your mattress."
Tucker "Dude, knowing my luck that will just turn her on, and then it'll get weird."
Nils "Yeah, THAT'S when it'll get weird."
Ben "Make for a better story, either way."
Tucker "Stop it. You know pussy is like a good crane kick to me: If do right, no can defense."

That night, on purpose, I had my friends in the living room with me. I was legitimately afraid she would still want to sleep with me, and I needed them there to impart enough shame on both of us to prevent it. She got to my place and texted me from her car.

IncontinentSlut: "im here"
Tucker: "you know where the door is youve been thru it twice"

She walked up the steps and tried to push the door open. It took her a legit five seconds to figure out that she had to PULL the screen door open. It was like that famous *Far Side* cartoon where the kid is pushing on the door that has PULL on it, trying to get into Midvale School for the Gifted. Except less funny and more sad, because she's not gifted, just a slutty bedwetter.

Once she finally got inside, she saw all the guys there smiling at her and turned bright red. She crossed the 15 feet or so from the door to where I was sitting on the couch in complete silence, with all eyes on her like the worst possible walk of shame. She handed me a small manila envelope—not something a college girl would have had handy, but more like she had to go to her dad and ask for the money, but not say why.

IncontinentSlut "Sorry."

She turned and almost ran to the door. I think she would have broken into a jog, except she had to figure out that now she needed to push, not pull the screen door, and that confused her.

Ben "She came into the house the same way she left it: stupid and confused."

Nils "You only did half your job, Tucker. She's broken, yes, but is she *house*broken?"

Jeff "I don't think she is. You have to rub their nose in it before you put them outside, or they don't learn where it's OK to go."

Whoring for Charity

Occurred—January 2010

As I was working on this book, I got this email:

> From: [redacted], [redacted]
> To: tuckermax@gmail.com
> Date: Nov 15, 2009
> Subject: Sex Traffic Us
>
> Dear Tucker Max,
>
> This is Angela and Heidi, and we are the co-chairs of the junior board of [charity redacted]—a diverse group of young profes-

sionals who share a common goal of promoting universal girls education and human rights.

We are having a fundraising cocktail event on January 7th in Manhattan and would be delighted for you to attend. We read your manifesto and we found it appalling, so of course we want to fuck you . . . Thoughts?

We've got the time if you've got the inclination. Let's meet for drinks sometime before then to coordinate the specifics.

We look forward to hearing from you soon!

Love,

[redacted]

From: tuckermax@gmail.com
To: [redacted], [redacted]
Date: Nov 15, 2009
Subject: re: Sex Traffic Us

First off, I need pics of both of you.

Second, am I correct in interpreting this as you two wanting to fuck me . . . for charity? How does that work exactly?

From: [redacted], [redacted]
To: tuckermax@gmail.com
Date: Nov 15, 2009
Subject: re: Sex Traffic Us

Well Tucker, pics attached.

And since you ask . . . For every minute you last with the two of us, every member of the Junior Board will donate 10$ to [the charity]. Bonus donations to be made for bondage and/or sex traffic role playing.

Does this sound like something you might be interested in?

Before we go further, I need to stop and point something out: Though I am not going to name the specific charity, it is a charity that is . . . how do I put this without giving it away? . . . very concerned about the welfare of poor and powerless women around the world. Considering that, go back and read the emails again. Pay special attention to the third email, notably the specific request that we role-play SEX TRAFFICKING.

You almost expect pious religious leaders to be supreme hypocrites and eventually be discovered as closeted homosexuals or pedophiles, but do you really expect people who volunteer for a charity dedicated to empowering women to ASK to be sexually exploited? For fun? Not only that, they want to use this sex game as a way to get their friends to donate to the charity. It's so hypocritical it's cartoonish, like a factory that pumps pollution into the air but doesn't actually make anything.

Perhaps the saddest part is that my life has become so fucking weird that this didn't even strike me as unusual at the time. Only when I mentioned it in passing to my friend Geoff, and he freaked out, did it really dawn on me how abnormal this was. He asked to come out with me in NYC when I met those two, because he wanted to meet them and see what the hell was going on.

Back to the important parts: The pics were good enough. Neither were what I would consider hot, but both had good bodies and were definitely fuckable, so I set it up for a time when I would be in NYC, and with my buddy Geoff tagging along, met them.

At dinner, it became obvious that these two could have been the poster children for what happens when rich people ignore their children. It was like we were in a real-life Bret Easton Ellis novel; what little soul these girls retained was taken up with drug use, disaffected sex, and a complete lack of meaning, all hidden under the façade of having the "right" job and belonging to the "right" social circles.

I have wiped the memory of that dinner conversation out of my mind because it was so banal, so I had to get Geoff to remind me with his Cliff Notes version:

> "My basic remembrances:
>
> —They showed up fairly bombed already. They had split a bottle of wine before dinner. Classy.
> —The brunette was pretty cute—a solid 7, 7.5. The blond less so, like a 5. You wouldn't have slept with her alone (at least I wouldn't have).
> —They were fairly annoying and not that bright.
> —They'd never done a 3 way before but had made out with each other in Europe or some shit. They were obviously nervous about actually hooking up with each other, but not really. As if they knew they were supposed to be nervous but were too jaded to actually care.
> —The charity thing had come up as a joke originally when they suggested you as a speaker for their charity event. It's for young women, so you're obviously not right, but then one of them said she thought you were cute and someone else did too and then a third suggested the 3 way for charity, daring them, and everyone chimed in.
> —Very long discussion about the actual scoring methods for the threesome, and how they would determine who had to donate what based on what happened. None of it made any sense.
> —The brunette's sexual history was ridiculous. She kept dating 21 year old guys who couldn't get it up. As much coke as she and her trust fund friends do, this is a shock?

—The brunette wanted you to be mean to her and you didn't care enough.

—Brunette was testing you and asked (regarding me), "Why don't you share?" You were annoyed with them and said it was time to go. She refused, trying to be coy. You said fuck it, told me I was welcome to have them both, and left.

—They were shocked that you actually left the bar without them. They couldn't believe you didn't know they were "just joking."

—They texted you, you responded, and off they went to your hotel . . ."

Geoff pretty much summed it up. The worst part is that I STILL fucked the brunette that night. Actually, I should say that the worst part is that the brunette was such a jealous cunt, she made the other one leave before she got to my hotel, so I didn't get a threesome. Whatever. At that point, it was like a home invasion; I just wanted it to be over.

About a month later, I got this email:

From: [redacted], [redacted]
To: tuckermax@gmail.com
Date: Feb 11, 2009
Subject: Charitable Sex

Okay new proposition . . . how would you feel about being put up for a DTF auction at the [charity's] cocktail party?

From: tuckermax@gmail.com
To: [redacted], [redacted]
Date: Feb 11, 2009
Subject: Charitable Sex

A DTF auction? You mean Down To Fuck? Where women bid money to have sex with me?

Are you seriously asking me to prostitute myself . . . for charity?

> From: [redacted], [redacted]
> To: tuckermax@gmail.com
> Date: Feb 11, 2009
> Subject: re: Charitable Sex
>
> Think of it as an act of selfless humanitarianism.
>
> It's a win-win-win situation: the [charity recipients] get $, you get karma points, and the highest bidder can have tax deductible sex with a best-selling author and cultural icon!
>
> We'll fly you in for the event . . . and it would definitely make good material for any future literary endeavors you might pursue . . .

Like I said earlier, it's not an easy thing to creep me out. It takes a lot to make me feel queasy and uncomfortable and morally repulsed. Well this did it. In a BIG way.

Even if a hot girl wins the auction, I'm still, on a core level, having sex for money. Once I step up on that podium and let the bidding begin, I essentially give up all choice, and I become nothing more than a slave to the person who buys my sex.

I may endure all sorts of nonsense because of my dick—I may even properly be referred to as a slave to my dick—but at least it's MY dick. I can accept being a slave to myself and my own desires, I can accept that because of this I have to do things to get pussy, I can even accept having to endure some bullshit for pussy . . . but I cannot accept being a slave to pussy. Not even for an anti-slavery charity.

You may be laughing, saying something about how I should not be surprised, that this is the logical consequence of the path I have chosen in life. And you may be right . . . but fuck you.

Baby Mama Drama

Occurred—March 2008

No one likes condoms. They're awkward to put on, they require you to interrupt a passionate act in order to unroll a latex tube onto your dick, they diminish the tactile intensity of skin-on-skin contact at the most pleasurable location, and they fucking stink like a chemical factory. I hate condoms as much as the next guy, but here is the list of things I hate more than condoms:

—herpes
—chlamydia
—syphilis
—gonorrhea
—AIDS
—having bastard children with dysfunctional girls

If you're like me and have been doing things like this for a while—guy or girl—you know the worst thing on that list is the last one. Don't think so? Every STD on that list is either curable or not a big deal, except of course AIDS. And even that's debatable. Yeah, AIDS definitely sucks, but Magic Johnson has had AIDS for twenty years. Do you think he's spent more money on his medicine for that disease, or on child support for his numerous out-of-wedlock kids?

I always try to use condoms, but condoms can break. Sometimes I put them on wrong and they come off. Sometimes I'm drunk and just forget. Other times I can't find any, get impatient, and dive in anyway. If you are a guy and can always think rationally in that situation, please tell me your secret, because I have only enough blood in my body for one head to function at a time.

But even though mistakes with condoms are inevitable, the decision about using a condom is yours to make, and if you don't make it, you're stupid. Take heed and learn something important from my stupidity, and DO NOT EVER believe the following sentence:

"You don't need to wear a condom—I'm on birth control."

That is always a lie. Even if she's telling the truth about being on birth control, it's a lie that you don't need to wear a condom. Other than festering, oozing sores directly on her labia, there is no bigger red flag of impending danger than when you are putting on a condom and a random girl STOPS YOU. Abandon hope all ye who enter her.

This is not me moralizing. I tell you this from experience. The last time I foolishly believed that lie was in 2008. I did a book event, and during the Q&A, I noticed this girl in the corner, eye-fucking the shit out of me. I looked over at her—she was so hot my dick immediately turned into a railroad spike. She didn't just have amazing tits, they were better than amazing. I normally like fake tits the best, but hers were those gravity-defying natural tits that are one in a million, and even then exist for only a short window of time. Her eyes were a piercing light amber, like a lioness. She was some sort of indeterminate mixed race and had that hybrid vigor hotness that can be so great.

When she came through the line to get her book signed, she talked to me for a minute, but she was just too hot for me to listen to anything she said. What little I did hear made it clear she was young, immature, not emotionally stable in the least, and completely obsessed with me. I have a name for this: My wheelhouse.

I write my number in her book, tell her to call me, and I swear I could smell her get wet right there. She starts texting me before she even leaves the bookstore, and it's hardly dark before she's naked in my hotel bed.

We are getting ready to fuck when she seductively whispers in my ear, her warm, sour-apple-candy-scented breath wafting into my nostrils:

HotHybrid "I want to feel every inch of you inside me."

Without hesitating, I reach for a condom. There was no question this girl was as fecund as the Fertile Crescent; she was that type of young girl you can get pregnant just by looking at her.

HotHybrid "It's OK. I'm on birth control. I want to feel your cum inside of me."

I am a grown man who's been in the game for more than 15 years—I *definitely* know better. I hesitate, am about to do the smart thing and turn her down . . . but she finds my weak spot. She starts licking and kissing the back of my neck and shoulders. If you're a girl and can do that well, I'm as powerless as you were before the 19th Amendment.

All rational cognitive thought leaves my brain, and I push her on her back and hit the hole like Walter Payton: hard, focused, and unstoppable (though sadly for her, still white). I stayed an extra day in her city so I could fuck her more, spending essentially every waking moment the next two days firing it into her with reckless abandon. I pumped so much cum in her she could have stayed hydrated on it for a month. The sex was so primal and intense, her vagina took part of my soul that weekend, and I gave it up with aplomb. I am getting hard right now just remembering it.

Any retard can tell you what happened next:

Three weeks later she drives to my place, ostensibly to see me and fuck some more (she lived in a different city but close enough to drive). But instead of sex, she wants to talk.

HotHybrid "I took two tests. I'm pregnant."
Tucker "I thought you were on birth control?"
HotHybrid "I am."
Tucker "Then how did you get pregnant?"
HotHybrid "I don't know. I guess it happens sometimes?"
Tucker "Are you fucking anyone else?"

HotHybrid "OF COURSE NOT!"
Tucker "OK, well, do you need help paying for the abortion?"
HotHybrid "Abortion? I don't want to do that!"
Tucker "Are you morally opposed to it, or just don't want to do it?"
HotHybrid "I don't know . . . I just don't want to do it, I guess."
Tucker "You guess? You were on the pill, right? This means you have no moral issue with birth control and don't want kids. Well, if the oral contraception fucks up, this is the next option."
HotHybrid "It's gross and I don't like it."
Tucker "You'd rather have a child???"

I try to discuss this with her, to make her understand that I don't want a child with a 19 year old whose last name I don't even know. And that as much as she may want to have kids at some point, doing it with a committed husband is the right way to raise a child—not with a baby daddy who will be fucking lots of other girls and not returning her calls.

It goes nowhere. This girl is just not able or willing to think about anything beyond how sexy she'd look pregnant and all the cool baby stuff she'd get to buy. The idea that the child was not a doll, but a human being who was going to require two decades of care, was beyond the comprehension or interest of her 19 year old brain. And then she lets this slip:

HotHybrid "I mean, plus you're like famous and stuff. Everyone wants a famous dad."

I almost laughed. My childhood dream was to be an NBA point guard, but I am white, 6 feet tall, and have small hands, so that dream wasn't in the cards for me. Looks like having a kid out of wedlock with some groupie is the closest I'm going to get. Only 11 more to catch up with Shawn Kemp.

She sets the first doctor's appointment for a week later, and asks me not only to pay for it, but also to come along. I agree to drive the three fucking hours to her city, but only because I figure I can get the OB/GYN to make her understand what having a kid means, and discuss options other than keeping the child.

I pick her up, and she's giddy with excitement, talking about names and wondering what features of mine it's going to have and whether it's going to be a boy or a girl.

HotHybrid "What kind of name do you like? If it's a boy, I like more traditional names like Joseph or Mark, but if it's a girl, I like unique names, like Anastasia and Alyandra. Do you think it's going to be a boy or a girl?"
Tucker "I hope it's stillborn."
HotHybrid "I hope it has your eyes, you have the coolest blue eyes, but I want it to have my hands, yours are too stumpy and meaty."

At this point, it starts sinking in: This fucking girl is serious about having a child. OF MINE. It wasn't really real to me until this moment. This is NOT good.

By the time we get to the doctor's office and go into the ultrasound room, I am visibly and seriously depressed. Like, to the point where I am sick to my stomach and can't even make jokes anymore, because she is very serious about having this kid.

It's not just the money she's going to want that's upsetting me; this is more of a personal issue. I grew up in a single-mother household with a largely absentee father, and it sucked. That's not how children should be raised, and I do NOT want to be responsible for bringing a child into that situation. I definitely want to have kids, lots of them, but I want to do it in the right situation, when I'm in a stable, committed relationship and ready to be a father and provide a healthy, loving, safe environment for my children to grow up in.

Not to mention, I want to do it with a woman I love, one who is just as committed to being a good parent. God fucking forbid I do it with THIS girl. Yeah, she's hotter than a blast furnace, but she's about as smart and ambitious as one too. She goes to community college for massage therapy, works at the Abercrombie outlet, still eats Jolly Ranchers, and lives in an MTV reality for fuck's sake. I'm not even sure how she can pay her rent, much less expect to be a good mother. And now, because of me, she's breeding? And not only will the child be mine, but it's my fault that it's going to be cursed with this retard as its mother? FUCK. I want to puke.

There is a nurse and an ultrasound tech in the room. I have dated enough nurses to know that, as a group, they are pretty smart, and this one was no different. One look at my face, and no rings on any fingers, and she knew what was up. But they are pros, so they tend not to ask any questions beyond the immediate pregnancy. I'm really only half paying attention, trying to think about how to deal with this, until I hear the tech:

Tech "There's the yolk sac, and you can just barely see the heartbeat there, if you look. So it's six or seven weeks old. Everything looks good."
Tucker "Wait—what did you just say? How old is it?"
Tech "About six weeks."
Tucker "Are you sure?"
Tech "Of course."
Tucker "Is there ANY chance at all it can be" [*I pause to do the math in my head, counting back from the first day we fucked*] "31 days old?"
Tech "No. None at all. At 4 weeks, the baby looks very different. And this baby has a discernible heartbeat, which can happen after 6 weeks, but not before. It's definitely not younger than 6 weeks. It might be 7 weeks. Gimme a minute, I can do some measurements and tell you the exact number of days if you want."

I look at HotHybrid and see pure panic in her eyes. Instantaneously, everything becomes crystal clear. I can't believe I didn't think about it earlier.

Tucker "You fucking liar."
HotHybrid "No, Tucker, it's got to be a mistake—"

The knot in my stomach releases, the monkey hops off my back, and I jump so high in celebration I almost hit the ceiling. I didn't think it was possible to be any more excited than when you get a negative STD test back, but this tops it, big-time. It's like winning the whore lottery!

Tucker "We fucked 31 days ago. FOUR WEEKS!"
HotHybrid "No, wait, Tucker—"
Tucker "YOU BETTER CALL MAURY! BECAUSE I AM NOT THE FATHER!!!!"

I have a confession to make. I love daytime TV. Maury Povich, especially. Not only that, but music-wise, I am a huge rap fan. It's pretty much all I listen to, and even though I am very white, I was so exuberant that I went straight ghetto crunk Shawty Putt on her:

Tucker "DAT BABY DON'T LOOK LIKE ME!!!!"
HotHybrid "No, Tucker, not—"
Tucker "We were doin' our thang, but dat nappy-head baby lookin' like T-Pain!!!"
HotHybrid "Tucker, wait, Tucker, please wait, I can explain—"

The ultrasound tech is confused. She is white and clearly doesn't understand what is going on at all. The nurse is a middle-aged black woman and figures out what is happening and immediately starts laughing. Though she might be laughing at me butchering the lyrics and acting the fool more than at the situation.

Tucker "DAT BABY DON'T LOOK LIKE ME!!!!"

I actually run out of the hospital, yelling random rap lyrics, and high fiving people like it was some Weird Al Yankovich video spoof.

Tucker "You better call Petey Pablo, didn't he say yo name on 'Freek-A-Leek'?"

That was the last I ever saw her or heard from her. I have no idea what she did after that. I'm actually not sure how she even got home, because I was the one who gave her a ride to the hospital. I honestly hope, for her sake and the child's sake, she either didn't have it, or gave it up for adoption. Or got hit by a bus.

I learned my lesson about believing the "I'm on birth control" lie. Never again.

The Virginity Paradox

"What men desire is a virgin who is a whore."
—Edward Dahlbert

What if I told you that you could do something so awesome it would inspire hundreds of virgins to seek you out, and ask you to be their first sexual experience? And not only that, you'd actually end up fucking dozens of them?

If you're a guy, you'd probably think this was the coolest thing you'd ever heard, and you'd want to know how to get started, right? I felt the same way the first time I heard about drive-through daiquiri stores, but both turned out to be disasters, for different reasons. I'm here to tell you:

Having sex with lots of virgins is not as cool as it sounds.

I've already talked about how much of a pussy boon it was when *IHTSBIH* became a huge hit. The thing that shocked me the most about its success was not the girls who came to me for sex, but rather the girls who came to me to lose their virginity. And there weren't just a few of them. Hundreds, at least. I still get numerous deflowering requests each month.

At the time, I had no idea why a girl would want to lose her virginity to me. It's supposed to be a very special intimate moment, something she cherishes and remembers forever. I'd struggle just to remember her name while she was still in my house.

I used to ask every girl why she chose me, but I stopped inquiring after the first few dozen, because every girl—and I mean every single one, without exception—gave the same combination of three basic reasons. This is an example I pulled verbatim from a virgin email:

"1. I want to lose it to someone I am not in love with, so there are no emotional complications.
2. I want someone experienced, who will know what they are doing and get it right.
3. There is no one in my life like that now and I just want to get this over with, but I don't want it to be with some random creeper I don't know, I want someone who I "know" and can know what to expect from."

If you stop and think about it from the perspective of an 18–21 year old girl, these reasons do have a certain fucked-up logic to them. Most guys in their teens are fucking idiots and terrible in bed (that definitely included me at that age). They aren't going to have to worry about me getting emotional or falling in love or anything like that. There is no question they know what they'll get with me, because my writing has one subject: myself. And I'm probably one of the safest guys a girl could hook up with; being famous puts a target on your chest. You have to be extra careful, because you are easy to find and have a lot to lose.

I can't remember exactly how many virgins have handed me their innocence; I've ended up sleeping with at least a dozen, maybe as many as 15 or 20. When this first started happening, I got a huge ego rush thinking about how cool I must be to have all these virgins coming to me for their first times. It was like dying and going to teenage boy heaven, except you don't have to strap a bomb to your chest and blow up a Jerusalem falafel stand to get there. But at some point along the way, I realized two things:

1. The girls have no interest in me as a human being, and
2. They really, really suck in bed.

After a while, sex with all those virgins stopped being fun and started becoming a job, so I've pretty much stopped accepting their requests. A lot of the enjoyment that comes from hooking up is interacting with the other person: drinking with her, talking to her, getting to know her, fucking with her and exploiting her emotional weaknesses—all the normal stuff. None of the virgins really wanted to do that. They just wanted a dick stuck in them so they could tell their judgmental friends they weren't virgins anymore. Fucking these girls had nothing to do with interacting with me and everything to do with what I could do for them. In a weird way, it almost made me feel used. I didn't think it was possible to see sex with lots of random girls as anything other than awesome, but fuck enough virgins, and it happens.

Read that last sentence again and tell me if you thought you'd ever see anyone, much less me, say it in sincerity.

But even though it may not have been the greatest time for me, I always tried to be very cool and considerate with every girl who came to me to lose her virginity. It's only fair; if I am going to accept the offer, I feel like I have an obligation to do the best job I can. And from what I understand, all of them came away from their encounters having gotten exactly what they were looking for: a safe, enjoyable first time, free from any bullshit or complications.

Well, almost all of them . . .

Don't Fuck with Jack LaLanne

Occurred—June 2005

If you've never been so hammered you drunkenly ordered something from an infomercial, then you've either never been really hammered, or you don't own a phone. I've done this twice.

The first time was as a freshman in college. Drunk on cheap rum, I bought *Freedom Rock* on a dare. (If you are too young to get that joke, go to YouTube and search for "Freedom Rock." It might be hard to believe, but comedy memes existed before the internet, and in 1995 everyone thought, "Well turn it up man," was fucking hilarious.)

The second time was in 2005, when I was living in Chicago. My buddy D-Rock and I were always trying to get each other to buy stupid shit we saw on TV or the internet. One night, a lot of alcohol and too much rejection from girls combined to inspire me to purchase a Ronco Food Dehydrator. I think I may have actually said on the phone to the operator, "My luck getting ass tonight was dried up, so my food will be too!"

I didn't plan to buy it, but when it finally showed up I became obsessed with my new gadget. I could now make my own beef jerky—how could that not get you excited? I bought approximately 30 pounds of various cuts of meat and, over a weekend, turned it into 10 pounds of delicious beef jerky. For at least a week, I ate nothing but desiccated meat. I felt like a Mongol warrior.

Later that week, Bunny and I went to Costco, and I found possibly the only thing that could make me more excited than a Ronco dehydrator: the Jack LaLanne Juicer Pro. On sale! I went nuts. I had to have it. I'd seen too many infomercials about how great juicing was for you, and since the last infomercial product worked so well, then they all had to be that good, right? Juicing was going to change my life!

We bought it and went straight to Stanley's produce market, where we bought pounds of carrots, mangoes, apples, and copious amounts of veggies like cucumbers, greens, tomatoes, and a ginger root the size of my head. The more we piled into our cart, the more excited we got. It was like being contestants on a really healthy episode of *Supermarket Sweep.* We bought so much fruit and vegetables, it was like a strongman workout carrying all that biomass to the car.

Once we got home, our plan was to juice only a few apples. But after we drank the delicious fresh apple juice, Bunny and I went nuts; we juiced and mixed EVERYTHING. We consumed the enzymes of pounds and pounds of fruits and veggies, more raw plant matter than either of us had consumed all month, probably.

You should have seen the leftover mulch. It was half the volume of a contractor trash bag. I could have made a hippie's year if I'd composted it. But Mother Earth has never done anything for me, so we just threw it away.

After drinking almost a gallon of pure fresh-squeezed juice each, Bunny got sick and went to lie down. She's such a wuss. While I was cleaning the counters, I heard the doorbell ring. Who could that be?

Oh shit.

TheVirgin "Hey."

I TOTALLY forgot that a virgin was coming over. And this was only the second or third one I had done it with, so at this point, I still thought deflowering virgins was the pinnacle of cool and was concerned with making sure this girl had a good time.

I invite her to sit down and hang out for a minute. I'm my normal relaxed self, but TheVirgin is so nervous and anxious, she's almost shivering. I offer her a delicious glass of carrot/apple/ginger juice, but she shakes her head.

Tucker "Are you OK? You sure you're up for this? We don't have to do this if you aren't feeling cool about it. There's no rush at all."
TheVirgin "No, I want to. I really do. I'll be OK in a minute. Do you have a beer?"

The girl is 18, so we can fuck, but I'm not serving minors. The last thing I need is some teenage girl coming over to my place to lose her virginity, get hammered, and slingshot her car in a school bus full of retarded children on their way to help out at a soup kitchen. Good-bye rest of my life.

We keep chatting and she finally calms down, so we decide to have sex. Everything starts normal; kissing, clothes off, foreplay, I start playing with her pussy a little. She's pretty wet anyway, but you never know if a virgin has broken her hymen or not, so I use lube to make sure everything is nice and smooth, and to prevent as much pain as possible. I put the condom on, go slow at first and start up.

It's going great for the first minute, when I smell something. I smell it even before I feel it: the sneakiest little fart ever.

It was kind of rancid, but not that unusual for one of my farts. I pretend nothing happened, and she's pretty focused on the sex, so no problem.

A few more thrusts and I can feel another fart coming. I'm determined not to let this one out. I clinch my asshole up tight, but the fart starts pushing back. I focus on holding it in, but this thing is fierce. It was like Chinese fingercuffs: The more I struggle, the worse it gets. I clench every muscle in my core to defeat it—

TheVirgin "Are you OK?"
Tucker "Oh, yeah, sorry."

PPPPFFFFFFFFFFFFTTTTTTTTTTTTT

The second I let up vigilance, the bastard snuck past the bouncers. Motherfucker! This one is silent and smells bad, but still a pretty average fart. I relax, refocus on her, and start humping again.

We're going along for another minute or so, but it quickly becomes clear that the farts are lined up in my colon like planes on the runway at O'Hare, ready to take off as soon as I unclench my ass cheeks. I try to fuck, but in order to thrust, I have to use my ass muscles, and if I do that, another fart will fly out.

Finally, I make the Hobson's choice: I'll let out another fart or two, eat the blame, and that'll buy me enough time to finish her off with a locked sphincter. I just need to go fast and think about a girl I actually like, and I can finish up quickly.

I relax my ass cheeks, almost hoping the fart would make a loud, ripping noise. Then we can both laugh about it and move on. It doesn't. Instead, multiple farts machine-gun out, smelling like old, fermented trash, and sticking to our lungs like a blanket of rotten juice. They enveloped us, leaving no escape and granting no mercy. It was a fruity death mist.

I keep humping away, hoping she'll play along with my little game of "pretend you don't smell the fart." I look down; she is making the same face aerophobics make when their plane hits turbulence.

Tucker "You OK?"
TheVirgin "Yeah." [*cough*] "Fine." [*cough*]

The good news: I wasn't in gastric agony any longer. The bad news: Like a window-washing beggar at the world's longest stoplight, the fucking smell would not go away.

It gets so bad I can feel myself starting to get soft. I'm not sure if it is performance anxiety, lack of focus, or the fact that the room smells like I was Cleveland Steamered by the Jolly Green Giant. I refocus on her pussy and start humping again, hard.

Keep humping . . .

Don't think about the smell . . .

Focus on the pussy . . .

This works well for a second, until I feel an ominous rumbling in my abdomen. This is it, the big one. It starts in the small intestine, rips through my large intestine, and comes at my asshole so hard I wasn't sure if it was going to be a fart or a shart. If this had been a fuck buddy I was more comfortable with, I'd have quoted one of my favorite movie lines, "Everybody run, a shit storm is coming!" but this poor virgin was mortified enough as it was.

RRRRRRRRRIIIIIIIIIIIIIIIIIIPPPPPPPPPPPPPPPPPP

Tucker "Sorry about that."
TheVirgin "Uhh . . . it's OK."

I have to take a shit. And not a normal shit. This was going to be the type of murky, nasty shit you find in a backed-up toilet at a truck stop.

Tucker "Hold on, I'll be right back."

I shoot up off of her, sprint into the bathroom, and plop down about a nanosecond before a tsunami of pulpy poop juice comes flooding out of me, like my ass was an upended milk jug. For a second I feel like my very soul will discharge out of the back of me. After five minutes, I take a gander into the toilet—if I didn't know better, I'd think the shit was staring back at me, like it wanted to fight.

TheVirgin "Is everything OK?"
Tucker "Yeah, sorry. I drank a lot of juice earlier. Let's get back to it."
TheVirgin "Oh . . . OK."

You know how exhausted you feel after a really long, draining shit? Yeah, well try and get hard after that. I felt like Dirk Diggler in *Boogie Nights,* during the prostitution scene in the car, "I'll get there, just gimme another second."

We eventually get things going, and I get close to cumming . . . when I start to feel it again. This was not as urgent as the last one, but like an Indian with his ear to ground, counting the number of approaching horses, I can sense it coming.

What do I do now? Since I'm close, I start to pump more vigorously, thinking I can get my cum to beat my poop to the finish line. But it seems like the harder I try to cum, the more my poop gains. Have you ever tried to contract your sphincter as you're having sex? Try it. It's really fucking hard.

As I move my penis back and forth inside her, I have a brief flash of insight: It wasn't a good idea to eat exclusively dried meat for a week and then drink a gallon of freshly squeezed juice. This seems very obvious in retrospect. . . .

I jump off her and sprint to the toilet again.

TheVirgin "Are you OK?"
Tucker [*in a strained voice*] "Yeah. Be out in a second."
TheVirgin "Should I go?"
Tucker "No, no problem. Just chill for a second."

As my ass spends the next five minutes fire-hosing greenish brown juice into the toilet, I silently curse Ron Popeil, Jack LaLanne, Billy Mays, Anthony Sullivan, and every other petty hustler associated with anything sold on TV. Not even OxiClean and a ShamWow! would be able to get this stain off my soul.

Before I was done, it took two more shits to pass every ounce of waste and fluid out of my body. I had read the whole "more people die from the dehydration caused by diarrhea than the actual disease that causes the diarrhea" factoid, but I'd never understood the concept until that night. I was so dehydrated by the time we finished I think I ejaculated sawdust. I collapsed onto her in pure exhaustion, almost overheating because I hardly had enough water in me even to sweat, and so tired from all the shitting I couldn't even go to the bathroom to get water.

She pushed me off her, quickly put her clothes on, and scrambled out. She may have said good-bye, I don't know. It took me thirty minutes of recovery before I had enough energy to make it upstairs. I was unable to look at juice without a spasm of revulsion, so I started pounding Gatorade as fast as I could.

Bunny "Tucker, that poor girl had the worst look of shame and disgust on her face when she ran out of here. What did you do to her?"
Tucker "Gave her a magical first time?"

STRICT LIABILITY

Occurred—July 2006

This virgin had been emailing me for a while, and even though she typed in that annoying teen lol-speak shit (OMG, lulz, how r u, STFU), the pictures she sent were really cute, and she seemed eager and nice, so I agreed to take her virginity.

When the day came, she knocked on my door at about 3pm. I answered it, and I momentarily thought a Girl Scout was at my door to sell me some Thin Mints. She had a hot pink puffy jacket on, edged with frilly lace, a *High School Musical* backpack, barrettes in her hair, and those rosy pink, baby-fat cheeks you see on girls who scream when their town is added to a Jonas Brothers tour.

What the fuck? Most girls don't look exactly like their internet pictures, and I can adjust for this, but this girl had worked some incredible magic with her pics. It wasn't that she was bad-looking at all. She was just so young.

Don't get me wrong, young is a good look for women, but prepubescent is not, and this girl didn't look old enough to cross state lines. I can deal with a 20 year old girl wearing pigtails; that can even be kinda hot under the right circumstances. But this was not a barely legal girl; she looked too young for *Tiger Beat.* In the meekest, lowest voice possible:

YoungGirl "Hey."

Standing in the doorway looking at her, for a split second I seriously considered just closing the door. But I didn't—I mean, she was already here, willing to fuck, and it was still pussy. She might be disturbingly young looking, but she was not ugly, and I'd definitely fucked worse. Plus she was a virgin, so it was normal that she'd look a bit innocent and young for her age.

I invited her in and talked to her for a little while. But the more we talked, the more uncomfortable I felt. Red flags and warning bells were going off all over the place, like a disaster slot machine just hit the megajackpot. Nothing was right about this girl.

Over the course of our emailing, she had told me she was a freshman in college, and I told her to bring her ID with her because I was going to card her. I was half joking—it didn't occur to me that a college girl might not only be under drinking age, but under fucking age—but at this point I decided I needed to follow through on it:

Tucker "You brought your ID, like I told you, right? Let's see it."

She pulled it out sheepishly. I wish I had scanned it so I could show you; you'd crack up laughing. It was a fucking joke. The picture was of a girl with different hair, different-color eyes, and BRACES! It was so obviously someone else's ID, I wasn't even sure it would work on Bourbon Street. It also said she was 19. If this girl was a 19 year old college freshman, I was an 80 year old D-day veteran.

Tucker "OK, come on. This is the most ridiculous fake I've ever seen. You couldn't fool a blind person with this."

She tried to sell me for about a minute, but I was having none of it.

Tucker "Come on, just stop lying. You're getting nowhere. Seriously, how old are you?"

I expected her to say 17. Even though the age of consent in that state was 17, I don't hook up with girls under 18 on principle, so her being young was actually turning out to be good thing—I wasn't into her at all, physically or as person, and now I had a nice, nonpersonal excuse when I broke the news that I wouldn't be firing it in her.

YoungGirl "I'm 14."

You know that feeling you get when you know you're fucked, you can see it coming, but it hasn't quite hit yet? Like when you're sitting at a stoplight, and you see a car speeding toward you in the rearview mirror and the driver is looking down texting instead of at the road. That moment when you realize he's not going to look up in time to stop, that split second before the disaster happens, when everything slows down and you know for a fact you're completely fucked and there's nothing you can do about it? I had that feeling.

Tucker "OH MY GOD!! OH MY FUCKING GOD!!!! 14??? 14!??!?!!? PLEASE TELL ME YOU'RE KIDDING?!??!"

She shook her head. My whole body went weak. I had a huge adrenaline dump, my knees buckled, and I had to catch myself on the table. My heart was beating so rapidly I thought it was going to come right out of my chest. I tore into her purse to find her real ID. It wasn't a state ID, not even a learner's permit. You need to be 15 to get one of those.

It was a *high school* ID.

And she was a *freshman*.

Tucker "HOLY FUCKING CHRIST!!!!! WHY WOULD YOU DO THIS TO ME??"

This was the closest I'd ever come to a legit panic attack in my life. I ran to my window and looked outside for Chris Hansen. Even though this girl had sought me out, lied to me about her age, and arrived at my house under false pretenses, I still fully expected a SWAT team to be outside waiting for me. There was no one there, but if cops had been outside, I can say with certainty I would've collapsed into a puddle and cried like a little bitch.

The worst part was that even though this girl lied to me in every way, there was nothing I could do. It's not like I could call the cops on her—how the fuck would I explain this situation to the police? "So you see Officer, I wrote a book about getting drunk and fucking lots of girls, and because of this, girls come to me to lose their virginity." I would not make it through that sentence before the nightstick came crashing down on my skull.

And God forbid, what if this girl lied to them, about anything? I'd be fucked. The taint of just an accusation, even if you are completely innocent and are eventually cleared, never really leaves you.

All these thoughts coalesced inside my head as I tried to collect myself, making me angrier and more freaked out with each passing second. And this was happening in June 2006. You remember what happened in March 2006? The Duke lacrosse case. The fates of Reade Seligmann, Collin Finnerty, and David Evans were fresh in my mind. I couldn't stand the lacrosse players I knew when I was at Duke (I didn't know those three), but no one deserves to be falsely accused of anything, especially not a sex crime. It's wrong and it's bullshit—and here I was in a position to have exactly that happen to me.

Tucker "DO YOU HAVE ANY IDEA HOW MUCH TROUBLE I COULD GET INTO FOR THIS?!??!?! IF WE HAD HOOKED UP, I COULD GO TO FEDERAL POUND-ME-IN-THE-ASS PRISON!!!"
YoungGirl "I'm sorry."
Tucker "YOU'RE SORRY? YOU STUPID FUCKING IDIOT, DO YOU HAVE ANY IDEA HOW MUCH FUCKING TROUBLE I COULD GET IN???"
YoungGirl "I don't understand, why are you so mad?"

Really, she said this. Those were her words. I started stuttering, I was so flabbergasted.

Tucker "WHY AM I MAD?? DO YOU EVEN KNOW WHAT STATUTORY RAPE IS, YOU FUCKING MORON????"

And that's when the crying started.

I guess that reaction should be expected when you scream curses at a 14 year old girl at the top of your lungs . . . though I'm not really sure, since I haven't hung out with girls that age since I was in middle school.

Though I felt pretty justified in losing my mind, it wasn't helping anything. I took a few deep breaths to calm down.

Tucker "OK, stop crying. I'm sorry I yelled, but this is fucking serious. Statutory rape is no joke."
YoungGirl "But . . . I want to sleep with you. That's not rape."
Tucker "Let me explain something to you. Statutory rape has nothing to do with consent. I can get notarized, filmed consent from you, and it wouldn't matter. If you are under the age of legal consent—and you are, by a wide WIDE margin—I'm fucked. End of story, I go to prison, no discussion or argument, and I'm labeled as a sex offender the rest of my life, all because you lied to me."
YoungGirl "But if I'm the one who lied, how can you get in trouble?"

It's funny. At Duke Law School, I never went to class, I never studied, I never did anything but drink with my friends and fuck UNC sorority girls. My friends call me all the time asking for legal advice, and most of the time, I have no idea what the answer is, so I just quote a scene from *Law & Order* that seems to be on point. Yet, there is ONE thing I did learn . . .

Tucker "Statutory rape is what's called a 'strict liability' crime. Unlike most crimes, that means that the intent of either party to the crime is irrelevant; all that matters is the act. Your mother and father could come in here and swear on a Bible in front of a judge that you were 18, and if I fuck you, and you're actually 14, it doesn't matter what they said, I STILL GO TO JAIL. That's why it's called STRICT liability."
YoungGirl "But that's not fair."
Tucker "NOT FAIR?!? SORT OF LIKE YOU FUCKING LYING TO ME ABOUT YOUR FUCKING AGE AND PUTTING ME AT RISK FOR PRISON???"

She started crying again. Bawling hysterically.

As I stood there watching her body heave with sobs, I briefly disassociated from my immediate emotions and began to reevaluate my life. I already knew this situation would take me months to recover from emotionally. In the meantime, there would be no more meeting girls off the internet. I was not gonna talk to girls without first carding them, even at bars, and I didn't care how much of a fucking weirdo people thought I was being. The next roommate I got would be a bouncer or work for the DMV. I'd have him card every girl I brought home, even if she was so old she looked like a catcher's mitt with lipstick.

These thoughts calmed me down, and I eventually got her to stop crying and listen to reason.

Tucker "We can debate the fairness of the law later. I can't have a 14 year old girl in my apartment. I think even this is breaking the law, I'm not sure, and I have no desire to find out. You have to go home right now."

She had taken a Greyhound bus to come see me, so I walked her down to the bus station to go back home (being as she was 14, she couldn't even drive a Vespa). We ran into one problem: It was two hours until the next bus was set to depart, and she was scared.

YoungGirl "Can you stay with me until the bus comes? These people creep me out."

It was like a scene straight out of *Adventures in Babysitting.* Whatever it took to get this girl safely away from me—other than having sex with her—I'd do. I was petrified that other people would notice the 30 year old guy with the 14 year old girl, but I guess they were just as fooled as I was, because no one gave us a second look. Though, if you've ever been to a bus station, you know it takes a LOT to stand out.

As we sat amid the bums and assorted other vagrants who ride Greyhound buses, something dawned on me.

Tucker "Wait a minute—your ID said you were 19. You can't even buy alcohol with that. Why did you get it?"
YoungGirl "Uhhh . . . I . . . uhhh . . ."
Tucker "You went out and got a fake ID for the SOLE purpose of fucking me?"

She didn't say anything.

Tucker "Oh. My. God."

I got up to walk around, as walking usually helps me think. I couldn't process all the traumas that were happening to me at once. A 14 year old girl . . . got a fake ID . . . to lose her virginity to me . . . and rode for an hour on a bus to do it.

What the fuck was going on? Is this really my life?

As I was trying to work through this emotional minefield, she came up and tugged on my arm.

YoungGirl "Oh look, there's a Pinkberry across the street. I love Pinkberry! Can we get some?"

She looked at me with those googly eyes that presexualized girls use to manipulate their parents and sexualized girls use to manipulate their boyfriends. Hers were both.

I knew this wasn't my fault. I knew I hadn't done anything wrong. I knew I hadn't touched her. I knew that she sought me out, emailed me first, sent me very misleading pictures, and lied to me multiples times, but still . . . I'd never felt dirtier in my life than that exact moment.

I looked at her in complete disbelief, weighed my options, and did the only thing that made any sense considering the events of the previous two hours.

I ordered a large green tea frozen yogurt with Cap'n Crunch and strawberries, because that shit is delicious.

Then I went home, took the longest shower I'd ever taken, in the hottest water I could bear, scrubbed myself raw, and drank beer until I passed out.

THE TUCKER MAX SEX-RAY

Occurred—August 2009

When the movie based on my first book came out, Nils, a crew of assorted miscreants, and I rode around the country in a huge tour bus, attending premieres in various cities and causing all sorts of havoc. There were many, many hilarious incidents, but one incident stood above the rest, an incident that was so awesome that it shocked even Dr. Drew.

It all started the night of the premiere in Raleigh, North Carolina. I was sitting on the tour bus, exhausted from a long day, sipping a beer and talking to Jeff and Nils. These two girls I had talked to earlier came on the bus, and they were pretty, but to be honest, I was fairly unenthusiastic about them. Still, they were girls, and they were there, and they wanted to fuck, so I tried to find something compelling about them.

Tucker "So what do you do?"
Girl "I'm an x-ray tech."

OK, that's interesting. Jeff had hurt his shoulder the day before—in a fit of rage, he tried to use it to dent an elevator door—and now he thought he might have a serious problem with it.

Tucker "Really? Jeff has a bad shoulder. Can you get it x-rayed for him?"
X-rayTech "Of course. I can x-ray anything."
Tucker "When can we go? Tomorrow morning, maybe?"
X-rayTech "Right now, if you want."
X-rayFriend "She has the keys to the place."

Jeff and I perk up like meerkats and share a conspiratorial glance.

Tucker "You have keys? To an x-ray clinic? How?"
X-rayTech "I'm the head tech there, and the boss wants to fuck me, so he lets me do anything I want."
Tucker "So we can go and get an x-ray right now?"
X-rayTech "Yep."
Tucker "What else can you x-ray?"
X-rayTech "I can x-ray anything you want."
Tucker "So . . . can you get an x-ray of you and me fucking?"

X-rayTech and her friend flash their best 3am Cinemax grins.

X-rayTech "I can do you one better. I can get an x-ray video of us fucking."
Tucker "You shut up! There is no such thing as x-ray video! That's only in *Total Recall*!"
X-rayFriend "There is. We can go now."

Jeff and I leap to our feet, I take X-rayTech by her hand, Jeff grabs the other one, and we sprint from the tour bus out to the van and race to the clinic.

X-rayTech unlocks the door and disarms the alarm, and we get situated in front of the x-ray machine. We quickly figure out that an x-ray video of us having sex is pretty much impossible, because it's just a mass of bones. I have another idea: I put X-rayTech on her knees and have her fellate me in front of the x-ray machine. Jeff and the other girl immediately crack up laughing.

Jeff "That's awesome! Holy shit!"

He is laughing so much I almost think he has to be playing it up.

Jeff "OK, that's good, you got plenty of video, I want to go now!!"

We switch places, they get in front of the x-ray machine and start going, and X-rayTech turns it on.

I literally fall on the floor laughing. The hardest I'd ever laughed in my life. The video is the best. Google "Tucker Max Sex-ray" and it'll come up, but here are some screen shots:

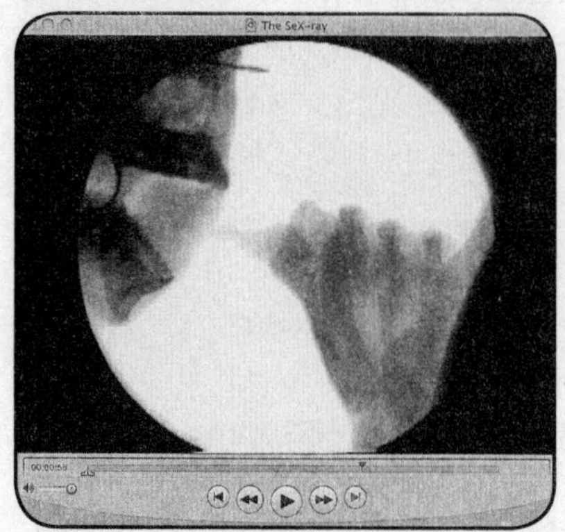

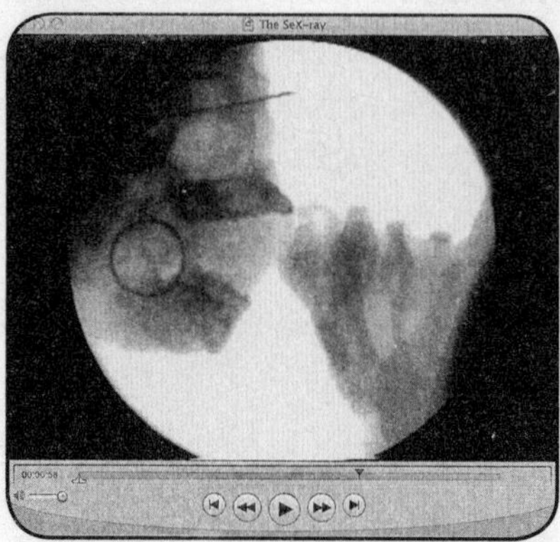

I Shock Dr. Drew

That's not all there is to this story. I went on *Loveline* a few weeks later, and I was really excited about it because I am a huge Dr. Drew fan. During a commercial, we were talking about things that shock him, and he said that after being a doctor for like 25 years, and doing *Loveline* for over 20, nothing shocked him anymore. So I showed him the SeX-ray video.

I will try to not overstate this, but there is no doubt Dr. Drew was shocked. He kinda stammered for a second, and then we came back on the air. This is the exact transcript from that point forward:

Dr. Drew "We're back . . . I was just exposed to a video of, I guess oral sex . . ."
Tucker "I knew that was gonna throw you for a curveball man."
Dr. Drew "It's oral sex on a Cinescope."
Tucker "No no, on x-ray video."
Dr. Drew "Yeah but a fluoroscope it's called. That's a ton of x-ray exposure buddy, right to your nuts."

Tucker "She had metal hoop earrings on too Dr. Drew! It was an x-ray tech who I hooked up with who put me in front of that thing . . ."

Dr. Drew "Is she out of her mind?"

Nils "Yes."

Tucker "Well . . . she said it was a lower level of exposure than . . ."

Dr. Drew "It is, but it's still a . . . we doctors are a very cautious . . ."

Tucker "And a doctor emailed me after I posted this. He's like, 'You cannot say who did that because they'll lose their license.' Like it's a big deal or something."

Dr. Drew "Yeah it's a big deal! And especially shooting across your testes. I mean, that's f-ed up. I'm sorry, but that's not a cool thing."

Nils "She might actually get an award from the National Organization for Women."

Dr. Drew "I guarantee that she was as narcissistic as you, or a drug addict, to be able to want to take that kind of risk."

Tucker "She's a nice lady!"

Dr. Drew "I'm just saying."

Tucker "It's really that bad?"

Dr. Drew "Is it bad? You know, when we use fluoroscopes, you put them on for just a second and then turn them off, because it's such a high level of radiation. It's continuous radiation exposure. It's not just a single picture."

Tucker "So I can go without a condom for a couple months?"

[*Dr. Drew glares at me.*]

Tucker "I'm just kidding. No but it's not permanent, is it really?"

Nils [*laughs*] "It's not permanent."

Dr. Drew "Well, risk of testicular cancers, risk of all kinds of stuff. That's why they wear those **big lead shields** when they're working there!"

Tucker "So you're saying that skeleton porn's not going to catch on."

Dr. Drew "I don't think so. What they've done is MRIs and CT scans and things like that."

Tucker "But have you ever seen x-ray porn like that?"

Dr. Drew "No."

Tucker "The best part is that she had hoop earrings on, did you see that?"

Dr. Drew "Yeah, so the x-ray was also firing into those and going all over the place."

Nils "That's the best part. Not the infertility."
Dr. Drew "Oh Tucker. This is not good. Not good at all."

I'll just say it: When you can shock Dr. Drew, you've really accomplished something. Whether it's good or bad—or causes testicular cancer—is a different issue. But it's definitely something.

Hot, Sane, Single

I have been dating, fucking, and otherwise dealing with women as an adult for 16+ plus years now, and for the most part, I've found one rule about them to be depressingly true:

1. hot
2. sane
3. single

Pick two.

Of course there are exceptions—all those amazing married women obviously had to be single at some point. Unfortunately, hot, sane women stay on the shelf for about as long as the new iPhone on release day.

Of all the various permutations from that list, I seem to attract the hot, single, and not sane ones the most. Actually, I shouldn't say I attract them more; it's just they're the type I'm most enthusiastic about fucking, because, you know—they're hot. Yes, it would probably be better to go with sane, single, and not hot, but I'm a guy—we're visual creatures. Like all guys, I want to fuck the hottest girls I can (unless of course, it's a one-off thing and no one is going to see me with her, then, whatever feels best in the dark works too).

Plus, I used to think the hot, single, crazy girl was awesome; her unpredictability, her spontaneity, and her promiscuity all appealed to me. Who doesn't want to be with that hot girl who's totally into you, always wants to get drunk and party, and loves blowing you in the bar bathroom? She can be really fun because in the beginning, the ride on that crazy train is a blast.

But what you DON'T see at the beginning is what becomes unbearable in the end: the codependency, the intense emotional traumas that replay themselves over and over in her life, the irrational mood swings, the dangerous self-destructiveness, the wanton whorishness. It all eventually catches up to you, and when you have to pay the price for it, the fun stuff doesn't seem that fun anymore. For me, the trips to Hot Crazy Land got to be too expensive.

What follows are a few of the funnier stories from some of the nuttier girls I have dealt with recently. Now, mind you, these are NOT the stories of the absolute craziest. I have several in my past that are really, seriously fucked in the head; the girl who tried to move into my apartment when I was at the gym, the Canadian sisters who killed their mother, etc. I am not writing about those types for three reasons:

1. Some of them are legit crazy; I'm talking about schizophrenia or other brain disorders. If someone has a genuine, biological disability, it's not cool to shit on her for it. If you're a bitch, or fat, or a lazy shithead, that's your fault. Your decisions have led to that result, and you can change that if you want to. But if you have a genuine issue with your brain chemistry that makes you crazy—that's not a choice. I have no desire to hurt or humiliate people for things they didn't choose and can't change.

2. They might stab me. Crazy people do crazy things. I have zero desire to spend my life looking over my shoulder wondering when the girl who flew me to Barcelona is going to come out of the shadows and stick a Ka-Bar knife into my liver (that girl was so nuts, even SlingBlade was afraid to make fun of her—seriously). If you've ever dealt with a truly crazy person, you know what I mean. If not, just look at a picture of Gary Busey and ask yourself, "Is that a person I want to have a dispute with?"

3. Perhaps most important, if I delve too deeply into the issues of the authentic crazies, I will inevitably run headlong into my own issues. I don't really feel like doing that. No matter how much I may tease or mock some of the girls I sleep with, I can't escape the fact that I am CHOOSING to fuck them. If you stick your dick in someone and then turn around and claim you are better than she is and don't share anything in common with her, well . . . you're probably just fooling yourself.

I'd prefer to keep fooling myself, at least for a little while longer.

The Fresno Vet

Occurred—March 2007

When I lived in LA, one day I got a pretty funny email from a woman named Tara, a 30 year old doctor living in Fresno. She complimented my book and all the other standard bullshit, and asked me what project I was working on next. My response:

> "What's next? I'm going to fuck a hot 30 year old doctor who loves my book. Send me a pic, so I can see if it's going to be you."

She sent a pic, was pretty cute, and we went back and forth for a while until we settled on a time for her to come to LA and hang out. The first night, I started to see the crazy come out. Not enough to prevent me from fucking her, but the seeds were planted.

- She wasn't just a doctor. She actually had TWO doctorates: A PhD in biochemistry and a doctorate in veterinary medicine. No one stays in school for that long unless she's hiding or overcompensating.

- The fact that she did all this before she hit 30, points to overcompensation. No one puts that sort of insane pressure to succeed on herself if she isn't overcompensating for some external trauma (in this case, probably a judgmental and overbearing father who tied love and acceptance to external indicators of achievement).

- She'd never heard of Cesar Millan. That by itself is not weird, except that she's a vet and he's the most famous dog trainer in America.

- She was what I call emotionally constipated. Some subject would come up in conversation that was clearly sensitive to her, but she would pretend it wasn't there and just smile and move on. When a girl's mom leaves her and her dad at age 3, and she laughs about it and then asks about the Redskins defense this year—that's not a good sign.

- She was the worst storyteller of all time. Literally the worst. She claimed she had some stories that were almost as good as mine. They may have been, but judging by the way she told them, they were about as exciting as a Boggle tournament. One story was so long that we drove from the east side of LA to the west side ON AN LA FREEWAY DURING RUSH HOUR, and by the time we arrived, she had still not gotten to the point. By the end of the story, I'd forgotten what my life was like before she started talking.

We hooked up that first night, and it was not good sex. She was not just emotionally constipated in conversation, she was the same way in bed. It was like trying to fuck an ice sculpture.

For some reason, many guys think crazy girls are better in bed. This is for two reasons: (1) they hear it from other idiots who don't know anything and mindlessly repeat it, and (2) they mistake promiscuity for skill.

Just because you've had more dicks in you than a detective agency doesn't mean you're good at sex. I've fucked hundreds of girls in my life, at all different points along the crazy spectrum, from completely sane to completely batshit insane, and I can tell you from a position of authority that crazy girls are NOT better in bed. There is no relationship between sanity and sexual skill.

In her defense, though, the first time you have sex with someone, it's not always that great. But she was really smart, which is a huge turn-on to me, so I was more than willing to give her another chance. We hung out and hooked up a few other times, but she got weirder, the sex got even worse, and I eventually lost interest and moved on.

I didn't return her calls or talk to her for a week or so, then one day she texted me like four times telling me what she was doing that day at work, asking what I was doing. Not realizing the level of nut job she actually was, I tried to be polite and responded that I was out with Nils, doing nothing, and then went back to ignoring her. This is not the right way to deal with crazies. A little attention is the worst thing you can do; they interpret it as meaning you still care, and all they have to do to get your attention is try harder.

Nils and I went out to dinner, came home—and found her there. Sitting on my couch. Watching TV and petting my dog. Like it was completely ordinary for her to be casually waiting for me.

I froze. Nils is normally a really calm guy, but he got this look of terror on his face. He immediately went and looked in the kitchen. Later on, he told me why: "I fully expected to see a rabbit boiling on the stove."

Tara "Hey, I was in LA, and I thought I would stop by and see how you were, because you know, you said you weren't doing anything."
Tucker "How did you get in?"
Tara "The back door was open, so I just came in. Murphy seemed happy to see me, so I figured I'd hang out with her for a while."

This was just so fucking weird. Not funny weird, like some hilariously peculiar prank Bam Margera would pull on Don Vito. This girl DROVE OVER THREE HOURS without making any plans with me. Then broke into my apartment. This was creeper weird.

Of course, I still slept with her that night. Come on, be reasonable—there was pussy in my apartment. What else am I supposed to do, throw rocks at it?

The next morning she got her stethoscope out of her purse and did an exam on Murphy.

Tara "I think Murphy has tachycardia."
Tucker "She's a healthy dog with a normal dog life. How could she have an irregular heartbeat?"

Tara "It's mild, but there are a few things that can cause it. Stress, diet maybe. Next time I see you, I'll bring more of my stuff with me, check more into it."

Of course, this freaked me out. I do not mess around with the health or happiness of my dog. I immediately took Murphy to the vet, even though she'd been there only two months earlier. Our normal vet couldn't hear any sort of irregularity, but he's old, so I didn't trust his hearing—this is my dog's health we're talking about, I'm not taking chances. I had them bring in the two other vets who worked in the office, a nurse, and a vet tech to listen to her heart, but not one of them could hear anything unusual.

Then it hit me: She didn't hear anything. She was looking for an excuse to come back to my place. Instead of "forgetting" a toothbrush at my place, she was using my dog's health as the leave-behind.

Holy shit.

I quizzed the vet about canine tachycardia, and it was exactly as I suspected: It's a rare problem in dogs, has no definitive treatment, and can require multiple visits over a period of time to monitor it.

Are you fucking kidding me? This woman, WHO IS A VET, is going Munchausen by proxy—on MY DOG—in order to stay in my life?

That set me off. You can fuck with me all you want—I'm a pro, I can handle it—but you do NOT mess with my doggy daughter.

I was enraged, but since she was a woman, I couldn't just go kick her fucking ass, so I did the only thing I could do: I immediately and permanently cut her out of my life. No more contact in any way for any reason whatsoever. She kept emailing me and texting me, I don't know how many times, but it was enough that I redirected her email to my spam folder.

Maybe a week later, I was out drinking with my buddy Ben, and told him this story, and he thought it was just uproarious. Yeah, it's real funny when it's not YOUR place she breaks into. We got really shit-faced, and he spent the night on my sofa because he was too drunk to drive home. The next morning we woke up hungover, decided to go to my favorite breakfast place, and walked outside my apartment . . .

. . . to find Tara, in her car, pulling up at my place.

Tucker *"Tara??"*
Tara "Hey."
Tucker "What are you doing here?"
Tara "Uh . . . I was in the neighborhood, and . . . uh, I just came by to see what you were doing."
Tucker "In the neighborhood? You live in Fresno."

Ben gave me the most pitiful look I'd ever seen on his face, like a toddler whose parents are yelling at each other. The dude was terrified. I could see the fear in his eyes as he wondered if this is how it would end for him, catching a stray bullet because he was standing next to Tucker Max when one of his crazies finally lost it.

Tucker "Um . . . OK, well, we're going to breakfast. See you later."

I didn't wait for an answer, just got into my car. Ben was so scared he ran to the passenger door, almost dropping into a combat roll on the way there.

That was the last time I saw her in person. But here's the thing with my crazies: They're like emotional burglars. After I cut them out of my life, they seek out other people in my life in order to sneak back in. I sent this story to Bunny to proofread for me—mind you, Bunny had never met this girl—and she called me right away:

Bunny "Tucker, is Tara's real name [redacted]?"
Tucker "YES! How did you know that?"
Bunny "Oh my God! She's been emailing me intermittently for years, asking me about you!"

Wilfred Brimley's Daughter

Occurred—May 2007

When I lived in NYC, I was kinda seeing this model, Crissy. She was hot in the way that fashion models are—angular features that are very photogenic but didn't stand out that much in person—and loved to have sex, which was nice. But, like all models, she was WAY too thin. The girl was so skinny you could have put cotton on her head and used her to clean your ears.

Hot and likes to fuck is cool, but you can find that plenty of places. The best part about Crissy was that, unlike most models, she had an actual personality. She was legitimately smart (she dropped out of an Ivy League school to model full-time) and was funny too. Not double-over gut-laugh hilarious, more funny in that I'm-trying-too-hard way that smart girls usually are.

But still, making me laugh at all is hard, so I liked her. It meant I could enjoy her as a person instead of just using her as a fuck hole when I was horny. Of course, there is a cost to combining those two attributes, funny and female—show me a truly funny girl who doesn't have emotional issues, and I'll introduce you to my stable of unicorn thoroughbreds ridden by leprechaun jockeys.

But shit, it's not like I can't deal with a girl who has some emotional issues. I call that Tuesday. The problem was, that wasn't the only thing that was off about her. She was just always . . . weird. Her version of weird wasn't like the quirky or peculiar stuff you can sometimes get with smart girls. Hers was more, why is she always slurring her speech and passing out at inappropriate times? I've hung out with enough drunks to know the signs of real alcoholism, and she didn't really have many of those: most notably, she didn't drink all that much. There was just something about her that didn't fit.

I didn't think too much about it though, mainly because ALL models are fucked up in some way. I just chalked it up to whatever unique cocktail of mood-altering substances she used to help her to deal with the pain of having an overbearing and unloving mother who pushed her into a soul-crushing profession where she is judged almost exclusively on how unhealthy she can look.

We were out drinking one time, and she was bitching because I never go down on her:

Crissy "Why don't you eat me out? I suck your dick. And I'm good at it. It's bullshit!"
Tucker "You're good at it because all your purging has made your throat all slippery. It's like an oyster cave in there."
Crissy "So? You should still go down on me."
Tucker "We aren't dating. I don't know where your pussy has been."
Crissy "Well, I don't know where your dick has been!"
Tucker "Right, but you go down on me anyway. The difference is, I have self-respect."

We eventually came up with a bet to settle the issue: I had one week, and if I could get us a key to Gramercy Park, she had to give me head in the park. If I couldn't, I had to eat her out in Battery Park. She picked that park because it's at the tip of Manhattan and she thought it'd be romantic to look at the Statue of Liberty as I performed cunnilingus on her. Weird, I told you.

If you don't know, Gramercy is a gated park in NYC that can be accessed only with a special key. Because it's New York City and everyone there obsesses over the most ridiculous status indicators, the only people who have keys are the fancy ones who think they're better'n everyone else. Well, Crissy didn't know it when we made the bet, but I had a friend in

NYC who is one of those fancy people with a key. He agreed to let me borrow it on the condition that I set him up with a female friend of mine he liked. He didn't know I'd already fucked her—easy trade for me (I guess he knows now; sorry man).

We met at a bar right next to the park and had a few drinks, waiting for it to get late enough and dark enough to not get the police called on us by some old lady. After a few drinks, she started acting . . . off. Not even necessarily drunk, just somehow off.

Tucker "You sure you're OK? You're acting even weirder than normal."
Crissy "No, I'm fine, seriously . . . I want to do this. Besides it'll actually help."
Tucker "Help you? With what?"
Crissy "With . . . whatever . . . Let's go, I want to suck your dick in Gramercy Park."

And that she did. I sat on one of the benches and she blew me under the stars in the middle of Gramercy. Take that, you fancy park-locking snobs!

As I got close to cumming, I started looking around for a good place to shoot my load. Maybe on the bench or the raked gravel paths or maybe on the big statue of Edwin Booth. You know, as a *Fight Club*–esque "fuck you" to their pretentious little private park. She felt me getting up and grabbed my hips, pushed me back down and deep-throated me. Her gag reflex was like her appetite: nonexistent. She kept her mouth on my cock as I came, slurping up every bit of my cum.

Even though I was proud of shooting my load in Gramercy Park, I really I wanted to shoot it *on* Gramercy Park. I wasn't pissed off or anything, but it was just another weird thing about Crissy—I know girls who like swallowing, but how many girls insist on swallowing to the point where they grab your hips so hard they leave bruises?

Afterward, she actually did seem a little better, so we went back to the bar and had a bunch more to drink as we bragged to everyone about getting head in Gramercy (no one cared), before going back to her place to fuck.

During sex, she liked being on top. I hated her being on top because, like every anorexic girl, her sharp ass bones get pile-driven into my thighs. Fucking her was like falling into a pile of brooms. As she was hopping on my cock and bruising my hips for the second time that night, I tried everything to distract myself from the pain on my legs and ended up just focusing on her pussy. It's not like she had tits I could distract myself with.

Then, out of nowhere, she began kinda . . . bugging out. Like she was having a seizure or something. At first, I thought she was just getting ready to cum, but this wasn't how she came normally. It was like watching *Aliens*, but in real life—she was moaning, drooling, and foaming at the mouth. I half expected something terrifying to explode out of her chest. Instead her eyes crossed, rolled back into her head, and she fell off the bed.

I'm not going to lie, I freaked the fuck out. All I could think was that one of two things happened:

1. I killed her with my dick, which would ruin my whole night, or

2. She is possessed. Which would make this the part of the horror movie where I need to get the fuck out of there.

Twitching on the floor, she managed to crawl to her side table, yank the drawer open, pull a full hypodermic needle out, rip the top off with her teeth, slam it into her thigh, depress the plunger, and inject the entire contents into her body.

Tucker "WHAT THE FUCK IS GOING ON!"

She lay there panting heavily with her eyes closed for what seemed like forever, but was probably only 15 seconds in non-I-just-killed-a-girl-with-my-dick time. I was about to pick up the phone and dial 911, when she said:

Crissy "Sorry, I didn't tell you . . . I'm diabetic."

Holy shit, of course! That explains everything about her! She acts so weird because she's in a constant state of mild diabetic shock! Every time I see her, she is either drinking or starving herself. Her weird behavior, her slurred speech—it all made sense now!

OH MY GOD! That's why she insisted on swallowing in the park—she was trying to regulate her blood sugar with my cum!

WHAT THE FUCK!?!?!!

What the fuck is wrong with her? That's not going to work! Is she nuts? The questions were flooding my head. I would have asked her myself, but she had already passed out. Right there on the floor. The combination of alcohol, extreme exertion, and a huge insulin injection were apparently too much for her to handle.

Even though her pulse was OK, I was still seriously worried. If she died, I could only imagine how I was going to explain this situation to the cops. "No Officer, even though she has my cum in her stomach and an empty hypodermic needle on the floor, I had nothing to do with this girl dying." Yeah, right. Even the best-case scenario sees me spending a night in The Tombs while they sort it out. I've read *Bonfire of the Vanities.* No thank you.

I called an old fuck buddy of mine who is a nurse:

Tucker "OhMyGod, AngieYouHaveToHelpMe, ThisDiabeticGirlUsedMyCumToRegulateHerBloodSugar, IThinkSheMightBeDead!"
Angie "Tucker, I can't understand a word you are saying. Slow down and explain this to me from the beginning."

I took a deep breath and went through the whole story. After Angie stopped laughing hysterically (thanks again, bitch) she broke it down:

Angie "If she has a steady pulse and is sleeping peacefully, she's going to be fine. But she's a complete idiot. You cannot play roulette like that with diabetes; she could easily go from diabetic shock to diabetic coma and potentially die. That is very, very dangerous."

Tucker "But she's going to be OK?"

Angie "Now she is, yes, but she could have died. Tucker, where do you find these girls?"

Tucker "They find me, Angie."

Angie "Keep telling yourself that."

I contemplated what to do next. It's not like I was going to fuck her while she was passed out. I'm not Armenian. I decided just to go home and try to finish off to MILF porn.

I moved her to the sofa where her roommate would see her in the morning, turned her on her stomach in case she puked up my cum, got dressed, and left.

She called me a few more times after that. She was hot and smart and fun, but I couldn't hook up with her again. If she wanted to be a fucking nut job and risk going into a diabetic coma, that's fine, but I have no desire to watch a girl die while impaled on my dick, not even for a story.

LA Girls Have Their Own Category

Occurred—September–November 2006

Living in LA is weird for a number of reasons: The weather never changes, the people are all malignant narcissists who live in a fantasy world, and no one drinks at bars, they all do pills or coke. But to me, the weirdest thing about LA is the women.

LA women are not like any other women on earth. It's hard to truly understand LA girls without interacting with them, sort of like describing what it's like to eat a raw jalapeño to someone who's never had one. You can say it's hot, but that doesn't really capture the *richness* of the experience. This is the closest I can come to making someone understand without going there yourself:

No matter what you want to say about women from any other part of America, good or bad, you would still never think to describe them as inhuman. Well, that's LA girls. They aren't human, at least not in the way that other women are. They seem to lack some of the most fundamental characteristics of all the women in the rest of the world: empathy, compassion, sweetness, caring, consideration for others, attentiveness, etc. It's as if they lack a soul. This is fine if you are looking to cast reality show contestants, hire contract killers, or staff a death camp, but not so great when you are looking for someone to interact with on a human level. It is not a coincidence that Paris Hilton, the Kardashian whores, Heidi Montag, all the girls from *Laguna Beach* and *The Hills*, Octomom, and basically every talentless, famous-only-for-being-famous celebwhore on earth lives in LA.

I'm sure there are countless men from other parts of America who will dispute my claim and hold out examples of specific girls they know who are like this. The answer to this challenge is simple: Where do all those girls end up moving to? That's right, Los Angeles.

I'd heard about LA girls before I moved there, and people had told me all these awful things about them, but it didn't register. I'd spent much of my youth in south Florida and had no problem running circles around the shallow women in the South Beach club scene during my college summers. Not only was I much older and wiser now, but how different could LA girls really be?

Oh boy, was I wrong. That's the equivalent of thinking you'd have no problem in real battlefield combat because you're awesome at Call of Duty. The difference between shallow and soulless is like the difference between chicken salad and chicken shit. I learned my lesson about LA girls the hard way—by dating one of them. One and one only; that was all it took.

Her name was Alexa. She was the worst kind of LA girl, because unlike most of them, she wasn't a transplant. She was born and raised there. The thing to understand about transplants is that, while they are despicable in their own right and have every opportunity to rise through the ranks of the LA Girl Sociopath Mafia, they will never reach the level of depravity achieved by born-and-bred LA girls. It's like a bunch of Tom Hagans in a sea of Corleones. If you're not Sicilian, you can work for the family, but you'll never be a don. Same principle applies.

My first contact with her was when she emailed me to fuck. This isn't unusual, except that she emailed me while she was at a funeral. Seriously, her family was on a boat, dumping her grandfather's ashes in the ocean, and she was on her Sidekick, setting up a hotel sex rendezvous with me.

Over the course of several emails, I learned more about her and realized she embodied almost every LA girl stereotype:

- She grew up in Malibu (the most "LA" place in the greater LA area).
- She had been in rehab. Twice. By age 21.
- She dropped out of USC because of some preposterous euphemism for being a slut (a car wreck or exhaustion or something like that).
- She had dated a few celebs, notably some midlevel TV star from some crappy show.
- Her dad was an agent and her mom was an actress who married her dad after her career flamed out.

One of the biggest stereotypes of LA girls is that they're all hot. It's true. That's the one benefit to having no soul: They're forced to pay a lot of attention to what they do have—their appearance—because it's the only currency soulless people have and care about (other than power).

Thankfully, she did not let me down in that regard either: Alexa was REALLY fucking hot. Big, glittery, audacious tits paired up with a small waist, tight ass, soft blond hair, and a face that stopped traffic—the valets actually stopped cars to stare at her as she entered the hotel. I can still get hard thinking about seeing her walk into the lobby in that practically see-through designer dress. We fucked three times, and it was really good.

Afterward, I just assumed she'd text all her friends about it, go shopping on Robertson, do coke at the Standard, and then fuck Mickey Avalon or some other D-lister. I thought I knew what to expect.

But instead, she was the complete opposite of what I expected from an LA girl. She stuck around and hung out with me, and acted very normal. None of the LA girl bullshit, in fact, I thought she was kinda cool. She didn't seem shallow or bitchy or anything like that. She was brutally honest about herself and fully admitted that though she participated in it some, the LA culture was bankrupt and absurd. She hated it as much as I did, and being that she grew up in it, she could deftly articulate its problems better than I could. She couldn't stand celebwhores and fameballs, had no desire to be one or to get into that scene at all, and she seemed to actually have plans to do something legitimate with her life. It was a bit of a shock, but in a good way. I decided we'd hang out a little longer, so we drove to get some food.

This was when I was right in the middle of selling my TV show a second time (what ended up being the Comedy Central deal), and in the car, I had to take a call from my agent. While I was on the phone, she undid her seat belt, leaned over, and started blowing me. Right there in the car, as I was driving and talking. This girl's a gamer, I like that.

But that's not all. She was kinda listening to my conversation, overheard me asking him a question, realized that he didn't know the answer, came up off my dick and said to me:

Alexa "No, HBO won't do deals with Sony. Chris Albrecht and Sony's CEO hate each other. They got in a huge fight at a party a few months ago."

I looked down at her in shock. She coyly smiled and then went right back to sucking me off.

I'm not kidding. She knew ancillary details about various networks and producers that my agent didn't know, and she related all of it while blowing me, as I drove down the 405 talking to my agent. If I hadn't been there, I wouldn't have believed it.

Tucker "Jesus Christ, Jack, there is a 21 year old girl sucking my dick right now—literally sucking my dick—and she knows more about this than you do. Get on it and call me back."

Granted, Alexa's dad was an agent, so it makes sense that she'd know about the entertainment business, but still, that was ridiculous. Let's check the scorecard:

1. So hot she literally stops traffic
2. Down to fuck and good at it
3. Cool to hang out with and hates fake LA people
4. Smart and wants to do something with her life
5. Knows more about internal TV politics than my agent
6. Fellates me while I drive, and is good at it

This girl can't be real. She must be too good to be true, right? I considered that, but I didn't care. With that list of attributes, she could be in Al Qaeda and I'd still be down.

Keep in mind, not only was this my first LA girl, but I was still *just* young and foolish enough to think that I was different, and the rules for women didn't apply to me. I mean, I'm Tucker Max. Those other guys may get fucked up by LA girls, but they just don't know how to handle women like I do . . . right? I can always succeed where others fail, right?

We started hanging out pretty much every day. She began perfect and somehow got better. She loved watching basketball. I could take her anywhere; she knew how to handle herself at parties and functions just as well as she knew her way around a dick. Even better, she was bisexual, but she didn't use it as a selling point, which would have been a bad sign. Instead, she just casually asked if I knew any hot girls in LA for us to fuck together. Well, hello. It was like someone had gone to Build-a-Girlfriend and got all the best parts.

And this girl was INTO me. The way to tell if an LA girl really likes you is if she *doesn't* introduce you to her female friends. In most places, this is a sign that you are either a fuck toy or an embarrassment. Not in LA. In LA, all the girls are evil, catty, deceitful whores. If an LA girl keeps you away from her female friends, it means she is afraid they will try to fuck you and steal you away.

At the beginning, I thought maybe I was just getting swept up in the hype, and that LA girls weren't that bad. But at the same time, I was still going out and meeting other LA girls, and Alexa wasn't like any of the rest. They were not only shallow, they were soulless and transparent in their career climbing; Alexa seemed to have depth and authenticity. She had me convinced that she wasn't like them at all. And those tits. Fuck me running.

By the third week of us hanging out, she had completely hooked me. The girl even manipulated me into DATING her. How? Well, aside from everything else I've already listed, she understood that I was still not ready to be with one girl. She really wanted to date me, but more than that, she wanted me to be happy. She told me that as long as she knew she was my actual girlfriend, she was more than willing to share my dick with other girls every now and then. I was so taken by her evolved perspective, she even convinced me to change my Facebook/MySpace status to "in a relationship." That night.

If nothing else tipped me off to her craziness and the inevitable disaster that would result, this should have. I should've known that the "I'm cool with you fucking other girls" shitck was a bad sign, and ANY girl who claimed to be cool with it was not only very delusional but also self-abusive and bug-fuck crazy.

In fact, I DID KNOW THAT. Of course I did, it's obvious. I just convinced myself that this was different. She wasn't crazy, this was just a sign that she recognized how awesome I am. Clearly all these hot girls should want to be with me this much, no matter what the cost. I'm Tucker Fucking Max!

The idea that she was an emotionally unstable codependent train wreck, who would do anything and pretend to be anything in order to attach herself to a high-status man who showed her even basic decency never occurred to me. I was too addicted to the constructed image of my own transcendent awesomeness to see the grains of truth starting to assemble themselves, but they were there, if only I'd had the courage to see them.

Gentlemen, listen to me: What seems too good to be true, is. It's never different, and you're not different. You may be really awesome, you may even be more awesome than me, but there are some inviolable rules of life that none of us can escape from. I've made a career out of breaking every rule there is. Most are easily breakable, without any consequence. But some are not: gravity, death, taxes, and the fact that no sane woman—no sane HUMAN—would subject herself to that degree of disrespect from her partner. These are just not changeable. I may be awesome, and I may have all the game on earth, but a disaster is a disaster, no matter who you are.

I did not always know this. I used to think I could get everything I wanted without having to pay the price for it. You can't. Life is a trade-off. This relationship taught me that the devil doesn't come dressed in a red cape and pointy horns. He comes as everything you've ever wished for, which is exactly what this girl held herself out to be: everything I could ever want in a girl . . . but with a hidden cost.

Once we actually started dating—only three weeks or so after we met—with each passing day it became a little more obvious what that cost was: delusion. I had not found the perfect girl for me. What I had found was an LA girl who quickly figured out what I wanted her to be, then masterfully changed her external self into that. I was dating an actress, except this wasn't a movie, it was real life, and she wasn't playing a role, she was playing me.

There's one problem with playing a role: It works for only a limited time. Your real self comes out eventually. For Alexa, it started with some minor crisis, like she couldn't start her car and needed a ride to school. Then she had a fight with a friend. Then her mom threatened to cut off her credit cards (yes, her parents still paid her bills). Then came some issue with an ex-boyfriend stalking her. The crises started small but kept building, kept getting bigger and bigger and more and more time-consuming. Before I realized what was happening, she turned me into Captain Save-a-Ho. Me. *Tucker Max.*

This perpetual state of crisis allowed her to probe the emotional landscape of the relationship. What I would tolerate, how I responded to issues, and where my weaknesses and vulnerabilities were. Guys, let me explain something else to you: A woman in constant crisis is a Charybdis to be avoided at all costs. I know that sometimes it can feel nice to be the problem solver or the white knight, but her problems are a way to (1) control you, (2) soothe and reassure her insecurities, and (3) use you as a shield from the world so she doesn't have to face her inability to deal with reality. Alexa was doing all of this to me and, like a pussy-whipped teenager, I was falling for it.

Once she figured out what worked and what didn't, she knew how to run me, got secure in her position, and shifted from playing the role I wanted to being who she really was. The cool, mature girl became a petulant child, who pouted and whined about everything. The fun, carefree girl who was always down for a good time became insufferably selfish and evidenced a complete lack of empathy for anything or anyone. The mature, grounded girl with ambitious plans for the future started to display a soul-sucking insecurity about everything in my life, becoming petty and manipulative about even the smallest things.

A specific incident really sticks out in my mind as the moment I began to recognize that this girl wasn't who I thought she was. When I met Alexa, I was living in NYC; I was only staying in LA for a few months to sell the TV show. My last night in LA before I went back, Alexa and I went to a really nice sushi dinner with Bunny and a few other friends. Alexa was a fucking brat all night because she wasn't the center of attention—this was mainly because the people at the table were really smart and she had nothing to add to the conversation, since it wasn't about celebrity relationships or haute couture or any of the five or so topics she could speak about intelligently. Afterward, trying to be nice, I decided we'd go to her favorite dessert place. Like any spoiled child who manipulates the situation into her way, this cheered her up immediately.

Alexa was one of those girls everyone hates because they can eat the worst shit and still have amazing bodies. Because of this, she was always eating candy and cereal and pizza, but her favorite thing in the world is a dessert called a Bazookie. It is a freshly baked chocolate chip cookie served in a round baking tin, with two scoops of vanilla ice cream and fudge on it. She LOVED that thing, even ordering it delivered to her house.

We got one to share for the table. When it came, she attacked it. Not in a funny or playful way. She was—and I cannot be more literal about this description—knocking people's spoons out of the way with her spoon and taking their bites away from them. Her selfishness was so aggressive, I half expected sparks to fly off the colliding metal utensils. It was almost inconceivable that an adult would act that way.

I'll never forget the look in her eyes. She got this expression on her face that was equal parts rage, greed, and malice. You know what it reminded me of? The look that Gollum, from *The Lord of the Rings* movies, got when he was jealous of Samwise's relationship with Frodo. The CGI in that movie did an amazing job capturing the evil, soulless eyes of a sociopath, and as Alexa ripped fudge-drenched cookie out of my spoon, I saw those eyes in her. The curtain on her soul was pulled away for a brief second, and it was awful: no capacity for true emotion or love, no empathy, not even the remotest possibility of consideration for others. There was nothing human there, only someone who knew how to pretend really, really well. It was spooky.

Even though I felt all of this that night, I didn't have the courage to fully admit it to myself. I couldn't accept what I had seen and then act on it accordingly. I had built her up in my mind to be what I wanted her to be, and she had played that role so well, that even when I saw something that made me know in my heart it was all a sham . . . I just couldn't face the harsh truth. I should've learned my lesson, broken up with her, dealt with the fallout, and moved on. But I didn't. Instead, I ignored my intuition, pretended it didn't happen, and went back to NYC, still believing in my fantasy.

It was stupid, weak, and cowardly, I know. But it's what I did.

A month later she came to NYC with her parents and her brother, to visit her sister (who went to Columbia). Alexa was staying with me in my new apartment in Chinatown. Alexa was even worse when she was around her mom—where do you think she learned how to be a soulless sociopath?—and she was an insufferable cunt as soon as she got to my place.

Of course, it probably didn't help that my ex-girlfriend Bunny was staying with me at the time also. This was a recipe for disaster that a kindergartner would have enough emotional intelligence to avoid, but I was far too narcissistic to recognize it. I mean, yeah, Bunny and I had dated, but that was four years ago, and we hadn't slept together since that time, and Bunny was my best friend. How could this possibly upset Alexa?

No, really—that was my fucked-up thought process at the time.

All Alexa and I did the whole week was fight. And not good fighting. It was the bitter and hurtful type of arguing that people do when they won't face what they're really mad about. My place became like an episode of *COPS*: empty bottles and cans; abusive, vitriolic, top-of-your-lungs screaming; neighbors pounding on the walls; exes and current girlfriends in the same apartment. All we needed was some dirty underfed children running around in diapers and the redneck milieu would have been perfect. And of course, no matter how much we yelled or screamed or what we said to each other, Alexa and I always ended up fucking like rabbits anyway.

Bunny "Tucker, if you're going to break up with her, you shouldn't keep sleeping with her. It sends the wrong message."

The second to last night she was in town, Alexa, Bunny, and I went to meet my agent and his wife at the Mercer Hotel for drinks. Alexa was mad and said nothing all night. She just typed on her Sidekick, ignoring everyone. I was so embarrassed at what a childish brat she was being that we ended up fighting some more, and I took her home early.

Back at the apartment, we argued more, and Alexa threw her Chanel bronzing powder onto the marble tiles on my floor, smashing the container into a thousand pieces and casting a permanent golden hue into the mortar. Considering the tiles were black, it was actually kind of pretty.

This momentary pause for reflection was very short-lived. We picked up the arguments with renewed vigor. I honestly don't know what we were arguing about or what was said, but I do remember that she flew into a rage at something . . . and took a swing at me.

No, seriously: She struck me.

It wasn't like she could cause substantial damage, and she didn't use a weapon or stab me or anything like that, but she unquestionably physically assaulted me, in anger, during an argument.

Tucker Max, victim of domestic violence.

I hope you are laughing as hard reading that sentence, as I just did writing it.

Jokes aside, arguing is one thing, but physical violence is something entirely different. By then, I knew we were going to break up, but there is nothing that will harden your resolve and force change quicker than someone putting their hands on you in anger.

Tucker "That's it. We're done. You need to go stay with your parents at the Ritz. You can catch a cab outside."

She tried yelling again for a second but stopped when I calmly told her that if she didn't leave in a timely manner, I'd call the cops. She got really quiet and creepy, put on tons of makeup, and then loudly started telling me about how she was going to hurt herself.

Alexa "I don't even know how to get to their hotel. I'll just sleep in the street."

I ignored her.

Alexa "And I'm going to buy drugs from homeless people."

Kept ignoring her.

Alexa "And I'll probably get raped and die. I don't care anymore."

Whereas this sort of emotional manipulation might have worked to some extent as recently as 30 minutes earlier, I was now unreachable. Much later than it should have been, I had finally admitted to myself who and what Alexa really was.

She packed up all her stuff and stood in the living room staring at me. I watched *Arrested Development* and pretended she didn't exist. No matter what she said, I just ignored her. Depriving her of attention was too much for her to take, I guess; she eventually exploded again, throwing her iPod at me. I have to say, she has a good arm, and good aim, because it hit me hard, square on the chin.

It's weird, but super-high-stress situations seem to bring a calm over me. If my vacuum cleaner won't start, I get enraged and freak out and can't deal with it. But put me in a ten-car pile-up or bar fight or something like that, and I'm calm as a baby on Benadryl. That's one of the few benefits of having parents who are yellers; you learn at a young age how to stay calm in the face of serious stress and trauma.

I stared at her for a second, picked up the iPod, walked casually out onto my deck, took a little crow hop, and launched that thing like Ichiro gunning out a runner from right field. The blue face lit up and pinwheeled away into the night, making an audible *ping* as it bounced off the lower level of the Manhattan Bridge. It was beautifully symbolic, watching Alexa's dysfunctional playlist spin its way out of my life. A very Zen moment.

I know it wasn't the most mature way to deal with my emotions, but it worked. I came back into the apartment smiling and happy. Alexa wailed:

Alexa "You're buying me a new one! Oh my God—at least you didn't throw the Chanel case."

Addendum

It would be nice to end the story here and be able just to blame everything on her and make myself out to be a hero, fighting the good fight against the crazy, fucked-up LA whore.

But we all know that's not the whole story; this coin obviously has two sides. I'm a guy, and I'm weak in the face of pussy, and I have my own issues that led to me dating this girl . . . and because of this, I ended up fucking her two more times.

The first time was about a year after we'd broken up. I was living in LA and hadn't really talked to her at all since we had broken up and she left NYC, even though she called me every few months. She had just broken up with a famous guy she was dating, and being the emotional vampire she was, she needed a soul to suck life out of. She was so persistent and still.so.fucking.hot, in a moment of weakness and stupidity, I told her what bar I was at. Once there, it only took twenty minutes before she got to the point:

Alexa "I want to come home with you."
Tucker "No chance."
Alexa "Why not?"
Tucker "Because fucking you is a bad idea."
Alexa "WHAT? Why?"
Tucker "Let's see—you're a toxic, codependent sociopath. And like every girl in LA, you have herpes."
Alexa "I DO NOT! Whatever. You don't want to fuck me anyway."
Tucker "Why, you on your period?"
Alexa "No! Gross!"
Tucker [*bored at this point, so totally kidding*] "What . . . you pregnant?"
Alexa [*overdramatic, soap opera pause*] "Yeah."
Tucker "Are you fucking serious?"
Alexa "Yeah."
Tucker "You fucking whore! YOU WERE GOING TO FUCK ME AND NOT EVEN TELL ME YOU WERE PREGNANT??"
Alexa "I was going to get the abortion today, but I decided to wait—BECAUSE I WANTED TO FUCK YOU!"

This can't be happening. This can't be true. She didn't just say that. This is not real. No one is this fucking evil!!!

If I really thought about it, and fully processed this statement and what it meant, both to me and her, I am fairly confident the resulting insights would collapse the balance of cognitive dissonances I have about many aspects of my life, and emotionally obliterate me. So instead of thinking about these things, I just started laughing.

Tucker "HAHAHAHAHHHAHAHAHAHHAHAAHHA."
Alexa "That's not funny!"
Tucker "HAHAHAHAHAHHAHAHAHAHAHHAHA."
Alexa "Stop it! Why are you laughing?"
Tucker "I'm just *so happy* that it's not mine."
Alexa "FUCK YOU! I HATE YOU!

I mean, it can't get worse than that, can it?

It can, and it did.

Because I still fucked her.

THAT night.

I know, I know. Let's just focus on the good things I do.

What I thought would be a one-time fuck turned into her staying at my place for two days. My roommate at the time thought it was great, because she would walk around naked. I didn't, because I knew what kind of scar touching this flame would leave.

Tucker "This is great and all, but don't you need to go get an abortion?"
Alexa "Stop trying to push me out. I think you like your dog more than you like me."
Tucker "Of course I do. I love my dog. She's loyal, affectionate, and caring."
Alexa "You love your dog more than you ever loved me!"
Tucker "Of course I do, probably because I don't even like you. If I thought it would make Murph one percent happier, I would throw you off a building."
Alexa "I HATE YOU!"
Tucker "Hate and love are emotions. You are a sociopath. You don't feel anything."

After this, I didn't hear from her until early 2009. That encounter is told in the final story in the book, "Good Game, Great Game, and No Game."

To this day, she still tries to get back in my life. Using any excuse she can, she'll text me or Facebook me. I'm not really sure why she keeps trying. Probably because I am the only person ever to be decent to her and treat her like a human. Or maybe she does it because it worked a few times in the past.

There might be some shred of humanity still left in her, I don't know. As much as I saw flashes of evil, I thought I saw flashes of good too, deep down. Maybe it'll come out later in her life and she'll turn it around, like Darth Vader. But as of now, take my warning:

LA girls aren't human, they have no souls, and they'll steal your soul from you if you let them.

Tucker Max: Baby Killer

Occurred—various 2005–2010

Due to the potent combination of my sexual recklessness and the slutty nature of some of the girls I have slept with, I have accumulated so many stories and anecdotes about abortion that they could name a Planned Parenthood clinic after me. A normal person might feel bad about that and examine his decision-making processes, but instead of doing that, I decided to put them all together into one story for the entertainment of millions. Let no one say I'm not a giver.

While writing this intro, I was having problems with striking the right balance between being funny and making a point, so I emailed Nils, possibly the world's best abortion joke artisan, for help.

Nils "There are so many ways to go with this. I mean, just think about the history of how you looked at abortion as a human being? When you're younger, you think of abortion as this huge shameful, painful ordeal that happens to girls with bad parents in nondescript buildings in the bad part of town. Now you're older and you're writing them off your taxes. That's funny."

Tucker "Yeah, but I think I need to make a point too, not just tell jokes. You're the one who loves abortions and thinks they're hilarious. I can find the humor in them, but I'm not the aficionado you are. I'm more of a midget guy."

Nils "Any procedure that can erase a massive lapse in judgment while at the same time saving hundreds of thousands of dollars and no fewer than 18 years of responsibility for the welfare of another human being, and can be performed with what amounts to a Black & Decker wet/dry vac from your local Home Depot—that's a procedure from which I will derive countless hours of entertainment. Don't forget the coat hangers either. Can't forget them."

Tucker "I'm thinking about doing something about how all the assorted haterz try to accuse me of things I don't do, like rape people or hate women, whereas they miss the one thing I actually do: kill unborn babies. Or maybe I'll do something with the process by which I discuss abortion with a girl who is pregnant. It's not always an easy thing to bring up or talk about. Though I'm not sure how to make that funny."

Nils "I'm at the gym right now and laughing out loud like a retard because for some reason all I can think of is some girl deciding to keep the baby just to spite you, and you going over to her house with a bullhorn and a picket sign yelling, 'HEY! HEY! HO! HO! THAT UNBORN BABY HAS GOT TO GO!!' Maybe do something with that."

Do something with THAT?

I can't. I'm just going to move on to the stories:

—One night I met a random at a bar. We got real drunk and had sex, and the next morning we realized that we had sex at least once without a condom.

Girl "Are you going to come with me to get the morning-after pill?"
Tucker "No. Why would I do that?"
Girl "Because I don't want to go alone."
Tucker "Don't you have friends?"
Girl "I'm not asking them to come with me! You fucked me, you have to come."
Tucker "Not happening."
Girl "What if I get pregnant? I don't want to get another abortion."
Tucker "That's fine. If you get knocked up, I'll just kick you in the stomach until it dies."

Girl "What?"
Tucker "Technically, that's not an abortion. It's a miscarriage. Problem solved."

—This happened in bed, with a girl who was ridiculously into me at the bar.

Girl "We can't have sex."
Tucker "Why not?"
Girl "Uh . . . umm . . . I don't want to?"
Tucker [*looking at her like the lying, eager slut she was*] "You and I both know that's not true."
Girl "OK, fine . . . I'll tell you why, but don't judge me. I had an abortion a week ago and the doctor said I can't have sex for another week. But we can totally fuck on, like, Tuesday."
Tucker "All right . . . well, they didn't vacuum the baby out of your mouth, did they?"

—We were ready to fuck, but like an idiot, I was out of condoms.

Tucker "I don't have a condom."
Girl "I'm not on the pill."
Tucker "Aren't you pro-choice?"
Girl "What? I mean, yeah, but I am not going to purposely use abortion as birth control!"
Tucker "What a waste. Why support *Roe v. Wade* if you're not going to use it?"

—This girl and I had a . . . tumultuous relationship. We would have sex, she would claim to be pregnant, I would call bullshit, she'd cry and apologize, I'd get pissed and ignore her . . . until I was horny, then I'd call her because I'm weak in the face of pussy. Rinse and repeat. The first few times it was just a pregnancy scare. Then she actually got knocked up, and I paid for the abortion. The next time she wanted to fuck, I picked her up.

Girl "Why'd you insist on coming to get me? I have a car."
Tucker "I know. But we have an appointment I want to be sure you make."

We pulled up to Planned Parenthood.

Girl "Why are we here?"
Tucker "If you want to have sex with me today, you have to get a Depo shot. Or NuvaRing or something. Right now."
Girl "You want me to get birth control right now? I'm already on birth control!"
Tucker "And we've already established that you're a liar. If you want to fuck me, you have to do it."
Girl "Why don't you just use condoms?"
Tucker "I did, and you STILL claimed to be pregnant."
Girl "Oh yeah. Whatever, I'm not going in there."
Tucker "You're welcome to say no, but you're going straight home. No penis for you."
Girl "This is ridiculous!"

She bitched and complained . . . but she got on birth control that day. And there were no more pregnancy scares (mostly because I stopped fucking her and moved onto some less demonic sluts, but whatever).

—I fucked a girl, and afterward we realized the condom had broken.

Girl "Oh no. Please, please don't get me pregnant."
Tucker "You think I want you knocked up? If you're pregnant, I'm going to kill someone."
Girl "THAT'S NOT FUNNY. I'm Catholic! And I'm not on the pill!!"
Tucker "Why weren't we just having anal, then?"

She informed me that she was morally opposed to abortion, so it was a long, shitty couple of weeks until I got this text from her:

"Hey great news! My pussy is bleeding! You home? Celebratory blowjob?"

Clearly abortions are the least of this girl's problems.

—Sometimes I fuck younger girls, 18 or 19, and for some reason, each one is convinced she's the first.

Her "I bet I am the first girl you've ever fucked who was born in the '90s huh?"
Tucker "Oh honey . . . I've not only fucked girls born in the 90s, I've already had to pay for an abortion for a girl born in the '90s."

I should mention that exchange took place in 2008 . . . March of 2008. Do the math.

—This girl was a Hooters waitress, came over to fuck a few times, and we used condoms pretty much every time . . . except for one time we didn't. It's not really my fault, though. You see, I can be a sleep fucker. Sometimes I'll wake up horny at 3am, and if I am next to a girl I'm fucking, I'll roll over and just start humping. I'll only be half awake and usually won't fully wake up until I cum. While sleep fucking is pretty common for me, sleep-putting-on-a-condom is not. It wasn't long before I got the call.

Girl "Hey, uh . . . it looks like I'm pregnant."
Tucker "Is it mine?"
Girl "Yes!"
Tucker "Of course it is."
Girl "It is!"
Tucker "Whatever. I guess you want me to pay for the abortion?"
Girl "I can't afford it. I work at Hooters."
Tucker "Fine. There's $1000 down the drain. Literally."
Girl "What?!?"
Tucker "Of course I'll pay for it. Just make sure to get me the receipt."
Girl "A receipt? For an abortion? What for?"
Tucker "Aside from the fact I want to make sure you go through with it, I'm going to write this off my taxes. If I write a story about this, I can claim it as a research expense and take it as a deduction."

Nils made a joke about this up top, but it's true: I really do write abortions off my taxes (as a research expense). And it's perfectly legal.

I'm like Sweden: Free abortions for everybody!

THE MIDGETS STRIKE BACK

Occurred—November 2009

Part 1: The Tiny Little Setup

After my first book got popular, colleges started asking me to come give speeches. These college speeches are kinda ridiculous; I get paid well into the five figures to talk for an hour, answer questions, autograph shit, and have young hot girls hit on me. Sign me up.

I gave one at a college in late 2009, as I was finishing this book. Afterward I was signing autographs and taking pictures, and a female midget came up to me. I never know how things like this will go. The vast majority of people who approach me in person are cool and nice, but of course every once in a while you get some nut job who wants you to save her from the fucking aliens or something.

Well, she waddled right up and said in her high-pitched, squeaky voice:

Midget "Would you ever fuck a midget again?"
Tucker "Are you offering?"
Midget "Maybe. If you're man enough to handle me."
Tucker "Handle you? You're lucky I don't stuff you in my carry-on and stow you in the overhead bin. Gimme your arm."

I wrote my number on her arm with a Sharpie.

Tucker "That's my real number, let's see if you're serious. But if I agree to hook up with you, you have to introduce me to Willy Wonka AND the Lollipop Guild."
Midget "Done."

After she left, I turned to one of the security people working the event.

Tucker "Did that just happen?"
Guy "Yeah. I never seen any shit like that before."

I'd never had a midget hit on me before. I didn't even know that was possible. Even though I'd slept with one, part of me still believed that midgets were mythical creatures, like unicorns and educated guidos.

She came out to meet me at the big campus bar. I am a sucker for a good midget joke, so I started in on her immediately.

Tucker "Who brought their kid to a bar?"
Midget "Hey!"
Tucker "What, did my joke go over your head?"
Midget "Enough with the midget jokes!"
Tucker "Sorry, I'll try to be the bigger man."

Tucker "Be honest; midgets have night vision, don't they?"
Midget "You're not supposed to call us midgets."
Tucker "So do you prefer to be called an LP, dwarf, or freakish little munchkin?"
Midget "LP is the correct term, but I know you're too much of an asshole to be corrected at this point, so I'm not even going to try."

Tucker "You're not mad at me, you're mad at those kids who keep trying to steal your Lucky Charms."
Midget "I'm not even Irish, dumbass!"
Tucker "Well, you're a half something."
Midget "Fuck you, jerk!"

The best part was this admission, when we were talking about the changes she had to make to her dorm room:

Midget "I had to buy a different bed too, one that was closer to the floor."
Tucker [*jokingly*] "Was it a dog bed? I bet those things fit you perfectly."

[*Midget blushes visibly.*]
Tucker "OH MY GOD! NO WAY! I was kidding! You actually sleep in a dog bed!"
Midget "It's a really nice special one! I only bought it because I couldn't climb into the bed that came with my dorm room. Stop laughing, it's actually really nice!"
Tucker "REALLY NICE?! IT'S A DOG BED! HOW NICE COULD IT BE? IT'S MADE FOR DOGS! If it's so nice, where did you buy it?"
[*Midget says nothing and looks embarrassed.*]
Tucker "Oh my God. You bought it at Target didn't you?"
Midget "NO!"
Tucker "Where then? Petco? PetSmart?"
[*Midget looks ashamed and hits me.*]
Tucker "Oh my God!!! You sleep in a bed you bought at a PET STORE!"
Midget "You better not write about this!"
Tucker "How can I? I don't believe half of what you say."

This was the only real bar on campus, and it was a college crowd, so there were a ton of young and hot girls out to meet/hook up with me. It was so fucking funny to watch the midget fight with them for my attention. Every time a girl would start to move in and monopolize me, the midget would scamper under her legs and tug on my shirt to get my attention back.

Fucking a midget is sort of like watching the "Two Girls, One Cup" video; you want to do it once to say you have, but after that, unless it's a fetish of yours, there's not much of a reason to do it again. So even aside from all the cute college girls into me, I wasn't all that into the midget. If I was going to do this, there had to be another reason.

Tucker "All right Midget, if you want to be the one to go home with me, you have to give me something cool. I've already fucked a midget once, you gotta up the ante."
Midget "I guarantee I'm better in bed than her."
Tucker "Probably, but that's not good enough. I know you can take a dick in your vagina . . . but can you take one in your ass?"
Midget "Goddamn right I can."

The bar erupted in cheers. It was awesome.

Tucker "Nice. OK, what about ass to mouth? Will you do that?"
Midget "OK, but let me get more drunk."
Tucker "Someone get her a thimble!"

Using this leverage, I got her to take a Master Blaster pic with me:

I SO regret not getting a pic where I held her by her ankles, like a catch of the day or something, or dangling her over a railing like Michael Jackson's baby. Opportunities squandered.

As you may be able to see from the picture, she is Hispanic. Midget jokes + race jokes is almost too easy.

Midget "You don't even remember my name, do you?"
Tucker "Of course I do. It's Midget."
Midget "That's not my name! I knew you didn't know it!"
Tucker "I know, I know, that's not your full name. It's actually wetback Midget."
Midget "NO! I'm Argentinean, not Mexican!"
Tucker "I'm not using wetback as a racial slur. I'm using it as a verb."

Midget "I don't get it."
Tucker "You will later, at the hotel."

I was staying in a hotel about a mile away from the bar, so I had walked to the bar and was going to walk back. With any other girl this wouldn't be an issue—but the midget's legs were so short, and her knees and hips were so bad, she said she couldn't make the walk to my hotel. And since there is no way to get a cab at 2am, I could only think of one solution.

I put her on my shoulders and carried her. The whole way. Just like in the pic. I'm in good shape, but carrying 80 pounds of mini-whore dead weight for a mile is not easy. And she was shifting around so much, it made it that much harder. It was like doing a sandbag CrossFit workout.

When we finally got to the hotel, even though it was 45 degrees outside, I was sweating like a whore in church and collapsed at the hotel door trying to set her down. She stepped off my shoulders and fell over like a bowling pin. Midgets are so uncoordinated.

Tucker "I've never worked this hard to fuck a girl before. How is it possible I have to work ten times harder for half a girl?"
Midget "I'm not like most girls, it'll be worth it, I promise."

I have to give her credit: She lived up to her word. Whereas the first midget had been awful in bed, this one was really good. Everything you dream of doing with a midget, we did. She even got on top and spun HERSELF in a circle on my dick. Turns out it IS possible to do, you just need a cooperative midget.

And when I say everything, I'm serious. Months later, I was still laughing about the text I sent to Nils:

"Just went ass to mouth on a midget. Time to retire. Jesus Christ hasn't even done that."

Part 2: The Greatest Threesome of All Time, and the Boomerang

Occurred—January 2010

Fucking a midget is awesome. I did that. Going ass to mouth on a midget is legendary. I did that too.

Before January of 2010, I didn't think it was possible to top those two things. How could I top them? It would take a team of Hollywood hacks to invent some ridiculous scenario that is literally impossible in real life—like stealing Mike Tyson's tiger and putting it in a Vegas hotel room—in order to top fucking a midget at a midget convention, and then going ass to mouth on one, right?

Wrong.

I topped it. By having a threesome . . . with two midgets.

And I have PICTURES.

This is the story:

The ATMMidget from the above story kept in touch with me after she slurped her poop off my dick. In mid-January of 2010, I went to NYC to meet with my publisher to finalize the release plans for this book and posted about my trip on Twitter. She called me and wanted to get together.

ATMMidget "I'm going to be visiting NYC with my friend when you're there. She's cute, let's get together."
Tucker "Eh, I don't know. I already went ass to mouth on you, what else is there to do? Get to know you?"
ATMMidget "Well, she's a midget too, and she really likes you."

Take a deep breath, Tucker.

Tucker "Are you . . . offering me a midget threesome? Do not tease me about this, woman."
ATMMidget "Well, she's a midget. I can't promise she'll want to hook up with you, you have to have good game, but she'll be with me and she's fun. If she's down, I'm down."
Tucker "Let me get these facts straight: You are going to be in NYC when I am there. You will be with another female. She is a midget. You are willing to have a threesome with her and me. You believe she may also be willing, assuming I have game. Are these statements correct?"
ATMMidget "Yes."

OH MY GOD. Stay cool Tucker, don't overplay your hand.

Tucker "OK, I'm in. But if you're fucking with me, I will feed you to a lion."

I didn't tell my friends about this, because I was certain it was going to fall through. I'd already fucked a midget at a midget convention, then went ass to mouth on a Mexi-midget. It was expecting too much from life to have a midget threesome. No way. These things don't happen, not even to Tucker Max.

The fateful night came. ATMMidget assured me that she and the other midget were on their way to meet me at dinner. Secure that they were in a cab on their way to me, I decided to inform my dinner companions what was up. I was eating with my buddy Mike, my book agent Byrd, and his boss Scott.

Tucker "OK guys, you want to stick around after dinner. I have a surprise for you."
Mike "Oh Jesus. What is this?"
Tucker "Just trust me. This is epic, even for me."
Byrd "Am I going to come back from this alive? Should I call my wife and tell her I love her?"
Tucker "Oh, you'll be alive. But you won't be the same."

An hour later, the four of us were sitting in the lobby bar at this super-nice NYC hotel, packed with pretentious NYC hipsters. I could tell the midgets got there before I saw them; a hush descended over the crowd, all the fancy hipsters not wanting to stop and stare but not being able to help themselves. I mean, two midgets were actually walking into a bar, and it wasn't the start of a joke—it was really happening.

As they came into view, Mike started laughing, Byrd audibly gasped, and Scott just stared, as if he couldn't believe what his eyes were seeing.

Scott "Are they real?"
Byrd "Every time I think you can't top yourself . . . I just, I know I should never doubt you . . . but, how does this . . . ?"
Mike "Tucker Max."
Byrd "I no longer have words."
Tucker "Gentlemen, the best part is that I'm going to fuck both of them."

Actually, the very best part was that the friend of ATMMidget was legitimately cute. I didn't realize it was possible to judge midget looks on any scale other than "for a midget," but she was cute even for a real human.

We all hung out and talked and drank and had a great time. They wanted some food, so I brought over the waiter:

Tucker "This is the normal menu. Do you have a children's menu?"
Waiter "A . . . children's menu? Uh, no, we don't."
Tucker "All right, but they won't be able to finish the normal portions. Bring us a grilled cheese and some of the chicken kebabs."
ATMMidget "And two apple martinis!"

The waiter was so befuddled by this scene he didn't even ID them.

ATMMidget "We never get ID'd. I don't know why."
Tucker "I think the drinking laws are different for mythical creatures."

Once everyone was sauced up and having a good time, I pulled out my ace in the hole: a bag of lollipops.

Tucker "OK, I want you two to go around the bar and hand these out to people."
ATMMidget "OK, cool!"
Tucker "Say they're gifts from your union."
CuteMidget "Union?"
Tucker "The Lollipop Guild."

Off they waddled, handing lollipops to people. Easily one of the proudest moments of my life.

I didn't think it could get any cooler than midgets giving people candy at a bar, but it did—because of how the people reacted. Hipsters are generally humorless idiots, so offending them isn't very hard. But hipsters are also a bunch of condescending, limp-wristed, panty-waisted, pacifist dilettantes, so getting them angry to the point where they will be confrontational is difficult. Well, these people got PISSED. I could've stood up and called Obama the N-word, and they wouldn't have been more upset than they were with the midgets. I guess these hipsters knew what was offensive to midgets . . . even better than the midgets *themselves*.

ATMMidget "Why were those people getting pissed? They have a shitty sense of humor."
Tucker "What can I say? If they can't take a joke, fuck 'em."

When two midgets say you can't take a midget joke, you know you suck.

We left there and went to another bar. On the street, the midgets pulled out cigarettes. I could not stop laughing at that sight. Midgets smoking looks so ridiculous, like chimps wearing tuxedos.

We ended up at a bar called BlackFinn. Cool place, very chill, and everyone there loved the midgets. Of course, there were only ten other people there, but still, it was fun. As we were drinking and hanging out, the subject of midget strength came up.

Tucker "Be serious. You can't even reach the counter to sign in at a gym, how can you be involved in a discussion of real strength?"
ATMMidget "Shut up! At the LP convention there are strength contests and stuff like that, and we beat regular people all the time!"
Tucker "Regular? You mean cripples and people with MS? Get the fuck out of here with that shit. Just because you can lift tiny little weights doesn't mean you have real strength."
Mike "I don't know man, they only have to move the weight half as far. They have an advantage."
ATMMidget "I bet we're stronger than you!"
CuteMidget "Yeah!"
Tucker "How many push-ups can you do?"
ATMMidget "I've done 60 before!"
Tucker "You can't even count to 60—it's too high for you to reach."
CuteMidget "We'll beat you!"
Tucker "HAHAHAHA. OK, let's have a push-up contest. Right here. I will do more than both of you COMBINED."

We got on the ground in push-up position. ATMMidget started first, and I went movement for movement with her. I have to say, she knocked out 20 pretty fast, and then CuteMidget got right down and knocked another

20 out like it was nothing, and ATMMidget followed her right up with 20 more.

Shit. They were not slouches.

Thankfully, they crapped out at 40 apiece, and I was able to keep going, so I won. To their credit, though, I'm in good shape, and they pushed me pretty close to the limits of my consecutive push-up ability. But, like all midgets, they came up short.

Mike "You know who wins a midget push-up contest? We all do."

Then the midgets started dancing on the bar. I wouldn't even mention it if I didn't have pics, but it was so fucking funny. The Mexican busboy comes up to Mike and me, and kinda looks at us confused:

Busboy "Amigo . . . chicas pequeños?"
Tucker "No no, amigo. Las MUJERES pequeñas."
Busboy "Ohhhh, duendes!"
Tucker "Sí, sí. Y . . . estoy chinga los dos."
Busboy "Ohhh! Muy bien!"
Mike "I didn't know you spoke Spanish."
Tucker "I don't. But I've spent enough years working in restaurants, I can talk to Mexicans."

[The translation for you monolingual retards who are too lazy to type this into Babel Fish:

Busboy "Friend . . . are those little children?"
Tucker "No no, my friend, they are small women."
Busboy "Ohhhh, elves."
Tucker "Yes, yes. And I'm fucking both."
Busboy "Ohhh! Very nice!"]

Some pics of them dancing on the bar:

Last call came and it was time to roll. My hotel was six blocks away, so I put ATMMidget on my shoulders, took CuteMidget by the hand, and wished everyone well.

New Yorkers think they're so jaded that it's impossible to shock them. They think they've seen and heard it all, and that may be mostly true. But I can tell you from experience that at 2am in Midtown, pretty much every person on the street will stop and gawk when they see a guy holding hands with one midget and another midget on his shoulders yelling out:

ATMMidget "WHO RUN BARTERTOWN? I RUN BARTERTOWN!"

Mike is friends with everyone who works at BlackFinn, and he tells me the Midget Push-up Contest has already reached legendary status there. And even though there were only 10 people in the bar when it happened, Mike tells me it has become like Wilt Chamberlain's hundred-point game—everyone swears they saw it.

The actual threesome itself was pretty basic. The thing I really wanted them to do was what I call "the totem pole," where they get on each other's shoulders and face me as I stand up, and one kisses me while the other sucks me off. The problem is midgets have frail, weak knees, and neither could support the other's weight. Oh well, not every fairy tale can have a perfect ending.

Wait, did I just bitch about a midget threesome?

Though I definitely had sex with two midgets, I am not entirely sure if I get to count it as a threesome. Maybe in midget math 1 + ½ + ½ = 3. I'll have to ask about that.

Lying in bed, basking in my incredible accomplishment, ATMMidget and I had a conversation that brought me down a notch or two:

ATMMidget "I like hanging out with you. It makes me feel good about myself."
Tucker "Why?"
ATMMidget "Hanging out with you is cool, but what I really like is that, back at school, that first night, you picked me out of all those other girls."
Tucker "Really? I don't mean to be a dick—seriously, I don't—but you know I picked you that night BECAUSE you're a midget. I mean, I ended up liking you and I think you're a cool girl and all . . . but that's pretty much the definition of objectification."
ATMMidget "Of course I know that, you idiot. Why do you think I fucked you?"
Tucker "Because I'm awesome."
ATMMidget "Uh . . . no. Because now I can mark 'fuck a celebrity' off my Sexual Bucket List."
Tucker "Are you fucking serious?"
ATMMidget "You're not the only one who can objectify someone."
Tucker "You nefarious little munchkin! I feel dirty and used!"

Who knew such big lessons could come from such little people?

I FUCKED TUCKER MAX!

It's funny, I started out my writing career by going out and finding girls to have sex with, and then writing about it. I got all this success and fame because of my stories, and as a result, girls came to me to have sex instead of me having to go out and pick them up. But now the tables have turned, and all kinds of girls are writing about what it's like to fuck me.

I am not going to bore you with speculation about what this means. I don't even fucking care what it means. I am sure there is some lesson about karma in there, but I don't give a shit about karma. Karma may be a bitch, but it's because I fucked her and never called her back.

Morals learned or not, the stories involving girls fucking me and writing about it are pretty funny.

THE PENN STATE LEMONDROP GIRL

Occurred—September 2009

This whole incident happened on the premiere tour for the *I Hope They Serve Beer In Hell* movie. Instead of going back and writing about it from my current perspective, I'm just laying it out as it happened. First is my write-up of the event, then her article about sleeping with me, which was published on Lemondrop.com, then my response.

Part 1: My Initial Write-up About the Penn State Premiere (as Posted on the Movie Blog)

At the end of the night, there were two girls who were kinda vying to go home with me. There was a really hot blond girl—like seriously smoking hot—but she was playing the I'm-too-sexy-for-this-shirt game. Not the best play with me. Then there was another really cute girl, also blond, like a year or two younger and very fun and eager. She was the type you just KNOW likes to fuck.

I would have been down with either, and I was willing to let everything play out, but of course Bill Dawes, a friend and comedian who was traveling with us on tour, decided to fuck with me. I went to the bathroom, leaving the two girls sitting there with an empty chair between them. Bill went up to the cute one and said:

Bill "I don't think you're going to win this one, Baby Fat. You better step up your game."

She got a panicked look on her face and raced to the bathroom to find me. Inside, she got her friend to promise to sleep with Jeff if I fucked her. With that in my pocket, I went back to the table and sat next to the superhot one.

Tucker "You coming home with me or not?"
HotGirl "Let's stay here for a while, see what happens."

Don't check raise me, honey. I will come over the top and go all in, and I will always win, because I don't care about the result.

I told the cute one to call a taxi for us, and when the hot one was in the bathroom, I left with the cute one. The hot one came back and sat down, to find Dawes in the seat I used to occupy.

HotGirl "You can't sit there, that's Tucker's seat."
Bill "Not anymore. He just left with that other girl."

Bill's description of her facial expression: "Like someone who just saw her puppy get run over."

Ladies, there's a lesson here: Playing games and acting like a coy bitch works with a lot of guys. Not with me.

As we were leaving the bar and getting into the taxi, someone yelled out to the cute girl, "You're going to be famous!"

We went back to the hotel and had sex, no big deal. After we hooked up, she said this:

CuteGirl "I have never hooked up with a guy outside of a relationship."
Tucker "Um, hello—we aren't dating."
CuteGirl "You don't count, you're not a real person."

The next morning in the lobby:

Nils "What's your girl's name?"
Tucker "Wait . . . shut up, I know this one!"

Part 2: I Slept with Tucker Max, the Internet's Biggest Asshat

by Courtney A., a senior at Penn State

Reprinted from Lemondrop, September 23, 2009

Tucker Max. If you're in college, you probably know him and his infamous stories.

If not, let me enlighten you. Tucker Max is a blogger-turned-author-turned-movie-producer who's basically famous for drinking to obliteration and having sex with girls whom he later savages in graphic detail on his site, TuckerMax.com.

Why does anybody care? Unfortunately, he happens to be pretty smart and a funny writer, so he landed a book deal. A few years later his collection of tell-all drunken sex essays, *I Hope They Serve Beer In Hell*, was made into a movie.

I met him at a bar after his premiere in State College. And I slept with him.

This is my story.

It was a Monday night, about a quarter to 11, and I was watching TV with my roommates. I'd asked a few people to go out but no one was feeling up to it. Then, I got a text from my friend Steph: "If you want to meet Tucker Max, come to Cafe 210."

I was a longtime fan and I'd been dying to meet him, so I got dressed as fast as I could and ran out the door. It was only the second week in school, and in my apartment I was already getting teased for my promiscuity. My roommates laughed as I left and told me to make sure to bring him back! "Yeah, like I'm gonna have sex with Tucker Max," I thought.

I was expecting a huge line at the bar, but when I showed up, it was totally dead. I asked the bouncers if they'd heard anything about Tucker Max coming there. "I hope not," one of them replied. Inside, I found some of my friends and some girls who were clearly Tucker's tour groupies assembled. We waited a little while, and just when I thought he wouldn't show, Tucker finally arrived.

Immediately a drunk girl latched onto him, hugging and kissing and falling all over him. She was cute, and I was just about to sigh, "Well, he's already got his hook-up tonight," when my friend Rosie snarled, "That's pathetic. Who wants to be that girl?" Regardless, we worked our way into the crowd surrounding Tucker, until we were face to face with him. I shook his hand, and told him I was a huge fan. His response? "Will you fuck a virgin?"

"Yeah," I said, "I'll fuck anyone." Big mistake.

Tucker yelled for his friends to go get some kid, apparently the aforementioned virgin, because he'd "got one" for him.

"Wait, wait, wait," I interrupted. "Is he cute?"

"No," said Tucker. "He's fat."

I replied that I had standards; Tucker replied that I was a whore.

Well, this was off to a great start. Tucker continued to try and get this kid laid while this drunk girl continued to follow him around like a lost puppy. My mission forgotten, I went back to chatting with my friends. Finally, Steph handed me her camera and suggested that Rosie and I ask to take a picture with him. We did, and this time, Tucker blatantly looked me up and down.

"34 C?" Tucker asked.

"32 C," I replied, "but good guess. What, are you trying to touch them or something?"

"Oh, I know I can touch them," he said. "But I like to guess first."

When I went back to sit with my friends, they'd been joined by a couple of Tucker's tour guys. Eventually, the man himself showed up.

"So," he asked, scooting in next to me. "Are you coming back with me tonight?"

I have two options. One: dignity. Two: a good story to tell later. So I snuck off and texted my best friend, Matt. "Should I fuck Tucker Max?" His response: "You will be a GOD in my eyes."

It's done. Around 1:30, I told Tucker that I would, in fact, go home with him. "Oh, I know," he replied. "We have a cab waiting, let's go."

We got into the cab with everyone at the bar waving and giving the thumbs up. The best part? I didn't even know most of them. Tucker took me back to the Hampton Inn where he was staying, showed me his tour bus (which was pretty sweet) and I met his dog, whom he talks to like somebody's aunt talking to a baby, except that he told him, "Say hello to the new slut!"

Finally, in his room, he wasted no time getting completely naked. Like, no foreplay at all. Well, girls? Here's everything you wanted to know about Tucker Max: His body is nice, but a little too hairy. He's a great kisser. He screws like he's jackhammering a sidewalk. I faked orgasm to get him to stop. After he was finished he told me we were going to do it again in the morning. Great! I should have gotten up and left, but then he wanted to chat.

We talked about normal things, like how he eventually wanted to get married and have kids, which was a shock.

"You're 33," I said. "Shouldn't you get a move on?"

He said that he wasn't interested in being in relationships, and I told him I liked being in them, at which point he totally misunderstood me and proceeded to tell me that we couldn't date.

"You're not a real person," I replied, by way of explanation. I also told him about this guy I was kind of hung up on and he was surprisingly nice and insightful, telling me that I was a cute girl and that I shouldn't pin my hopes on some dude at my age.

The next day, he woke me up for sex, as promised. It was worse, because he was panting this time, and when he was putting his clothes on, he farted loudly, multiple times. I called a cab, and he gave me 20 bucks for the cab which I gladly took. (Hey, I'm in college.) He hugged me and said, "I'd totally hook up with you again. Call me if you're ever in L.A."

Eh. I think one episode of stunt sex is all I'll ever need.

Part 3: Tucker Max Responds to Courtney, His One-Night Stand Who Told All

Reprinted from Lemondrop, October 1, 2009

If you're reading this, then you've probably read the "I Slept With Tucker Max" piece that started it. Basically, a girl I fucked in State College wrote her account of what happened. I have to say, I applaud young Courtney for two things:

1. Using her real name and picture. I would have had very little respect for her if she'd written all of this anonymously, but she didn't. If you are going to kiss and tell, be honest and open about it, and she was. Very cool.

2. Being pretty fair and honest about everything. For the most part, she left out all the insecure editorializing bullshit that girls usually put into those things, and basically told it like it was. I was very impressed with her fairness and objectivity.

In fact, I was so impressed with the whole piece that I didn't even feel the need to write any sort of comprehensive rebuttal. Though I disagreed with a few things, and she left a few things out, I was going to let it all lie, because it was far more true than not. The fact that she was fair and reasonably accurate and actually spoke from a position of experience instead of just assuming what I was like secondhand, that immediately put her ahead of 95 percent of the people who write about me.

Yes, there were a ton of details she left out. Like when this other hot girl was all up in my shit, and Bill Dawes went up to her and said, "Hey, Baby Fat, I think you've lost this one," and she took off and got her friend to promise to fuck my friend Jeff if I left with her. I had actually forgotten about that until Jeff reminded me, but it's an irrelevant detail. The basic point is that she came out to fuck me, and she readily admitted that, so whatever. It's a story not a police report; she got enough right.

But when Lemondrop asked me if I wanted to write a rebuttal, I took them up on it. I couldn't help it. Not for the reasons you might think. But I couldn't stop myself from writing this, because of one thing she wrote:

"He screws like he's jackhammering a sidewalk. I faked orgasm to get him to stop."

I don't have any beef with her description of me in bed. I would prefer the phrasing "dominant and aggressive," but whatever; you can call me a jackhammer, the difference is semantics.

The thing that pissed me off is that she said she faked an orgasm to get me to stop. I mean honey, really? Did you think I was paying the LEAST bit of attention to you or your "orgasm"? You know why I stopped? Because I came. That's always when I stop. I couldn't tell your orgasm from pixie dust, I don't even know if either are real, and neither would make me stop if I wasn't done, that's for sure.

Courtney, I know you're only 21, so that explains a lot, but baby, please understand: We all reap what we sow. Just like I have to be OK with the women who come to fuck me Twittering about it or writing about it for millions to read, you need to be OK with me not caring for or considering you in bed. I'm sure there are a lot of guys who will be sweet and gentle with you in bed and really pay attention to your needs, but the guys you come out to sport fuck probably won't be among them.

And for the record, two things she said I want to confirm as true:

1. I absolutely baby-talk my dog, Murph, and I am not ashamed to admit it. I love that goofy mutt, and she likes it when I baby-talk her and I don't care who knows.

2. She wasn't lying when she said I told her I wanted to eventually settle down and have kids. I do. Maybe not now, but soon enough that I think about it now. Of course, traveling around the country fucking all kinds

of college girls who throw themselves at me probably doesn't help accomplish this goal. Eh, what can you do?

Still single, ladies: tuckermax@gmail.com

Texts from Tucker Max's Night

I am a fan of the website Texts From Last Night, so much so that their book is one of only three I have given a blurb to. In thanks, Lauren Leto (the girl who started the site) sent me a selection of the funniest "I fucked Tucker Max" submissions they have received but not published:

From: Lauren Leto <lauren.leto@gmail.com>
To: Tucker Max <tuckermax@gmail.com>
Date: Mon, Dec 7, 2009
Subject: Tucker Max Texts

From our back end, a selection of just a few of the best. Impressive diversity of area codes, btw:

(301): i had sex with tucker max last night . . . my life is complete

(404): Last night I fucked Tucker max

(323): OMG . . . I think Tucker Max fucked me last night!

(301): i just fucked tucker max

(864): new life goal: to NOT fuck Tucker Max

(919): i just slept with tucker max. we're over.

(919): I'm fucking Tucker Max
(1-919): Really?
(919): Yep. Kayla and I are going to his hotel. Bahahaha

(860): my friend fucked tucker max!

(714): You fuck an asian from West Covina, I fuck Tucker Max. I win!

(469): My new goal in life is to be a "Tucker max" story . . .

(505): So I banged out a girl last night who slept with Tucker Max. WIN!

(513): I just hugged my friend that was with tucker max last night . . . im spending the night in the hospital. fuck.

(303): I just banged a chick that fucked Tucker Max. If my dick falls off I'm gonna be pissed!!

(443): remember when jo was screaming about how much she hated tucker max last week? she's making out with him at the bar. CALL ME.

(724): Tucker Max just asked me if my cleavage was going to the bar tonight . . . Over the microphone in front of everyone

(803): let's stalk tucker max's bus. I feel like there was a connection there last night
(1-803): um. Maybe I missed that? Connection? He was calling girls out about lawnmower hair and throwing rocks at dead hookers. I saw no "connections"
(803): he totally looked up my skirt. In Tucker, that means, you + me = true love. behind the bus!! LETS GO FOLLOW THE BUS!

(949): Tucker Max called me a stripper. Life is now complete.

(440): Tucker Max just gave me his number.
(330): This is the one time I will allow cheating—but get pics.

(410): In conversation she brought up that she slept with Tucker Max on the UF football field
(804): Red flag Red flag Red flag Red flag Red flag Red flag—the flag is RED bro

The Handprint Story

Occurred—September 2009

This also happened on the movie premiere tour, but in Philadelphia, with a different girl. First up is my write-up, then her article about sleeping with me, which was published in a UPenn student newspaper.

Part 1: The Handprint Story

We had half an hour to kill in Philly, and this one girl on the bus who had been giving "fuck me" eyes for hours, said:

Girl "You have a half hour? I live right across the street."
Tucker "No need to be subtle with me, let's go."

We got in the elevator, I grabbed her and started kissing her, and I put my hand in her crotch, and before I knew it I was knuckle deep inside of her. Very nice. This one came to play ball.

She told me she wanted me to tie her up, pull her hair, all of the standard BDSM stuff that some girls are into. OK, not really my game, but I can be physical if the girl is really into that.

I threw the Cumfy Cuffs on her and got to work. I have been with a good number of girls, I basically know my way around the vagina, and let me tell you: This girl was dirty in bed. And I mean that in the BEST possible way.

I flipped her over to finish (I like finishing from behind), and right as I was about to cum I decided to put an exclamation point on it by laying a slap on her ass that would make Ike Turner proud. She squealed, so I laid another one on her and finished.

As I stood there sweating and putting my clothes on, my only regret was that I had to leave to get on the bus. I fucked that girl pretty hard, but I was nowhere near her limits. But she wasn't done.

DirtyGirl "I want you to sign it."
Tucker "Sign what?"
DirtyGirl "Sign the handprints on my ass."
Tucker "For real?"
DirtyGirl "Yes. I've wanted to fuck you since I was 16, I want proof of this."

So I did it. And I took a picture, a picture she liked so much she told me to post it on my blog:

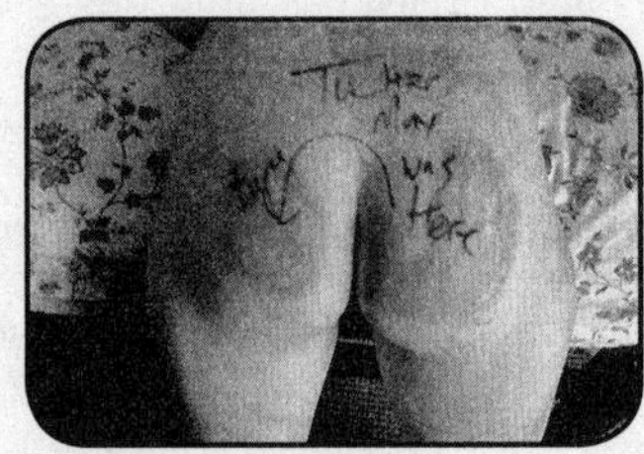

Part 2: I Did It with Tucker Max

by Anonymous (but it is the girl from above; she emailed me about this story before it was printed)

Reprinted from Pennetration, Edition 2, February 2010

Let me preface this with: Tucker Max is the fucking man.

I could try to describe his greatness, but I'd prefer to use his own words. As Tucker writes in the introduction to his website, "I get excessively drunk at inappropriate times, disregard social norms, indulge every whim, ignore the consequences of my actions, mock idiots and posers, sleep with more women than is safe or reasonable, and just generally act like a raging dickhead."

I've always sort of fancied myself the female equivalent of Tucker Max. He has unquestionably been one of my biggest influences, in both my personal conduct and my writing style.

When I was a sophomore in high school, one of my male friends introduced me to the Tucker Max website. Right away I thought, "This dude is awesome!" I read through his many chronicles of drunken debauchery, which many times made me laugh so hard that I cried, and found myself strongly identifying with Tucker.

I've never really had a filter, or what could be called a proper conscience . . . you know, that voice that tells you that the shit you want to say is inappropriate and will offend any decent human being in the immediate vicinity?

Furthermore, like Tucker, I'm a self-professed slut. I certainly have sex with more people than is safe or reasonable. I love sex, and I'm not ashamed of it. Society tends to frown upon women who fuck whomever they want, whenever they want, which is why I've up until now limited my sexcapade tales to oral retellings, rather than writing them out and posting them on the internet.

When I heard that Tucker was touring the nation in promotion of *I Hope They Serve Beer In Hell*, the movie based on his bestselling book, I immediately jumped at the chance to meet my mentor. I secured a seat at the movie premiere at the Bridge. And of course, I was banking on the possibility that I might be able to seduce him, and thus fuck the man who inspired my love of casual sex.

Tucker Max has sex for the conquest. He admits it. As Tucker writes, "Some things in life you want to do just so you can say you've done them."

I wanted to fuck Tucker Max for the simple fact that thereafter I could say, "I had sex with Tucker Max." Tucker Max is a legend. I consider it an admirable feat to have slept with him.

But I didn't want to be just another one of the hundreds of girls he's fucked. I wanted my own personal Tucker Max story.

If you're familiar with Tucker's writing you'll know that in order to be forever immortalized in writing, a girl will have to do something pretty extreme. In many of his stories, the girls he fucks are memorable for their utter vacuity or general whoreishness. I decided that if I was going to be the subject of a Tucker Max story, it was going to have to be an exchange of mutual respect.

I dressed for the premiere like a shameless slut. I wanted it to be pretty obvious that I was down to fuck, and the tight little black number that exposed my tits and rode up my ass made the perfect statement. I got a few disapproving looks from other female audience members, but whatever, I was there on a mission, and couldn't spare the energy to put the others in their place.

After the movie, I slipped into the movie theater's bar to get a drink. Tucker was signing autographs, and the line was a mile long. I had some time to kill before I could wrangle my way onto the tour bus. I ordered a vodka and Diet Coke, and not five minutes after I got my drink, I was invited onto the tour bus for a drink while I waited for Tucker. Fuck, they were going to booze me up for free and I just paid six dollars for shitty well vodka? I fixed myself a sugar-free Red Bull and Ketel One. Not top shelf, but certainly better than the cat piss I was drinking at 12 Lounge.

Finally Tucker arrived. He gave me an approving once-over. Sweet. This was going to be easy.

Like Tucker says in "The Handprint Story," I was indeed giving him "Fuck Me" eyes, and he returned them. After about 45 minutes or so, the rest of the bus guests took off and I was left to have a private conversation with Tucker. We made a bit of small talk; he asked me what I'm majoring in and all that standard bullshit. One of the guys on the tour bus told Tucker that they had to leave for Boston in about half an hour for early morning press engagements. This was no time for pleasantries. Point blank, I told Tucker that my apartment was kitty-corner to the bus, and we left.

The rest is pretty much exactly how Tucker tells it. I am, in fact, a dirty girl. Even without Tucker clarifying that he means this in "the BEST possible way" I take no offense at this appellation. I like kinky sex and have no problem expressing it. Like I said, if I was going to fuck Tucker it was going to be on my terms. So I told him in the elevator that I wanted to be tied up and smacked around a bit. And Tucker was very accommodating to my wishes.

The sex was enjoyable. We didn't have a lot of time, so we just had to make a quick go of it. As Tucker explains, I then told him I wanted him to sign the handprints on my ass. He complied. We took a photo.

After we fucked, I put my dress back on and accompanied Tucker to the door. But the night wasn't over. I only had about 4 or so drinks in me and was only slightly inebriated. So I went back out and met my friends at the bar across the street. The bus was gone.

The next afternoon Tucker texted me to make sure it was alright for the picture to go up on the blog. To which I replied, "Of course you can put it on the site! It's fucking hilarious. It better be a good story."

And I'm wholly satisfied with "The Handprint Story." It's short, but does the incident justice. More importantly, not once in the story does Tucker demean me. Only compliments. I couldn't be more pleased. I come across exactly how I am: an aggressive flirt, a freak in the bed, and a huge fan. I have no qualms.

Tucker told me that he wants to fuck again, so he can really work me over. If we have sex again, I can guarantee there'll be a tale to top "The Handprint Story." He has my number, and knows where to find me.

Objectification

Occurred—September 2009

I honestly forget in which city I met this girl on the movie tour—I feel like she might have been a Michigan State girl—but she was pretty persistent about fucking me, to the point where she tracked me down in my hotel room, woke me up from my nap, and did everything but pull my dick inside her.

As soon as we were finished—and I mean the very fucking second I rolled off her, before I even took the condom off—she picked up her phone and started texting on it.

Tucker "What are you doing?"
Girl "Texting my friends, of course!"
Tucker "What are you texting them?"
Girl "I just fucked Tucker Max!"

I looked over at her phone. She wasn't just texting some friends.

Tucker "You are MASS TEXTING your whole phone book?"
Girl "Of course; it'd take forever to text each of my friends individually and tell them that I fucked Tucker Max."
Tucker "You know, I'm an actual person. I'm right here next to you, in fact."
Girl "Wait, what? Hold on, let me finish this."

Good Game, Great Game, and No Game

Occurred—March 2009

Many people misinterpreted a lot of things about my first book. For example, a ton of people think that because I mostly wrote about my crazy nights out, that's all there is to me—that I'm drunk all the time and my entire life is a 24/7 party.

This just isn't remotely true. The book is only a small slice of my life, the absolute craziest things that happened to me over a ten-year period. Of course there is plenty more to my life, I just don't write about it because it's not entertaining. Who cares that I go mountain biking with my dog or that I'm an avid rap fan or that I am into paleolithic eating? None of that makes people laugh, so I keep it to myself.

Along the same lines, some people think that because I don't write about girlfriends or meaningful female relationships, that I've never had one. That's definitely not true. I get some variation of this question a lot, and it always confuses me: "Do you believe in love and/or do you think you are capable of love?"

I mean, OF COURSE I believe in love. Who doesn't? Getting drunk and having sex with a hot girl is awesome; getting drunk and having sex with a hot girl you love is even better. Love is amazing; it's one of the greatest emotions, if not the greatest human emotion there is. The only people who spout anti-love drivel are the defeated emo navel gazers who were hurt at some point in their lives and refuse to face the pain and get over it, so instead they spread toxic bullshit like a festering boil. Get over yourself, get past your pain, and quit being stupid. When it's right, love is awesome.

The only reason I am even bringing this up is that I have a story about something astounding that happened with a girlfriend of mine. But the entertaining part requires a proper setup, so bear with me for a minute. It'll pay off, I promise—this is the last story in the book for a reason.

The Backstory

From September 2008 to about July 2009, I had a girlfriend. This was not a bullshit fling; it was a real, committed, monogamous relationship, with a great girl I was very much in love with. Her name was "HotNurse."

At this point in my life, it is not only common for girls to email me to meet or hook up, it's how I meet the majority of women I interact with. I get so much contact from girls through email or Facebook or Twitter or whatever that I don't need to do anything else. Like I said in the intro to the second half of the book, I haven't had to go out and pick up a girl in years. HotNurse was no different. She emailed me to hang out. She explained that she was a traveling nurse who had just moved to LA from Michigan, didn't know anyone in town, and though she didn't really know who I was either, she had read my book on the plane to LA, loved it, thought I sounded like fun, and wanted to meet someone cool to hang out with.

Normally I am not eager to respond to emails from girls who want something from me but aren't obviously looking to hook up. This is for many reasons, the main one being a lot of girls who email me clearly suck; either they try to play bitchy (why would anyone think that would work with me?), they try some stupid call out or lame challenge, or they just ramble pointlessly about how cool they are or how much they drink or what a slut they are, but they'd never sleep with me, but please let's hang out anyway.

HotNurse didn't do any of that. She seemed like a normal, nice girl. We exchanged a few emails, and the more I interacted with her, the more I realized there was something different about this girl. It's hard to describe, but after reading hundreds of thousands of emails from strangers over the past eight years, I have developed a pretty sensitive radar for personality in email, and—though she might not be looking to hook up—she came across as a fun, intelligent girl who would definitely be enjoyable to be around. At the very least, it would be worth meeting her for beers.

On the appointed night, I walked into the bar, and though I don't believe in love at first sight—only lust at first sight—something about her just hit me in the right way. Of course she was hot; about a hundred times hotter in real life than the picture she had sent me. But hot is easy to find. And of course she was sweet; almost any nurse you meet will be a caring person, and HotNurse was the real deal. What made her stand out, what was so attractive about her, was the happiness that radiated off of her. Living in LA, I had forgotten what it was like to be around a real human, and here was the opposite of everything bad about LA: a fun, happy girl who was sweet and caring and compassionate, but still sexy and smart. I was smitten. Not only that, but her fake tits were incredible.

I'm not all that selective about who I fuck, but I am extremely selective about who I date. If you're a girl and want my dick in you, you pretty much only need to make it easy for me. If you want me to date you . . . good luck. Any sort of commitment from me, and there has to be a serious underlying reason; with her, there was. We clicked on every level. So much so that we had sex four hours after we met. It was incredible too. I think we had sex five or six times that first night/morning, and we hung out pretty much every free moment we had had from that day forward. I am not sure when we started officially dating, but it was basically a done deal before it happened. She was the only person I hooked up with from the moment we met until after we broke up.

A lot of girls ask me what it will take for a woman to tame me. That's not possible, and it's the wrong way to look at relationships. HotNurse did not tame me. I was ready to be in a relationship—I had been for a while—and she was the right person at the right time. She didn't try to change me or alter me. We just fit.

HotNurse and I dated for ten months, which is a long time (for me, at least), and this was a real relationship, built on shared experience and meaningful connection. I'd had other meaningful relationships with great girls in the past, but this one was different; it was the most intense, meaningful, and rewarding romantic relationship I've ever had.

We did break up, though. It was not a nasty, angry breakup, but was difficult to get through, for both of us. We probably broke up and got back together three or four times before it stuck, as is common in situations like this.

Why'd we break up? I could write 10,000 words about that, but it comes down to the fact that we weren't exactly right for each other. We connected deeply on many levels, but not all the levels you need to for a sustainable, long-term relationship. That's the hardest relationship to break off, the one that is right in so many ways but not quite all the way right. The specific reasons aren't that interesting, except to know it wasn't because either of us cheated or betrayed trust or did anything bad to the other. Sometimes two people can be very much in love and, despite their attempts to make the relationship work, still don't get there. That was the case with us. Sucks, but that's life sometimes.

You are probably expecting me to reverse this and come back with a snappy one-liner that puts her down or whatever. It's not coming. She's a wonderful, caring, compassionate woman whom I deeply and truly loved, and I'm glad we dated. We're still friends, and she'll always have a positive place in my heart.

If that was the end of our story, I would NEVER have put it in the book. I mean, as great as it was for me, none of that part is funny or entertaining—so who the fuck cares besides me and her?

Well, our otherwise boring love story got very weird and astounding at the end. What happened to us I didn't even think was POSSIBLE, and when you can shock me—Tucker Max—that is something I have to write about.

The Good Part

In March of 2009, we held our biggest distributor screening for the movie at a theater in Beverly Hills. The house would be packed: half film executives, half friends and family. At the time, HotNurse and I were officially broken up, but we were still in love and still sleeping together, and she was coming with me as my date.

I stood with her in the lobby, meeting and greeting people. I saw some actor buddies of mine come in and went to greet them . . . and nearly had complete organ failure when I saw who tagged along.

Alexa.

Remember Alexa, the LA girl I dated, from the story "Hot, Sane, Single"? Yeah, exactly what I said: OH FUCK.

I immediately pulled one of the guys aside:

Tucker "Dude, what is she doing here?"
Friend "You said I could bring anyone, and she really wanted to come. I figured you wouldn't mind."
Tucker "You idiot. Just stay with her and make sure she stays away from HotNurse."

I wasn't that worried about Alexa making a scene in public with me—Alexa is far too worried about her Hollywood reputation ever to do anything like that. But she absolutely is the type who would be an evil cunt to HotNurse, or God forbid, corner her in the bathroom and do something worse. The stories I'd heard about the things she'd done to her ex's current girlfriends were insane. I did not want to find out if they were true now.

But I calmed down when I realized that there were 500+ people there. What are the odds those two will meet? Even I don't have luck that bad. Just in case, I made sure they sat far apart in the theater and entered it through different doors. Aside from that little scene straight out of a *Frasier* episode, the screening went very smoothly.

After the movie was over, we had a small after-party. Just to be double safe, I told HotNurse to head over to the bar as soon as the credits rolled and I would meet her there after I got done talking to people. Problem solved.

I got to the party a little late. HotNurse came up immediately, gave me a kiss, and told me how proud of me she was. And then, being the cool girl she is, she went off and did her own thing so I could have the space to talk to all the people I hadn't spoken to before the movie. About an hour later, I was still stuck near the front door talking to people . . . and Alexa walks in.

Alexa "Hey! I am so happy for you, the movie was so great!"
Tucker "Uh—what are you doing here?"
Alexa "Oh, I came with [ActorFriend] and we decided to stop by for a drink."

Yeah, that's great, why don't you just rape me with a buck knife while you're at it? How fucking ridiculous is this? I've dated only two girls in the past six years, and the one party in my life where I don't want drama is the one where BOTH of them show up. What the fuck?

I know only one way to handle situations like this:

Tucker "Bartender! I want Irish Car Bombs."

Bartender "How many?"
Tucker "How many clean glasses do you have?"

I chugged enough Guinness, Bailey's and Jameson to shame an Irishman, and just hoped for the best. I didn't watch what happened next, but Nils—who knows the history of both girls and was as worried as me that they'd cause a scene—did watch, and this is his recount.

> "I remember Alexa starting literally at the opposite end of the bar having drinks with some guy. She instantly spotted HotNurse and began tracking her from across the room, slowly making her way over by way of short chitchat with the people she recognized between her original spot at the end of the bar and where HotNurse was standing over by the jukebox. It was like the scene in a movie where you see the assassin, then you cut to the assassin's target, unaware. You cut back to the assassin and he's that much closer. Then back to the dignitary, shaking hands with his back to the danger. Back to a close-up on the face of the assassin as he raises his gun. The tension is ratcheting up, the music is crescendoing, and before you know it, the predator is upon its prey."

I look over a while later and see Nils with a bad, bad look on his face. He is standing straight up, face frozen in a mix of terror, apprehension, and concern. I'm afraid to follow his eyes.

Tucker "Is it bad?"
Nils "Look."

HotNurse and Alexa are standing about ten feet from each other, pretending not to notice anything, while out of the corners of their eyes they inspect and judge every physical and material aspect of the other girl. It reminds me of the mongoose and the cobra circling each other in *Rikki-tikki-tavi*; you know one of them isn't going to survive this face-off, you just don't know which.

Tucker "Fuck."

Nils gives me his judgmental eye, then looks immediately back at them. Nils is a big dude, like 6'5", 260, used to be a bouncer in college, and is wearing the most intense face I've ever seen on him. He is ready to pounce and pull them apart when the inevitable happens. Nils's wife, Jen, comes up to say something to him, and he doesn't respond to her, so she follows his eyes.

Jen "Oh no . . . Tucker . . ."
Tucker "It's not my fault! I didn't invite her!"

The tension is maddening. Alexa and HotNurse are two feet away from each other. You know they know exactly who the other one is, and you know they are aching to meet, but both are waiting for the other to make the initial move. Like two field generals, each wants the other to show her strategy first. At least five other people come up to me, each sees what's going on, and of course, all find it uproariously hilarious.

Sean McKittrick [producer of *Donnie Darko*] "This fight will wreck the whole bar. It's going to be awesome!"
Jesse Bradford "Oh dude . . . bad call."
Tucker "I did NOT invite them both!"
Keri Lynn Pratt "I don't know why people think your stories are fake. Your real life is much crazier than your book."
Sean McKittrick "Who wants to make bets? I'm putting money on the blond one, she looks like a dirty fighter."
Jesse Bradford "I don't know, HotNurse is skinny, but she's wiry and strong. She's a nurse too, she's used to fighting crazies in the ER."
Jen "Don't bet against Alexa. Crazy strength is formidable."
Tucker "Fuck all of you, this is not funny!"

It's Alexa who makes the first move. Unable to bear the suspense anymore she faces HotNurse and introduces herself. At that moment, almost the entire room holds its collective breath, waiting to see what happens. It gets so quiet, I swear to God I can hear their conversation down the bar:

Alexa "Are you HotNurse? I'm Tucker's other ex, Alexa."
HotNurse "Yeah, I recognized you from your pictures on Tucker's site."
Alexa "Yeah, I recognized you too. Nice to finally meet you."

You can literally hear the bar exhale and go back to normal noise levels. But not Nils. He's still watching them like a hawk as they start a conversation, tense, expecting the worst, ready to pounce at any moment.

Nils and I are both pretty good at reading body language, and after five minutes, we kinda come to a realization. This isn't a catfight. This is not even coming close to a catfight. This is unmistakably an animated, friendly conversation.

Tucker "Dude, are they . . . friends?"
Nils "For now."

I go back to drinking and talking to people, at first keeping an eye on them, then getting caught up in some conversation and of course, as soon as I let my guard down, it happens.

I hear this loud thud, then the crash of a dozen glasses hitting the floor. I turn and see HotNurse sitting on the floor, shards of glass all around her and an overturned table behind her, Alexa standing there right in front of her. Everyone else is frozen, staring at them, mortified. Great. I'm going to have to deal with the fallout of this fight for months or years, and I didn't even get to see the punch.

I take a deep breath and run over, grab Alexa and pull her away from HotNurse.

Tucker "What the fuck?"

Almost immediately everyone starts laughing. Not nervous laughter, but joyful, fun, haha laughter. Alexa, HotNurse, EVERYONE is laughing. A lot.

HotNurse "Whoops. Alexa, I guess we can't sit on these tables."

Before I can even help her up, Alexa reaches over and pulls her off the floor.

Tucker "Are you two . . . getting along!?"
Alexa "Oh my God Tucker, why didn't you introduce us earlier? HotNurse is so cool, we're like best friends already!"

I look at HotNurse, who just smiles and shrugs, and both of them start jabbering to me about how much they like each other and how great they are getting along and how they are BFFs forever. I barely have time to process this, they are talking so fast and animatedly. They are like excited children telling their parents about everything they saw at Disney World.

I didn't know how to react. I had considered scenarios and outlined responses to every possible outcome from this encounter . . . except this. I could not even conceive of this happening. Alexa and HotNurse are almost polar opposites in almost every way: one blond, pale, and light eyes, the other brunette, olive-complected, and dark eyes. One crazier than a shithouse rat, the other completely emotionally stable. One a toxic narcissist, the other so caring and compassionate she became a nurse, etc., etc. Yet here they were, peas in a pod.

The dynamic between the two was so weird I would have run away if the bar hadn't been so crowded. It was like wandering into a bad neighborhood and running into a couple of blinged-out thug gangsters . . . who then start joking around and treating you with respect. You're just waiting for the other Timberland to drop. When are they going to roll me? I'm going to feel the gunshot any time now. But the gunshot never came, and I could not, for the life of me, understand why not.

Then I thought about it from their perspectives, and there was a logic to it. In taking the measure of each other, they both breathed a sigh of relief because their biggest fears were put to rest: HotNurse realized that she didn't have anything to worry about competition-wise, because Alexa was just as fucked up and broken as I had told her she was, and Alexa saw that she now had a chance to weasel her way back into my life because I was quasi-dating a girl who liked her. It's like they each gave the other one hope. They were each other's Obama.

As strange as this was, I was cool with it, because now I could relax and go back to talking to my friends and getting drunker and drunker. About 1:30am, right before last call, I was content that they really were getting along and that there weren't going to be any ex-girlfriend eruptions. I felt like I could finally breathe.

Tucker "Nils, did you ever think that would happen? That those two would meet and not have an issue? I guess my life is starting to turn around. The crazy randomness is giving way to some semblance of normality."
Nils "Don't hold your breath."

He saw it before I did. HotNurse and Alexa came over to me, hand in hand, got right up close, and said:

Alexa "HotNurse and I have decided that you're going to take us home, and we're all going to have a threesome."
Tucker "Wait—what?"
Alexa "You're going to take us back to your place and have a threesome with us."

I understood each word individually. In the abstract, I assembled them to form a coherent thought. But it took a second for the implications to fully sink in: The only two girlfriends I'd had over the past six years met each other at a bar and decided—independently of me—that we were going to have a threesome.

This couldn't happening. This was something a teenager makes up and sends to *Penthouse Letters*, and it gets rejected because it's unrealistic.

I started looking at the people around me in the bar, searching for confirmation that this was in fact happening and not some drunken fantasy of mine. My assistant Ian just stared at me, completely dumbfounded. Nils shook his head and rolled his eyes. Sean McKittrick muttered something about hating me.

Tucker "You're telling me that you two decided, without asking or consulting me, that the three of us are going to have sex? Together?"
Alexa "Yep."
Tucker [*directly to HotNurse*] "And you are in on this? You told me when we were dating that you weren't into threesomes. But now you are?"
HotNurse "Uh-huh."

There is no playbook for situations like this, because before that moment, I would not have believed it was even possible. But then I remembered that I am Tucker Max, and I did the only thing that made sense. I went all in:

Tucker "Well then, let's get out of here and go fuck."

As they were getting their jackets to leave, this one movie guy I'd been talking to for a while—who was even more shocked than my friends—couldn't figure it out.

Guy "How'd you pull that off? You didn't even do anything!"
Tucker "Yes I did, you just didn't see it. The best game is being so good you don't need game."
Guy "What does that mean?"
Tucker "Sun Tzu said good generals beat their opponents in the field with superior tactics, great generals beat their opponents by planning a superior strategy, but the best generals beat their opponents without even having to fight."
Guy "You're quoting Chinese philosophy to me? I don't get it."
Tucker "Probably why you're going home alone, and I'm going home to have the most epic threesome ever."

Nils "The connection between Tucker Max and Sun Tzu is simple: Surround yourself with emotionally broken sluts, and they do what comes natural—act like sluts—eliminating the need for you to make it happen."
Guy "Ohhh . . ."

When I meet St. Peter at the pearly gates, I will offer this night as proof that my life was great. I've had many threesomes in my life. I even dated and lived with a bisexual girl for a year (Bunny is writing her own book about that), so I know my way around two pussies almost as well as one, and I am here to tell you that this was the hottest threesome, and maybe one of the hottest nights, I've ever had.

Everything you can imagine doing in a threesome, we did. I fucked one while the other watched, then switched. I fucked one while she ate the other out, then switched. I had one blow me while the other ate out my ass, etc., etc. Go to YouPorn.com or Pussy.org or whatever your favorite porn site is, watch all the MFF threesome videos, put it into one night, and that was what we did. Three hours of nearly constant sex later, we passed out in a tangled, sweaty heap of tits, dick, and ass. It was glorious. It was such an amazing sexual experience I'm going to be masturbating to it for the rest of my life. THAT'S how good it was.

Not only that, but the next morning I fucked both of them again individually, and then they got up, got dressed, and left. No barking from the dog, no smog, and momma cooked the breakfast with no hog. I gotta say it was a good day.

I walked out of my room to find my roommate, GeneralsDaughter, sitting on the couch, watching TV, and brooding.

GeneralsDaughter "I hate you so much. This is so ridiculous, I cannot even believe it happened. And to you, of ALL people."
Tucker "What do you want me to say? I'm just that awesome."
GeneralsDaughter "Go fuck yourself. You don't fucking deserve this."

Tucker "I guess assholes do finish first."

GeneralsDaughter "You're just saying that so you can put it in your book. Fuck you! END YOUR BOOK WITH THIS INSTEAD: FUCK YOU, TUCKER MAX, FUCK YOU AND THE WHORES YOU RODE IN ON!"

THE END

Prelude to *Hilarity Ensues* and *Sloppy Seconds*

When I signed the deal with my publisher for *Assholes Finish First* in early 2007, I thought it would be my last book. But when I sat down in late 2009 and started organizing everything I had written since *I Hope They Serve Beer In Hell* came out, I realized I was wrong; this wasn't just one more book, it was at least two more books, maybe even three.

It's now June of 2011, all my writing is done . . . and I can confirm that there will be two more Tucker Max books.

The third book will be called *Hilarity Ensues*. It will be released in February of 2012, and will have some of my personal favorite stories, for example:

—"The Cancún Story," about what that happened when I lived in Mexico during my second semester of law school, and how exactly I pulled such a feat off.

—"The Law School Weddings and Bachelor Parties," a collection of stories about the ridiculous shit that happened at the bachelor parties and weddings of all my law school friends.

—A full and complete re-telling of one of my most iconic stories, a story that quite literally made U.S. legal history: "The Miss Vermont Story." The very first iteration of that story is on my website, and because of that, you may think you know that story . . . but you don't. The version in *Hilarity Ensues* will be fully revised and updated, complete with artwork, legal briefs, and many things not in the original story. There is SO MUCH more that hasn't been told.

—"The Ex-Girlfriend Threesome Fallout," which is the follow-up story to the last story in this book. I left the aftermath of the story out of this book on purpose; primarily because I really wanted to end the book on the perfect quote by my buddy GeneralsDaughter, but also because . . . well, you'll have to read my next book to find out why. I'll give you a hint: Assholes may finish first . . . but nothing that good comes without a price.

My fourth book will be called *Sloppy Seconds: The Tucker Max Leftovers.* You won't have to wait for it, because it will come out at the exact same day as *Hilarity Ensues.* It's going to be the same style as my other three books, there will be one big difference that is really really cool . . . but you'll have to wait to see what it is. It'll be worth it, I promise.

You can pre-order a copy of both books on my website, www.TuckerMax .com (and if you're reading this book after February 2012, then the books are out, just go buy them). And if you want more info, updates, humor, and bullshit like that, you can also follow me on Twitter (@TuckerMax), or Facebook (facebook.com/TuckerMax).

Or, like SlingBlade used to say, "just follow the trail of Chick-fil-A wrappers and funny walking whores, you'll find Tucker at the end of it."

BONUS SECTION: OTHER PERSPECTIVES FROM THE PEOPLE WHO WERE THERE

What you've just finished reading is my part of *Assholes Finish First*. My work is done.

But there is more. Other people who were involved in these stories have perspectives of their own. Of course, they can't write as well as me, and I don't really care what their perspectives are, so I left them out of my part of the book.

But some of my fans may be interested in what they have to say, so I decided to include this bonus section of stuff that other people wrote about what it was like to be involved in the stories you just read.

The Sexual To-Do List

"The Midget Story" was originally on my website, and of course it caused a little stir. Here are my two favorite midget hate mails:

> From: [redacted]
> To: tuckermax@gmail.com
> Date: Aug 10, 2006 9:46 AM
> Subject: The Midget Story
>
> You said you looked forward to "tiny little emails, full of tiny little rage" telling you how awful you are for writing the "midget" story. Well, here's one:
>
> I have never been one of your fans, nor will I ever be. I heard about your "midget" story through a so-called friend who thought your story was hilarious. Well, I read the whole thing. I read it in utter disgust. I honestly feel sorry for you and the brain you have been dealt in life.

First of all, we "midgets" prefer to be called little people or dwarves. I equal the word "midget" to the word "nigger." It is offensive, and reminds us of days when we were considered beneath other human beings.

Secondly, the ways in which you describe little people are truly revolting. How can you rip on entire group of people who can't help the way they are? I can't even begin to fathom your sick mind. Finally, I was there at the Little People Convention in Milwuakee, and I wish that I had seen you and known what you were doing. I guarantee that you would have been thrown out of the hotel.

Oh, by the way, in case you haven't noticed, which I would not be surprised, I am a little person. I graduated valedictorian in my high school class this year, and I am majoring in film at college. I look forward to showing you what a real little person can do in life, but I am sure that whatever I accomplish in life, I will become more successful than you in more ways than one.

From: [redacted]
To: tuckermax@gmail.com
Subject: Midgets
Date: Aug 11, 2006 04:46 PM
Subject: fuck you

Hey asswhole,

Did you even go to college? Let me guess some fucking crappy college right because you are too fucking stupid for any good college.

Guess what asswhole, midgets are doctors, TV executives (btw—never want any gigs from CBS—you have just been banned), and lawyers (which I am sure you will come in contact with soon!). They have better jobs than you and obviously a better education.

You are an ignorant ass who should donate his time to the military. I heard Bush needs some good bullet shields in Iraq, your background matches the job.

The Tattoo Story

I promised Jess, the girl who got the "I fucked Tucker Max" tattoo, that I would publish her version of the events and any commentary she had along with mine, so here it is, totally unabridged:

> "Given the chance to refute a Tucker Max story, any friend of mine could tell you that I'd cum in my pants. But, alas, here I am, my Holy Grail before me . . . and I can't get it up. I am rebuttal-y impotent.
>
> Everything Tucker has said about that night is true.
>
> In my head, I feel as though I was less of a verbal dick-sucker than he makes me out to be (although that Jesus quote is actually verbatim). I'm also sure, though, that in his head, I actually was that much of a verbal dick-sucker. It is Tucker, after all; don't we expect him to think that way? It's pretty irrelevant either way—whether I was or was not fellating his ego as much as reported—but I make issue of it for one major reason: to illustrate the fact that, while he is, and for a long time has been, my idol, I am not in love with Tucker Max.
>
> Let me repeat that.
>
> I am not in love with Tucker Max.

That's not what this tattoo is about. It is not an attempt to charm him, wow him, make him my husband, boyfriend or even friend (though at this point, the latter is more or less inevitable; as Max himself has said, for better or worse, we are now inextricably linked). It is not, and was not, an attempt at anything, except proving to Tucker that I am a no-bullshit sort of girl. If I say I'll do something, I'll do it, even if I only said it in passing. Go back and re-read Tucker's story. He called my bullshit. That is the only reason that I now have a badass little, black, Bank Gothic inked brand of "I Fucked Tucker Max" crowning the kitten (that, coupled with the fact that I did actually fuck him). In no way was this tattoo premeditated. It was an impulse purchase. Kind of like gum. And, while I may one day choke on my gum and damn myself for ever having bought it, at present I have no regrets.

No bullshit.

Tucker left Sunday morning, and having had my tattoo for a full 24 hours, I decide I have healed well enough. The first booty-call I get, I am all too eager to comply. It's time to take my new puppy out for her first walk around the block.

I head over to this guy's house. Not because I come when he calls, but because I want to maintain some semblance of class and don't want to make the poor bastard lay in Tucker's and my sex sheets. I walk into his place and we start fooling around, when I suddenly realize I have not properly prepared myself.

I have a brand-new tattoo an inch and a half away from my vag. Razors and fresh needle-punctures do not mix. I haven't shaved. Fuck.

Granted, this is not a major embarrassment (and at least my legs are smooth). Nonetheless, as we grope our way into his bedroom, I hit the light switch on my way in. Stubble is slightly less noticeable in the dark. So are tattoos.

Again, I have not properly prepared. The events of the entire past 24 hours run though my head and I start to think that I may actually be mildly retarded.

He reaches over to his nightstand to get a condom when I stop him. "Let's do this with the lights on," I say. I am shameless, as well as on a mission; he has to see this tattoo.

I guess guys get kind of excited over the idea of fucking with the lights on, because he literally bounded to the wall and flipped the switch again. He was Bambi-bounding back to bed when he skidded to a halt, cracking his shins on his own footboard.

"Wha . . . what . . . what the fu . . . who the fuck . . . ? "

Mission accomplished.

I fake a confused look, when he turns around, sits down on the foot of his bed, and puts his head into his hands. At this point, I start to worry. I'm not afraid that this tattoo is going to cost me sex (and I plan to prove that in the coming months), but the prospect of having to deal with all of the guys' emotional issues upon revealing to them my little battle scar is more than I can handle. Just as Tucker said, I have serious emotional issues—mostly of the "attachment" sort. I'm not really interested in being attached to anyone at the moment, and as such have developed the lovely skill of being able to emotionally detach myself from sex. It's not love. It's fucking with a good friend, a drinking buddy, whatever. I like to tell myself that all of my fuck buddies feel the same way. But if this tattoo is going to shatter that illusion, if by turning on a light to show off my tattoo I have begun to drag their emotional issues out into the bright light as well . . . I have ruined my favorite pastime.

What have I done?

As I lay there sulking, the guy turns to me. Here we go.

"Who is Tucker Max?"

"This guy . . . he has a website."

Kid marches right over to his computer and Google's "Tucker Max," obviously pointing him in the direction of the site. At first I ask him what he's doing. He tells me to hush; he'll read some stuff and if he thinks "the guy is money, we can still fuck." He reads for a while, ten or fifteen minutes, snickering occasionally. Then he stands up, gets a condom, turns the light back off, and pounces. Crisis averted. After we're done (we fucked, in case that needed to be spelled out), he speaks for the first time since surfing Tucker's site.

"That guy is fucking funny. I'll take his sloppy seconds. And if you still talk to him, you can go ahead and tell him I said that."

Then we had pizza and watched SportsCenter, and I went home.

To wash my sheets."

The Virginity Paradox

When I sent this story to my friends to get feedback, almost to a person they wanted to know more—more about the virgins, more about why they did this, more about what it was like, more about everything. The problem is, I don't really have much else to write about the virgins other than what I wrote.

Then I remembered Sharon. She was the third or fourth girl who came to me to lose her virginity, and she was actually a really pleasant girl to hang out with, enough so that she became one of the few virgins I slept with multiple times. From my perspective, nothing really happened that was worthy of a story. But from HER perspective . . . well, you can judge for yourself.

These are all real emails she sent me outlining the results of her decision. This first email was a few weeks after she lost her virginity to me, the second was several months later, the third a few years later.

> From: Sharon
> To: tuckermax@gmail.com
> Date: April 15, 2005
> Subject: You were right
>
> Hey Tucker—
>
> I don't know if you're still on vacation or what, but when you get back do you want to do something? I promise it wont take me 2+ hours to get there this time . . . so when are you free?
>
> Also, something funny (more so sad really . . .) happened and it was exactly like what you said. This past weekend I had sex with some guy at my school. He told me he'd had sex before, so I expected it to obviously not be as good as with you seeing as you've had a lot of experience . . . but still somewhat decent. Let's just say, doing my laundry would have been more engaging; I think dirty socks might have turned me on more, and in the middle of one of the times we were fucking, I literally yawned.

And afterwards I thought of what you'd said about how high school boys just don't know what the fuck they're doing in anything, and started laughing because he's the epitome of this. It's not like I'm an expert either, but I don't claim to be, and he does. The first thing he said after we fucked was "So . . . I know those rumors about you having an abortion from Tucker Max aren't true and I know you've never been with Tucker . . . but in case something got screwed up from tonight you would get an abortion right?!" Exhibit A of retardness. And after we sat there for a few minutes he said, "So that was probably the best you've ever had, I'm assuming. You know, I almost wish you had fucked Tucker so you could tell him that I'm better than him in bed, haha." And that was my cue to exit. Yes, he's quite a retarded boy.

In conclusion high school boys suck. Let's have sex again.

From: Sharon
To: tuckermax@gmail.com
Date: August 20, 2005
Subject: My life is ruined

Heyyy Tucker,

I don't know if you even remember me, but we slept together (and yes, I even lost my virginity to you) a few times before the summer. Anyway, the reason I'm writing you is to tell you what happened to me, mainly because it is direct evidence of exactly what you claim on your website. I really can't believe how true it is, honestly. I have firsthand evidence of how if you are female, associating with Tucker Max is the clearest path to a ruined life. (I'm not blaming you in any way, don't worry, but just completely realizing why you tell people not to be involved with you. You are so aware and correct it's amazing.) You'll either find this sad, stupid, very funny, or some combination of the three. But I thought I should just tell you anyway how you ruined yet another girls life (completely my fault, as I said, but still, you like completely altered my whole life, even if it was inadvertently). I'll give you a summary of it all since the whole thing would be really long.

Basically, after the last time we slept together, I think it was May, I was late for my period and I'm usually really regular. This freaked me out because that last time, you were incredibly drunk and you woke me up in the middle of the night to have sex, which you didn't remember the next morning and we realized you hadn't used a condom, if you remember any of that. I took a pregnancy test and it came out negative, but 3 days later I still hadn't gotten it, so I took another one . . . and it came out positive. So, this was not good at all, and being in high school and only 18 made being pregnant pretty much the worst thing ever. I didn't want to call and tell you until I was sure or not. So I went to get information about some clinics to get tested at to know for sure. My friends were scared to death, and they thought I should tell my parents, but I wanted to wait to make sure if I was pregnant before I decided if I'd say anything to them or not.

The next day, my friends decided to take matters in their own hands and TOLD MY PARENTS because they are retarded and fucking crazy, and that caused obviously huge problems in our friendship but that's not really so important for this story. Anyway, I don't know if you remember, but you and I had conversations about how my parents would destroy me and everything I hold dear if they ever found out I had slept with you. Well, I was very correct in that statement. My friends went into a lot of detail because they were so worried (which I don't think justifies what they did at all but whatever)—they told them I was sleeping with a 28 year old I met from the internet and was possibly pregnant with his child. And just as a bonus they told them that I'd also been partying a lot and getting sick from drinking too much. That's pretty much something you never really want to hear as a parent.

Well I turned out to not be pregnant. But it almost made the situation worse because I had to deal with all the consequences anyway. My parents hate you very very much. I didn't really feel bad about sleeping with you or anything, in fact I thought the sex was better than with high school guys and you can actually have good conversations so I wasn't upset at all. So like a week later I went on your website, and my mom caught me on it and I'm pretty sure it was in that moment she realized I'm the worst daughter ever. She asked me why I was on your site. And I couldn't really say anything other than "It's just funny . . . ," and this didn't make her satisfied. My parents actually hired a computer guy to come and block your site, so I have no idea like what's going on with you for the past few months, but I remember you were going to do some pitches so I hope all that went well.

Anyway, my parents destroyed my entire social life and have no trust in me whatsoever anymore. They also sent me to therapy, but the good thing is I got out after like 4 meetings with her. It was pretty funny because I had to talk about you the whole time, and I just kept thinking, "I wish Tucker could just see this right now, he'd be laughing so hard at me and how I have to talk about solely him for an hour every week in therapy." It sounds pretty bad to describe your relationship as such, "Well, we're not at all dating and it's not at all exclusive. It was pretty much just sex. I mean we still talked and he's actually a really funny and nice guy, even though he has a website that's just about sex and drinking and being an asshole. And yeah, he was sleeping with a bunch of other girls. But I mean, I knew that getting into it. So that's basically what it was."

Therapist: And that's what you want in a relationship? Do you feel guilty about this, and do you think this is normal?
Me: Well, sex can be a fun thing . . . and no I don't feel guilty . . . ? [long pause] Please don't send me to a psychiatric hospital.

Anyway, she determined that there was actually nothing wrong with me and I just made poor decisions. It's still insanely awkward at home though. Like, my father knows I'm not a virgin . . . and that I decided to lose my virginity to Tucker Max. You just can't really look at your child the same way.

I'm allowed to like go out and do stuff though, so that'll be good. And then I'm off to college next year, so it's all fine. But I just had to tell you all that's happened. The lesson I learned is: don't tell your friends you're pregnant. Well, hopefully sometime again I can perhaps see you and perhaps we can fuck, but who knows if you'll still want to or when I can. Oh Lord, I really didn't take what I should have out of his experience . . . damn you.

Also—please don't post this e-mail on your website, only because people from school would figure out this was me, so I'm asking you as a favor to please not.

I hope all is well with you, and if you're in California (?) or wherever, that pitches or vacations or fuckings are going well!

Love,

Sharon

From: Sharon
To: tuckermax@gmail.com
Date: Nov 26, 2007
Subject: A Stupid Email (aka we used to sleep together)

Hey Tucker,

I'm not sure if you remember me, but a few years ago I lost my virginity to you when I was in high school and you were living in Chicago (yes, this is an email from one of those girls). I am writing you for two reasons:

1.) I just got tested for STD's once again and therefore reminisced about every questionable piece of ass I've ever gotten in my past, namely from when I was retarded/drunk/sleeping with 28 year old men from the internet. (Now only the first two are applicable—clearly signs of maturity.)

2.) I'm a creative writing major (yes, I am aware I will die penniless and alone on the streets), and I wrote a short story that is being adapted into a play. It's loosely about a girl in high school who loses her virginity to a man she meets on the internet named Tucker Max and then has a pregnancy test that comes out positive (if you remember that happening . . . it was just a fabulous time). Clearly it's a dark comedy. Anyway, I didn't think you'd care, it's just for community theater at my old high school, but I didn't want to use your name if you didn't want me to for some reason. (everyone at my high school knows who you are of course.)

Anyway this email sounded bitter and stupid but really I just wanted to I guess let you know that that was happening and check to see if it was okay with you, and if it's not I can change some small details and your name.

Hope all is well with you and LA isn't pissing you off too much,

Sharon

PS—Your book is at Urban Outfitters, and I dragged my boyfriend in there yesterday to go shopping. Needless to say he was less than thrilled to see your book there. He was a fan of yours though until he learned of my past involvements.

Whatever, everyone else thinks it's cool.

That's not all. I emailed another virgin I'd slept with and asked her if she wanted to write anything about her experience, what it was like and why she did it. Here is her take, again completely unedited:

> "There are a lot of reasons why it makes no sense that I wrote Tucker Max to take my virginity. I am routinely teased for being a Good Girl; I'm usually the one who is the first to quit drinking for the night; I stress out on everything; I'm oversensitive to everyone's feelings; I hate it when friends make our upcoming plans public on my private Facebook wall. Tucker Max on the other hand has openly declared in print that he's an Asshole, drinks like a fish, acts impulsively, has no problem dishing out sharp-tongued insults, and gleefully documents his doings for the entire world to read. So, why did I write him of all people to take my virginity? A few reasons. I mean, besides being 30. 30 years old. For fuck's sake.
>
> Why did I wait so long?
>
> Before you ask, no, I wasn't abused. To make a long story short, I blame a friendship with a poacher "best friend" that lasted from the 4th grade to Junior year of college. Back then, I didn't know she was an idiot savant in the "purposefully stealing guys to feel self worth" department. Instead, I thought that consistently losing guys to her meant that I was man-repellent (I look back at my photos, and I can honestly say I wasn't). Instead of speaking to someone who might have wisdom on the subject and could have clued me into what was actually going on, I gave up and adopted a lazy method of pursuing guys. Somehow, declaring my interest to everyone but the guy in question never worked out. Imagine that.
>
> In the meantime, I was already in self-image hell without her help. I had to wear a back brace for scoliosis from 5th to 9th grade, which of course is every adolescent girl's dream come true. Teenagers automatically feel completely awkward all the

time anyway, so you can imagine how psyched I was to add that thing into the mix. If I could go back in time, I would have told myself "Look. It's a piece of plastic. Big fucking deal. It'll be out of your life in 4 years." Even after I was liberated from the brace and my physical imperfections were unnoticeable, I still felt like a circus freak.

To make matters worse, any last shred of confidence I had left was annihilated through my own fault during my college years. Let's just say that although Taco Bell Value Meals and Grand Slam Breakfasts are not meant to be diet staples, they were for me. "So what? Heavy girls get action too!" you say. Well, yes even though I wasn't an appropriate weight for my height, a handful of opportunities still came up. But these guys were of your average bar sleaze variety. I wasn't going to fuck some gold toothed random who looked alright through 3am beer goggles just so I could check this off my bucket list. I wanted to at least be attracted to the guy! Eventually I formed a relationship with the elliptical at the gym and cut down on the junk food with the hope I would attract male attention that I would actually welcome. Mission accomplished.

By 30, I had just about enough of being the only virgin in my circle of friends. They would go out for the night and come back with tales of debauchery while I sat on the sidelines jealous. By that time I had hooked up, but still hadn't had actual sex. I'm not saying I wanted to go out and slut it up every weekend, but I did have biological needs that I wanted to act on and was extremely frustrated. Something had to be done before Judd Apatow got ahold of my life story and made a movie out of it.

Why Tucker?

There are various people out there who've addressed this question. They've all come up with the same basic answer:

Tucker's the quintessential Alpha Male. Well duh. Glad to see you paid attention in your Psych 101 class. But in my case, there was a bit more to it than that.

I am known for having a weakness for hot guys with substance abuse and/or personality problems. So my attraction to Tucker after reading *I Hope They Serve Beer In Hell* was surprising to no one. Personally, I blame Charlie Sheen's character in *Ferris Bueller's Day Off* for making 10-year-old me believe that hot drugged out jailbirds were not only ready to make out at any given time, but would also understand me on a meaningful level that no one else could.

Over time I've found that I'm better off keeping those types of guys to my pre-bedtime fantasies and have learned to stay away from them in reality. But since *IHTSBIH* vaguely hinted that there might be more depth to Tucker than the hellraiser that's mostly represented in the book, I went to his website to see what else I could learn about him. After reading present-day stuff from Tucker, I found that besides being hilarious and intelligent, he had drive, honesty and self-awareness on a level I hadn't yet seen among my own peers. All that plus the whole cliche bad boy thing, and how could I not be attracted? Oh and blahblah Alpha Male blahblah.

So, fine. Like tons of other females who've read his writing, I had an attraction to Tucker. So why didn't I just leave it at that, put a photo up on AdultFriendFinder.com and get it crackin' with a stranger? Well, I'll tell you. While wading through the stories on his site, I read one of the Book Tour updates from his stop in Ann Arbor, Michigan, where he talked about meeting up with virgins. The way he described their point of view about how they'd like their first time to go mirrored my own thoughts exactly: ". . . they want to lose their virginity to someone who knows what he is doing, who won't fall in love with them and who she wouldn't fall in love with, and they want to do it in a controlled situation under her terms, and not in a random or haphazard way." For a control freak like me, this sounded like a dream scenario. Besides understanding the emotional needs of the girl, he seemed so matter of fact about the role of being The First. Other guys I had tested the waters with before Tucker were up for sex, but had an irrational fear that being my first was going to wreak emotional carnage on both our lives, so it never happened. The fact that Tucker seemed so at ease with the responsibility made him even more of a prospect.

Going into this, the only real worry I had was being written about. In fact, I was almost hoping I was going to be completely unmemorable so that I would be left out of the blog. Tucker holds nothing back when it comes to his opinion, and this is especially true when it comes to women. I was worried that I'd log on to the message board later that night and see a virgin-hating blog directed at me or be greeted with a paragraph dedicated to how much I sucked at life in his next book. But the thing is, I often agreed with his evaluations of people. If he had something to say about me, I figured I might want to give his thoughts at least a little bit of consideration. However, if I escaped a post-sex trashing, my self esteem would shoot through the roof. I know I should have a high opinion of myself on my own, but right before writing Tucker I had just had my heart broken. I was in the middle of dealing with what I like to call "The Summer My Soul Was Murdered." So of course I was feeling like shit and needed an ego boost at the time.

After re-reading that paragraph, I feel a little gross that validation from Tucker had anything to do with motivating me. But I've heard Dave Grohl gush over Bob Dylan using "Everlong," Howard Stern fawn over Steve Martin, and I'm willing to bet that 100% of *American Idol* contestants really care what Simon thinks. So, I guess I'm not so much pathetic as I am human. If it wasn't in our nature to want approval, especially from people who are notorious for their low tolerance for bullshit, Simon Cowell would be out of a job. Wow. Did I just compare me and my sex life to *American Idol*, and Tucker to Simon Cowell? I guess I know what my next therapy session will be about.

Now that I think about it, besides wanting to give my recent Heartbreaker a big "Fuck you, I'm moving on," I actually think I was telling myself to fuck off as well. It was like I had a self-intervention. A voice that had been hiding inside for years finally showed up and kicked my ass: "Enough is enough. Stop being so fucking safe and do something adventurous. Fuck the Heartbreaker and fuck everything else that has kept you from doing this until now. Nobody puts baby in the corner!" Um, you get the idea. Basically, it was time to make a move and I knew it. Were there other ways I could have sought adventure? Of course. Did I mention I was 30?

Since Tucker made himself easily accessible to everyone, lived within a reasonable travel distance, and I was definitely attracted to him, I figured why the hell not. After sending photos and talking on the phone, successfully hurdling the obstacles of "Will he even think I'm cute?" and "Will we get along?" we made plans to meet up for a late lunch that weekend.

So how did it go?

Knowing how I am, and even how I was then, I still can't believe I didn't have a full blown anxiety attack on the way to see him. But like anything in life—a job, a relationship, or evidently a hookup with someone you've never met—when something's right, there's nothing to analyze or freak out about. You want to do it and it feels natural, like it's exactly what you are supposed to be doing right at that time. All that's left to do is let it happen and enjoy it.

It's funny. When someone complains to me that they're not getting any or they're having post-hookup drama, my response is: "I find that e-mailing someone and simply asking them if they want to fuck seems to work out pretty well." People think I'm joking, but I'm being serious. The experience really couldn't have gone better.

Offline, Tucker wasn't much different than what I expected, except that he was nicer and a bit more chill than I imagined he would be. And for all my worrying about facing decimation via blog, I actually ended up feeling pretty comfortable once I was with him and forgot all about the impending threat.

I remember when my chicken sandwich arrived at the lunch table. I was nervous there'd be some kind of freak disaster and everything between the bread would shoot out and hit Tucker in the face. I tried to be Miss Dainty and started to use my utensils to cut it in half instead. Tucker shot me a look as if I had two heads and asked "Are you actually going to cut your sandwich up with a fork and knife right now?!" I blushed and told him that normally I rip apart the sandwich with my hands like a neanderthal, but I didn't want to look nuts. "That would have been awesome!" he laughed. Sensing he'd rather I be myself than try too hard to be perfect, I put the utensils down and broke up the sandwich like I normally do. That was precisely the moment where I relaxed and the vibe changed from "interview" to "hang out with a guy I'm into."

After we finished lunch, we headed to his place. I sat on the edge of his bed while I watched him do a quick e-mail check. I was way too shy to make the first move and didn't know what to do. Should I lean back, motion to my lap with my hands as if I'm a *Price is Right* Girl presenting my virginity as a prize and say "I'm ready for you now"? Needless to say, I silently prayed that he would be the one to initiate.

When he was done on the computer, he turned around to face me and asked me about the first time I had been naked with a guy. While I babbled about that, he leaned back in his chair and rested his leg by my side. He slid the tip of his foot under my shirt and lightly grazed my hip as I continued to talk. I remember feeling the right corner of my mouth uncontrollably form a sly grin. It was such a random action, but it was enough to flip the "Oh it's ON NOW" switch in my head. Right after that discussion ended, Tucker thankfully released me from my initiation nerves and joined me on the bed to get things going.

I was happy with how things went in and out of the bedroom. Tucker showed an amazing amount of sensitivity towards me and respected the whole situation, even reassuring me on the phone that it was completely understandable if I wanted to back out at the last minute. When he gave me a heads up about what to physically expect during the event and the following day or two, I joked that I felt like I was at an appointment with the Virgin Doctor. But honestly, I appreciated it. He made the whole thing way less scarier than it would have been had I jumped in the sack as a high schooler with a clueless teenage boy, or if I had gotten drunk in college and let a party hookup get off and go home.

Any regrets?

A tiny part of me wishes I still waited for The One, just for the sake of adding some romance to the whole thing. But other than that, I don't have any regrets. I made the right decision for myself at the time, which is all anyone can really do in this life. I'm glad I can look back at my first experience with a smile. Partially because it's hilarious to me that I got the nerve to do that at all. But also because it went off without a hitch, which was all thanks to Tucker being a gentleman about the whole thing. There are a lot of people who can't believe that I can truthfully use the words "gentleman," "sensitivity," "respect" and "Tucker Max" in the same sentence. I don't know what to tell them. Maybe I caught Tucker on a good day.

Would I ever write an internet stranger for sex now? Definitely not. Back then I had different priorities: I hated feeling like the circus freak for the second time in my life, I needed to know what sex was like, I was at a low point because of a recent heartbreak, and well, I just wanted to bang Tucker. Now, my overall self esteem is in a different place. Hooking up, especially for self esteem reasons, isn't an urgent need. If I meet a guy at a party or wherever, and I feel like messing around with him, then I will. But as far as actual sex, believe it or not, Tucker was the last person. It's not that he ruined me for other men or anything like that. It's just that I place a higher value of intimacy on that particular act than I did then. So for now I'm fine to wait it out for The One. Unless of course Tucker calls. Because you know us ladies and our need for the Alpha Male."

I Fucked Tucker Max!

I didn't put the story about all these girls coming out to fuck me and then writing about it in the first draft. When Bunny finished proofing it for me, she asked where it was.

Tucker "I don't know . . . I don't want to put it in."
Bunny "How could you possibly leave that story out of a section that is specifically about your POST-FAME sex life?"
Tucker "I don't know . . . I don't want to deal with everything surrounding those stories of girls writing about fucking me."
Bunny "That is STUPID! You put those stories in that book this minute!"

Still waffling, I asked Nils what he thought about putting these stories in the book, and as usual, he perceptively and accurately summed up all the issues:

> "AHAHHAHAHAHAH, you are realizing this stuff is "kinda starting" to change your behavior?!!? Glad to see it's taken only five years of emotionally vacant sexual encounters to move the needle . . . kinda.
>
> I am not at all worried that this story would take on a braggart's tone. I'm more interested to see what insights you have and what conclusions you've drawn from it all. Because to me, more than "this is what happens when you get everything you want," it's a cautionary tale about reaping what you sow. When you spend 6–7 years cultivating a culture that promotes and celebrates meaningless, emotionless sex for sex's sake between consenting adults who, ideally, want nothing from the other person besides the sex, it's going to come full circle when you have moved forward and realized there is something better than random sex while a whole generation of young people are coming fresh to your material as this static piece of biblical philosophy divorced from time and place. It's no coincidence that these stories affected you in a way that you describe as feeling used (even if you are being partly tongue-in-cheek), and all three happened post-HotNurse.
>
> You can do this story without the HotNurse angle if you talk about these things in a way that doesn't deal with feeling used but rather how strange it all is seeing things come full circle (i.e., you used to say random crazy shit to girls to see what you could get away with all for the story. Now, because of the fame that lifestyle has brought you, girls are trying to fuck you for the story . . . but they're not actually doing anything other than making the first move and consenting . . . which I guess is the female equivalent of doing crazy shit to see what they can get away with).

What's so fucked up about this is that to the casual observer, the whole idea of YOU talking about being used for sex is just dripping with irony when the reality is that over the last four years or so, you never actually sought out one single girl for ANYTHING, let alone to use her for sex. The reality is that you have been getting used for sex for years. You made yourself openly available to all comers, and as your fame and notoriety grew, more and more of those comers had selfish motives unrelated to sexual gratification and a good time.

And the more important issue (at least personally and emotionally) related to that whole idea is that it profoundly affected how you viewed and related to women. I can say from first-hand experience that it jaundiced you toward women for a significant period of time to the point where you nearly became the woman-hating person critics made you out to be based on the book/site when, in fact, you weren't that person at all when you wrote it. Which, of course, is yet another irony to pile onto the other ironies."

Nils and Bunny were right. Fuck them both. Fine, I'll put it in. But I'm not happy about it, and I'm NOT going to draw any of the inevitable conclusions.

I know that with all things there comes a time to pay the piper, a time to tally the costs of your lifestyle. And I know that nothing lasts forever, nor is it supposed to. My time to step off the stage will come . . . but that time and that reckoning are not today. For now, I'm sticking to my position from "Hot, Sane, Single":

I prefer to keep fooling myself, at least for a little while longer.

PAPERBACK BONUS SECTION

In October of 2010, I went on a nationwide book tour to promote the release of this book. These are the best pictures from the tour:

There were supposed to be protesters at my Philadelphia signing. They were so fucking lazy, they just taped this sign to the outside wall of the bookstore and left.

That is me, with the midget from “The Midget Threesome” story on my shoulders, and a girl who is a giant (she’s 6’2”). I fucked both. Talk about a 1,000 words from one picture.

This girl asked me to sign her stomach. I signed it "Not Mine."

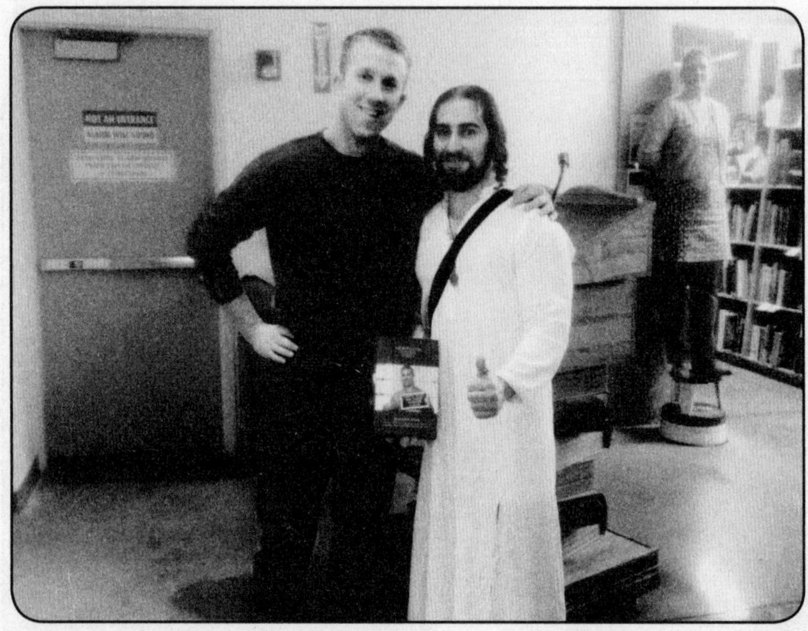

At first I wasn't sure if this dude was coming to protest me, but it turns out, he's a big fan. Even Jesus approves of Tucker Max.

During the tour, I stopped at the Walter Reed Army Medical Center and signed books for wounded soldiers. This is in the front of the hospital with one of the sergeants who helped set it up.

The hospital administrators asked me not to post the pictures I took with the soldiers, and trust me, you don't want to see those. War is awful. Thank a soldier.

I do a ton of media, but one of the only things I really like doing is *Loveline* with Dr. Drew (and now Psycho Mike). He's such a great guy, even cooler than he is on TV/radio.

Right before the Charlotte book signing, I got served process in a lawsuit. Here's the pic of me with the cop. Who sued me? Duke Law School. My alma mater. For real.

This series of pictures still flabbergasts me. This guy asked me to sign his back during the Denver signing. So I did. And then he got my signature inked onto him. I still don't know what to say . . .

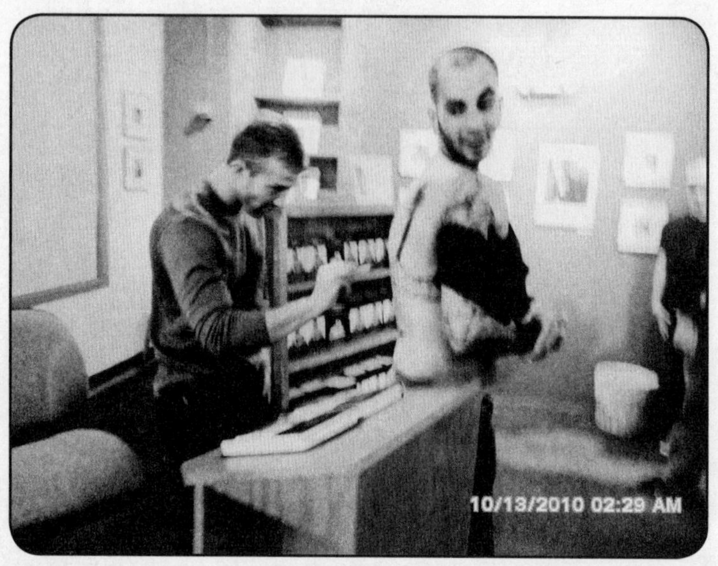

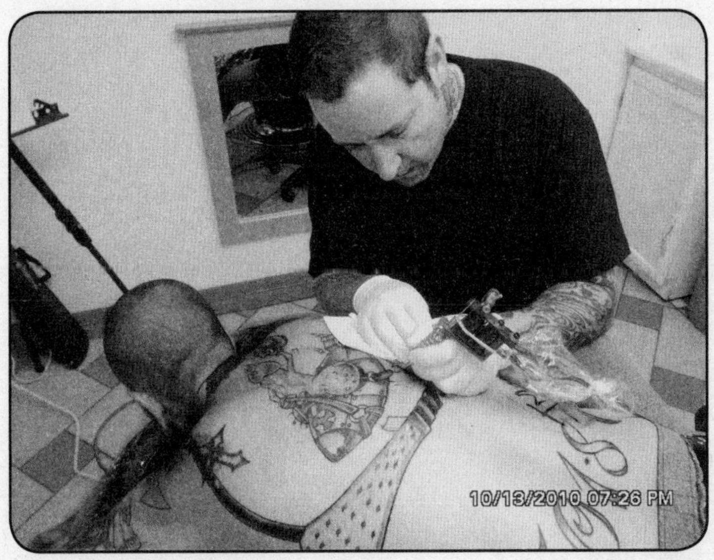
10/13/2010 07:26 PM

Max